Threes and Fours
Go to School

Prentice-Hall Series in Early Childhood

Bernard Spodek, *Editor*

Threes and Fours

Go to School

SYLVIA KROWN

With the Collaboration of Miriam Many

PRENTICE-HALL, INC., Englewood Cliffs, New Jersey

Library of Congress Cataloging in Publication Data

KROWN, SYLVIA.
    Threes and fours go to school.

    (Prentice-Hall series in early childhood)
    Bibliography: p. 227
    1. Nursery schools—Israel.   2. Compensatory
education—Israel.   I. Many, Miriam, joint author.
II. Title.
LB1140.2.K76   372.21'6'095694   74–12321
ISBN 0–13–920322–2

Much of the material in this book was previously published in Hebrew
by the Israel Ministry of Education and Culture. Funds for the project
were provided by research group number SRS/WA-ISR-20-66 of the
International Research Program, Social and Rehabilitation Services,
U.S. Department of Health, Education, and Welfare,
as well as by the Israel Ministry of Education and Culture.

Printed in the United States of America

10 9 8 7 6 5 4 3 2 1

Prentice-Hall International, Inc., *London*
Prentice-Hall of Australia, Pty. Ltd., *Sydney*
Prentice-Hall of Canada, Ltd., *Toronto*
Prentice-Hall of India Private Limited, *New Delhi*
Prentice-Hall of Japan, Inc., *Tokyo*

To Barbara Biber—

who has inspired me and a whole generation of people concerned
with the welfare of young children. Her original and clear thinking,
her warm humanity and deep concern for the child and his maximum
development in all areas of his life have created a profound philosophy
of education that will enrich future generations.

Contents

4   **Curriculum   89**

5   **Parents   208**

Epilogue   215

Bibliography   227

Foreword

During the past decade, one of the major efforts in the study and development of preschool programs for disadvantaged children has been launched in the United States. Project *Head Start* is one of the more visible results of that effort. In addition, new models and programs of early childhood education have been created and tested and programs developed from a range of theoretical positions.

Given the work of American early childhood educators, why do we need to turn to Israel as a source of knowledge about such programs? That small country certainly has many fewer educational resources. In addition, the problems of disadvantaged children are certainly different in Israel from the problems in the United States. Although each country has elements of its population that suffer from poverty and discrimination, the differences in income between affluent and underprivileged families are far less in Israel than in our country. The differences in culture, however, are probably far greater. The privileged in Israel include persons of European heritage, whereas the disadvantaged are more recent arrivals from North Africa and the Middle East.

Although the differences between the American experience and the Israel experience are great, there are similarities, similarities in concerns as well as in approaches to educational problems.

Sylvia Krown, in collaboration with Miriam Many, provides us with a vivid picture of an experimental program for disadvantaged children. The program is brought to life in this volume with narrative and anecdotal records so that while the differences between the American and Israeli experience can be noted, the similarities and commonalities among all young children also become apparent. The program is based as much on the traditions of American early childhood education as on the Israeli experience. We have here a case study of an educational program that can be easily understood by teachers and students of early childhood education. The program presented is distinctive enough to provide American educators with an important learning opportunity.

The model of curriculum development used in this project is significantly different from most of those used for disadvantaged children in this country. The program might be characterized as an emergent one. Rather than have content and method prespecified for each child by a group of university-based researchers, the program was allowed to grow differently in each center, based upon the identified needs and interests of each group of children. It represented a collaborative effort on the part of teachers, researchers, parents, and ancillary personnel. The teachers remained in control of program elements while the university personnel served as advisors and consultants.

The model of program development used was based upon a clearly articulated rationale as the basis of selection of activities. Psychodynamic theory provided one root of that rationale; progressive early childhood educational philosophy provided another. The teachers were concerned with the social behavior of the children and their emotional development, while intellectual and language activities also were provided. The program was activity-oriented, with play used as the basis for intellectual learning and each child's activities providing the basis for language acquisition. Formal teacher-directed activities also were provided when appropriate, and the content was organized into "areas of interest," not unlike the units found in many American schools.

Much of the program development consisted in helping teachers become sensitive to learning opportunities that arose in the daily life of a group of children and in the community that surrounds them. Teachers were helped to become involved in stimulating and directing children's play.

Even the celebration of holidays was carefully analyzed to make it more consistent with the purposes of the programs. Although these holidays are different from those celebrated in American schools, there is a lesson to be learned from the deemphasis of celebrations and the involvement of parents to the point of having the parents perform for the children rather than the other way around, which is too often the case in our schools.

Although no hard data on the effects of the program are reported in this volume, the impressions presented are that the disadvantaged and privileged children became more similar by the end of the program. Evidence is also provided of parent satisfaction in the program. In addition, the teachers reported that they too changed as a result of their involvement. The fact that teacher involvement in research provides excellent staff development is a lesson we have almost forgotten from the days when action research was popular in our schools.

There is much here that is of worth to the American reader. Although the names of teachers and children may seem strange at first, once the reader accommodates to them he will find much that is familiar in the educational setting and much that is worth study and reflection as well as application to the American early childhood educational scene.

BERNARD SPODEK

Preface

Background: The Research Setting

In September 1967, a two-year research study "The Effects of Hetero-geneous Grouping and Compensatory Measures on Culturally Disadvan-taged Preschool Children In Israel," began in Jerusalem. For the purposes of the study, four nursery schools with children of selected families were established. The children were all three years old at the beginning of the study and remained in the nurseries until the age of five, when they en-tered the national kindergarten system. This book is an account of the methods and educational approach used at the nurseries of the research study.

One objective of the study was to shed light on the question of whether integrating very young children of disadvantaged parents with children of middle-class parents in the same nursery school setting would stimulate the development of the disadvantaged group. Therefore, the children were studied in mixed, heterogeneous groups of advantaged and disadvantaged children as well as in a homogeneous group of disadvan-taged children exclusively.

Another objective was to identify and pinpoint more clearly the com-ponents of the deficits revealed by the disadvantaged children through ob-serving them together in close proximity under identical conditions in the same nursery schools. In this manner, it was hoped to gain more under-standing of the nature and causes of the intellectual gap and social distance between the two groups. The insights and knowledge gained by the con-stant comparison of the two groups were to be used in the process of developing and evaluating educational and emotional experiences which also would meet the specific needs of the disadvantaged children.

In addition, the study was designed to observe whether the educational methods developed by the project could be successfully applied to a homogeneous group of culturally disadvantaged children. The basic philosophy underlying the educational approach that was used is described in this book. Its goal was to integrate maximal intellectual stimulation with mental health principles and concern for children's emotional and developmental growth needs; it looked upon cognitive and emotional development as interrelated rather than as separate areas in a child's development. A self-motivated and "activity" approach to learning was the foundation of the educational philosophy. The program was basically designed to meet the normal needs of all children (on the premise that all children have the same fundamental needs). In addition, the program paid particular attention to alleviating the specific disabilities that the culturally disadvantaged child presented in his reaction to the activities and experiences of a nursery school that provided full opportunities for interaction with the people and events in his environment.

As stated above, four classes for three-year-olds were established. In three of these classes, one-third of the children were chosen from low socioeconomic, minimally educated, culturally disadvantaged families, whereas the remaining two-thirds were chosen from middle-class, relatively intellectual homes. In the fourth group all the children were from low socioeconomic, culturally disadvantaged families.

The same educational approach and compensatory methods were used in all four nursery groups. The children were all tested before and after the two-year program, and control groups of children in nearby neighborhood nurseries were similarly tested. The children in the program were under continual observation by trained observers as well as by the teachers, and there were written recordings of detailed and extensive observations of the children. These observations were used as one of the basic means of obtaining the qualitative information sought in this study.

Specifically, there were ninety-six children in the program—forty-eight from middle-class, culturally advantaged families, and forty-eight from culturally disadvantaged families. The families were chosen according to the following criteria:

CULTURALLY DISADVANTAGED

1. Both parents were of Middle Eastern or North African origin.
2. Neither parent had received more than an elementary school education.
3. Fathers were employed in semi-skilled or unskilled occupations, manual labor.

UPPER MIDDLE CLASS

1. Families were of Western or European origin.
2. Both parents were graduates of secondary schools, and one, at least, had continued beyond this.
3. Fathers (or parents) belonged to the higher occupational strata such as professions or business.

The children and families are referred to throughout the book as the D (disadvantaged) group—D children, D parents, D's, etc., and those of the second group as P (privileged)—P children, P parents, P's, etc. There were twenty-four children in each group with two fully qualified teachers. The heterogeneous groups consisted of sixteen P children and eight D children.

The project was sponsored by the International Research Program, Social and Rehabilitation Services of the Department of Health, Education and Welfare in the United States with the cooperation of the Israel Ministry of Education and the Municipality of Jerusalem and was carried out under the auspices of the Hebrew University in Jerusalem.

At the request of the Ministry of Education in Israel, this book was prepared for the use of nursery teachers and describes the educational philosophy, the curriculum and compensatory methods used as they evolved during the two year-period. The final report and the findings of the research are still in preparation and will appear at a later date.

ACKNOWLEDGMENTS

I wish to express my gratitude and deep appreciation to Dr. Dina Feitelson, of the Haifa University, the principal investigator of the research project "The Effects of Heterogeneous Grouping and Compensatory Measures on Culturally Disadvantaged Preschool Children in Israel," for her helpful advice and encouragement in the preparation of this work. I am deeply indebted to her and to the entire staff involved in the project from which this book stems. The coordinated efforts of all concerned provided the basic material upon which this book is built.

I am especially grateful to Miriam Many, who painstakingly sifted through the observer's notes, the teacher's diaries, and the minutes of meetings in order to gather the anecdotal material which is such a vital part of the book. Her involved interest and helpful suggestions during the writing process were a most valuable contribution.

In particular, I would like to express my admiration and appreciation to the teachers who contributed so much of their own personalities and creativity in developing the program described:

Leah Ben Zeev	Shulamit Morashti
Zipora Greenfield	Hadassa Nir
Yehudit Vandenberg	Rina Ephron
Shulamit Meir	Zipora Shier

to the music teacher, Leah Hellner, whose imaginative work provided us all with a unique experience, and also to Dr. Morton Kaufman, whose analytic insights added another dimension to our understanding of the children.

Many thanks to Shoshana Weintraub whose excellent observational records were invaluable. I am indebted to my dear friend, Shirley Lashner Spira, who spent many long hours with me reading and correcting the manuscript. I am especially grateful to Nizza Naftali, Chief Supervisor of Kindergartens in the Ministry of Education, who suggested that this book be written and who advised, encouraged, and prodded until it was produced.

My deepest gratitude to my husband and daughter who were so forbearing and helpful during the long hours when our normal family activities had to be curtailed.

S.K.

Introduction

TEAM WORK

This book is a report of two years of intensive work on the part of the investigators, teachers, and children. The nature of the project was such that it could not have been carried out in the spirit in which it was conceived without much good will, *joint* thinking, groping, and consultations. The definitions of the problems, the work that was done, the plans that were made, the successes and the failures were the products of the team.

Aside from the research staff, our working team consisted of eight teachers (two in each group), one music teacher, two investigators, one coordinator, and a child analyst who met with us occasionally.

The responsibility of the team was to observe the two groups of children, to analyze and define their differences, and then to plan and implement a curriculum that would ameliorate the problems of the D children and at the same time stimulate the P children toward maximum growth. This required much soul-searching, honesty, and self-criticism, as well as willingness to learn from others and to be ready to make changes.

The special requirement of our project demanded considerable readjustment on the part of our teachers. As nursery school teachers in Israel, they had been accustomed to much independence, since each nursery is a separate institution in a separate building with no principal or director. They now had to become members of a team. They had to accustom themselves to continuous observation, and accept the fact that project members dropped in frequently. They had to participate in intensive discussions and consultations and had to subscribe to the team approach as the mode of handling problems and of evolving a new approach to curriculum planning and practice. Specifically, two problems needed to be worked out before the team became comfortable in its new method of work: working in teams of two, and joint curriculum planning.

Working in Teams of Two

The need for two teachers in each nursery became clear as we decided on the format of the nursery groups. Deprived and privileged children were in the same nursery and were exposed to the same program. We wanted to give the deprived children optimal help so that they would derive full benefit from their contact with the privileged children. At the same time, the privileged children needed full teacher attention in order to function at their best. When team-teaching was originally proposed by the investigators, it appeared to present the greatest stumbling block to the project since it so directly countered the prized independence of each individual teacher. The teachers expressed much doubt and anxiety about how they would adjust to working in pairs. In the three-week preliminary orientation seminar for the staff, a block of time was deliberately set aside to air the feelings about this plan and to discuss why it was necessary to the project. Two American early childhood educators visiting Israel were specially invited to the seminar to relate their own experiences in working in teams and to tell how enriching work under similar conditions had been for them.

The warm personal relations that finally developed in each pair of the four teams of teachers proved to be one of the most positive forces of the project. Each day after the children left, the staff remained in the nurseries to discuss and record what had happened, to talk about a particular child or a challenging curriculum problem, and to make plans or preparations for the next day.

Joint Curriculum Planning

In spite of the fact that our teachers theoretically accepted the need for broad joint planning, thinking, and consultation, in practice it required considerable painful readjustment on their part. Every activity that as nursery school teachers they had previously offered as part of their usual program, every story they had been accustomed to tell, every holiday celebration they had carried out, was subject to joint scrutiny and evaluation, and often to change. It required tremendous good will and a sense of purpose and enthusiasm, as well as delicacy and sensitivity on the part of everyone, to make the changes palatable and even desirable.

The three-week intensive orientation seminar and workshop that took place at the Hebrew University before the school year began was an im-

portant step in demonstrating to each of us the fruitfulness of joint thinking. Together we listened to lectures and discussed characteristic three-
year-old behavior; aspects of cultural deprivation, of intellectual development and learning problems, of play and its role in the emotional and
intellectual development of young children; and specific cultural values of
the various ethnic communities. We conducted a series of workshops which
dealt with planning the curriculum, techniques of language stimulation and
sharpening perception, plans for the first days and mother-child separation
problems, relations with parents, purpose and methods of home visits, and
techniques and plans for note-taking and recording.

The seminar and the workshops succeeded in giving each participant,
including the investigators, the feeling that he had learned and thought a
great deal and that there were many yet unanswered questions. An especially important and exceptionally pleasant outcome was the formation of a
very real group that had gone through a unifying, joint experience and
was united by a common purpose. Naturally, in the course of the work,
there were difficulties, and the teachers moved at differing rates of progress,
but, in spite of this, the individual members of the team were ready to
accept each other.

A more subtle difficulty arose in the area of the joint educational
planning when it became clear that the teachers were requesting highly-
developed, specific modes of work. It was a slow process before they fully
understood that actual daily practice was to be developed according to
each one's initiative and the needs of the children, while at the same time
all would be adhering to a basic joint philosophy and point of view arrived at in our staff meetings. At first this tended to produce insecurities on
the part of the teachers, especially since cut-and-dried solutions and "lesson plans" were not specifically defined. The guidelines that were developed were a basic rationale of the hows and whys of program planning.
The teachers were not told *what* to teach but instead were helped to think
how to teach. They met the challenge beautifully. They were creative, in-
ventive, resourceful, and thoughtful, and together we hammered out the
program and the general approach which this book depicts.

In addition to regular individual supervisory sessions in each group,
an evening staff meeting took place once a week. At these meetings, we
discussed curriculum plans and difficulties, made equipment suggestions
and planned parents' meetings, and discussed home visits and approaches
to parents. Frequently we would spend an evening discussing an individual
child and trying to anlyze what the source of his difficulties were and how
the nursery could be of help. We occasionally invited guests who were
equipped to help us plan science and art programs or who could contribute a deeper understanding of an individual child and his emotional diffi-

culties. Occasional tensions among staff members also were aired at the meetings. At times we held these meetings in the respective nurseries so that we could see each others' work. The teachers always felt enriched by such visits and felt that they learned new techniques from each other.

When the two-year program ended, all the staff members felt it was difficult to separate. The teachers, especially, missed a forum in which to discuss problems and learn from one another, and they felt the need to continue meeting to exchange ideas. In the year following the end of the project, several meetings of the staff were held, as well as innumerable informal meetings.

It is our hope that the experience that was so stimulating and enjoyable to all of us will serve as a spur to others to organize themselves into teams in order to achieve more satisfying and effective work.

Rationale of the Program

TWO CHILDREN

Uri (P)[1]

Three-year-old Uri was round-faced, red-cheeked, blue-eyed, very sturdy, with a usually placid-to-happy and interested expression on his face. He walked steadily and unhurriedly, with deliberate movements; he seemed quite sure of himself but was not overly assertive. He was dressed cleanly and appropriately and had a scrubbed look when he arrived in the morning.

His first days at school seemed to be a pleasant and satisfying experience for him. He went directly to the blocks and began piling and then lining them up in a row, and within a few days he was making an enclosure of four walls and a very exact roof, usually with an automobile or bulldozer inside. He tried the paints, the plasticene, the sand, and the water box, listened to stories with great interest, and loved the rhythms period. Each new piece of equipment and material absorbed him.

The following is an excerpt from the observer's notes during the second week of the program:

SEPTEMBER 1967: Heterogeneous Group

When the others drift inside (after their first "trip"), Uri remains alone outside on the porch near the water box. He tries to fill his pail by placing it in the water, which is too shallow. He therefore does not suceed in filling it more than a a quarter full. He persists in this activity for 11 minutes; each time the water spills out as he tilts his pail to scoop up the water. Judy comes and fills her pail by using a small cup which she first fills with wa-

[1]See page xiv for definitions of P and D.

ter and then pours into her pail. Uri sees this but makes still another attempt at his own method. He then takes a small toy milk bottle, fills it and pours the water into his pail repeatedly, until it is full. He is pleased, looks at the teacher for approval, pours the water out and feverishly begins refilling his pail by the same method. As he continues filling and pouring he works faster and faster, very pleased at his success.

He successfully handles Ron (P), the "boss," who has also joined them at the water box. Ron has immediately "employed" the two children to fill his pail for him. He then takes the pails which the children have filled and waters the garden. At first Uri is glad to fill Ron's pail in order to be playing with him, but after he has filled it several times, he again fills his own and he too waters the garden. Ron gives him instructions to refill his pail, but Uri demurs and continues with his own watering. Ron continues to ask Uri to fill his pail and occasionally Uri does this (in order to maintain his relationship with Ron) and then continues with his own work.

Uri then goes inside to the block corner and sees Oded (P), who has arranged a line of automobiles and is building with blocks. Uri asks "What are we building?" and Oded answers "A bridge." At Uri's request, Oded gives him an automobile and Uri moves it about and then builds a garage around it saying, "This will be the roof, right?" No answer. He repeats, "This will be the roof, right?" Just then his building collapses. With teacher's encouragement, he rebuilds it. He is really playing alone but seems to feel very much in contact with Oded who is building near him.

At one point, when teacher admires and encourages Naomi (D), who is also building near him, Uri says, "I am making one too." Teacher asks "What?" He answers, "A bench." Teacher asks, "Who can sit on the bench?" Uri, with a twinkle in his eye answers, "An auto." When teacher asks, "Can an auto sit on a bench?" Uri laughs, shakes his head to indicate "No" and seems to be enjoying himself tremendously. Then he says "I can sit on it," and sits down very gingerly. The teacher makes a gesture as if she too will sit down on the "bench," then gets up and asks, "Why can't I sit on it?" Uri thinks a moment and then says, "Because it's too small." Teacher replies, "Right, it is too small."

Uri was able to separate from his parents and adjust to nursery with apparent ease. His mother and father brought him in the morning and then went off to work. Nursery school perhaps held fewer fears for him because the mother of the child next door, (who is a close friend) was still sitting in the nursery daily with her own child. Uri was delighted when his father came to pick him up, and showed him all the things in the nursery and what he had done.

Uri is the younger of two children, his brother being three years older. Both parents are sabras (born in Israel). His father is a businessman, and his mother is a teacher. They live in a large house with a well-tended garden. The atmosphere in the home is very child-centered. Mother spends most of the afternoons and evenings with the children, reads to them a great deal, watches them draw, encourages their play, and arranges for mutual visits with other children. The attic room is arranged as a playroom filled with toys. The family often takes trips together. Both parents seem to enjoy the children, and Uri's father is especially proud of Uri who resembles him. Uri's mother was concerned about Uri who had begun to stammer a bit. She said he is very talkative but could not seem to get the words out fast enough. The teacher indicated that it might be a passing developmental phase because Uri seems so well-organized and relaxed.

David (D)

Three-year-old David was small for his age and very wiry, with clever, shining brown eyes and sallow skin. He looked tense and fearful, hung his head, and darted suspicious glances at the teacher. He moved very slowly or even seemed to be glued to one spot, or else he darted about impulsively. He wore torn and patched pants and a sweater much too large for him, its sleeves covering his hands. He had sores covered with dirty bandages on his head.

In his first few days at the nursery, he frequently resorted to shrieking and running home. He also spent time observing the others from a distance. Most efforts of the teachers to reach him were resisted; he did not fight them, but he seemed to be untouched by their approach.

Here are some excerpts from the observation on David. Note the remarkable progress that the teacher's constant awareness of him, and her gentle prodding produced within a one-hour observation.[2]

SEPTEMBER 1967: Homogeneous Group

David is lying on the ground pushing an auto along the floor. Suddenly he gets up, goes to the yard, sucking at his sweater sleeve, and watches the children running about outdoors. He enters the room again, goes to his cubby, takes his bag of food (which he brought from home even though the families were requested not to send food), chews on the leather strap and then begins to head for the outdoor gate and home.

Teacher goes to him, gently removes his bag from his shoulder, explaining to him that it is not yet time to go home but that when the time comes, she will give him his bag.

She pulls out a sack of variously colored balls and shows him each one, asking which he wants to play with. He nods at one of them without saying a word. Teacher asks if he wants to play with her. He nods yes. Just then

[2]David became one of our "success stories," as a note from the teacher's diary only five months after the beginning of the project shows:

February 1968: David is much loved, he now has no sores. The children seek his company and he succeeds in attracting children to work; he is a real leader. He builds well and talks freely about what he has built. They are complicated, thoughtful buildings.

He seems to be much more trusting, especially when we remember his previous need to be closed and suspicious.

He participates actively in group discussions at his own initiative.

Ronit comes and asks for a ball. Teacher converses with her and David clutches his ball tight for fear it will be taken from him. Teacher later throws him the ball as she talks to him but he does not move, making no effort to catch it. She does this several times and then gives up. She picks David up in her arms and takes him to the slide, talks to him, and asks if he wants to slide but he doesn't answer. She lifts him to the top, gives him a starting shove and he slides down but he makes no move to pick himself up.

Teacher takes him by the hand as she picks up a large plastic basin, explains they have to fill it with water for the sandbox. They go in and teacher asks him to put the basin under the faucet and fill it. Teacher then goes out. David works very hard to get the basin into place, tongue out, but then can't reach the faucet because the basin is in the way. He glances at the observer, stands and waits for the teacher, then goes out.

Teacher meets him outside and brings him back to the sink. She says "Oh, you can't reach the faucet. I'll open it and you stand and watch till it fills." She opens the tap and leaves. David stands, looking at the basin from time to time as it fills, but when it has filled he makes no move either to shut it off or to ask for help and the observer has to turn it off.

Teacher returns, asks David to help her carry the basin because it is heavy but he stands motionless. She takes the basin alone and David walks after her. He does not play with the water that has been placed in the sandbox.

He wanders into the room and sees some girls dancing around beating on triangles and singing la-la-la. Other children are watching the "performance." David does not sit down with the "audience" but goes off to the side and watches out of the corner of his eye. When teacher comes in and offers him some castanets (after she has shown the children how they work) he takes them and begins to try them out. Yosef (D) sits down next to him with a tambourine and it is clear that David wants it. There is a wordless exchange between them, half-smiling, half-teasing. Yosef has no intention of giving him the tambourine, but there is a sense of communication and togetherness as they each play their instruments. Later teacher asks him if he wants a triangle and he answers "yes" clearly! He takes it slowly, but then he plays it with vigor in the manner the teacher had demonstrated.

He begins to wander again, following teacher about. She has offered to play ball with several children but they have refused. When she offers to play with David, he agrees. He actually throws the ball, catches it, and even kicks it at the teacher's suggestion. Teacher tells the children to see how nicely David is playing. However, he is not ready to run after the ball when it rolls far away.

He wanders again, and then agrees to play with a mosaic game. He plays with interest for a short while then suddenly gets up, takes his bag of food and starts for home. Teacher stops him, removes his bag smilingly and asks if he has had breakfast. He shakes his head. She gives him a piece of bread and butter which he eats ravenously.

He continues to wander, usually keeping the teacher in sight, but stopping at various moments to do things on his own initiative. He finds pliers on the workbench and works diligently and intelligently to remove a nail but doesn't succeed. He stops to play with a driving wheel which he is able to fix skillfully when it comes out of its drive shaft; at one point he shows sufficient interest in what Shmuel is doing with a wagon so that

Shmuel invites him to join in. David does not answer or join him directly, but when teacher asks Shmuel if he is playing with David, Shmuel answers "Yes."

The end of the observation finds him playing alone but vigorously with the ball, throwing it, kicking it, and running after it, a slight smile on his face.

David is the seventh of eight children, ranging in age from two to fifteen; he has one sister a year younger than himself. David's father works occasionally in a shoe factory; his mother was a cleaning woman at the university but stopped work. (There are many indications that she earns money as a prostitute.)

When the social worker went to visit the family, she was shown into a filthy two-room apartment with broken furniture and four very narrow beds for five children. However, there was an incongruously modern and expensively furnished kitchen. By accident she discovered that the family owned another two-room apartment on the same floor which was lived in by the parents only—the children were not permitted inside. This flat was luxuriously and newly furnished. The neighborhood is a bad one, with many large families, children out in the streets from morning until night, and the police called in every day.

David's family is known in the neighborhood as one of the worst. His oldest brother (15) is in a probation home; all the children older than David are delinquents and truants. Two attend a school for the retarded. Their mother blames the "bad kids" in the neighborhood for leading them into wrong paths.

The children are all filthy, neglected, and bruised from stone-throwing in the street. David's mother related to the children in an aggressive manner, screaming and snarling at them and telling them to "get away." (However, when a neighbor came in to complain that one of the children had broken a window, she came to his defense by signaling her daughter to say that he was away all day and could not have done it.) She was concerned about the children and their behavior, worried about their future and made unrealistic plans for them. She blamed all her troubles on the bad neighborhood, the mini-skirts, the external immoral forces in society; she had already moved twice to improve their conditions. Actually she had thrown up her hands about the situation, and hoped things would be better for the two younger ones but was pessimistic about it. She wanted to place all of the children, except perhaps for the two younger ones, in an institution (which she felt would make them into law-abiding citizens).

Neither parent can read or write. There were no toys for the children and no provision for their intellectual development. The most characteristic of the mother's statements, which were largely a constant recounting of the outside forces working against them, was "What really matters is Luck—Mazal."

DESCRIPTION AND COMPARISON OF THE PRIVILEGED
AND DEPRIVED CHILDREN IN THE EXPERIMENT

We have presented two children, both extremely different in their development and their home conditions. Both of them were in our nurseries. Both were typical of the children in their socioeconomic group and yet atypical in that they were extremes: Uri, the well-adjusted child of a well-functioning middle-class family, and David, the intelligent but frightened and enormously restricted little boy of a disorganized, asocial lower-class family.

At three years old, our two groups showed striking differences in behavior. There was great disparity in language facility, ways of relating to adults and to each other, play, interests, information, ways of learning, understanding, exploring, and degree of self-confidence. Within each group as well there were wide variations of ability, competence, and emotional health, yet each group, despite its range of variations, differed considerably from the other. There was a broad and very clear divergence between the two groups which made itself felt at every moment.

Since we had both groups together under constant observation, we were in an advantageous position to note the differences as the children functioned side by side under the same conditions. We shall attempt to outline here, in very general terms, the most outstanding characteristics of the two groups of three-year-olds as we observed them in our nurseries at the beginning of the program. The overall picture, despite the individual differences, looked very rosy for the P children, very bleak for the D's.

The P's, of course, were not all enthusiastic, outgoing, easy in relations. There were many in the P group with great difficulties in relating to other children and in utilizing and developing their innate abilities and capacities. There were many with neurotic manifestations—fears, bedwetting, separation difficulties, character problems; mother-child relations often were very strained, and this reflected sadly in the children's feelings about themselves and their relations with others.

The D's too were not all passive and uncommunicative. Even at the outset, a few were able to express themselves well; some formed friendships and played together in simple play, and some enjoyed the nursery from the beginning.

Nevertheless, when we look at each group as a whole, the outstanding characteristics outlined below, despite the wide range of individual variations, were typical of many of the children within the group.

Physical Appearance

This was the least outstanding of the differences, except at the extremes. At first glance, a newcomer to the nursery, looking at the children's outward appearance would be unable to distinguish between most of the P and D children. At a superficial glance, they appeared to be healthy, active, and happy.

Many of the D children were dressed well, often in new clothes (perhaps bought especially because the children were attending the "university" nursery). Many of the P children were casually, often sloppily dressed. At the extremes were a small portion of D children dressed in ill-fitting, torn, hand-me-down clothes with seemingly no attention paid to taste or weather changes (sandals in winter, no sweaters or rain clothes), whereas some P children wore expensive, imported clothing.

The health of the D children was not as well protected as that of the P children—many were sent to school with fever; when sent home with an infectious children's disease, they often would come back to school the following day; sometimes they had open, neglected sores; and most of them had continuously running noses which they made no effort to wipe. Yet for the most part, they were not undernourished or sickly. Often they were sent to school having had no breakfast and were very hungry during the morning, but some would arrive holding a large roll or piece of bread.

The P children were well cared for medically and were clean. A few of the D children were filthy, even lice-infested, smelling of urine and feces, but most of them were clean.

Careful observation of the D children soon revealed basic differences in their appearance from that of the P children. There was a tense guardedness in their stance and posture that was often characteristic; their body movements were tight and inhibited, lacking the freedom and gaiety so frequently found in the P children; their facial expressions were often dissatisfied, wary, and sometimes angry. There was a depressed quality in their general appearance which made itself felt in too many instances. They gave the superficial impression of being active because they were usually in motion, but actually their activity was aimless, unplanned, and lacked interest or direction.

Activity-Passivity

The most striking difference in the two groups was in the activity level. After the initial adjustment period, which lasted an entire month for some, a great many of the P children were lively and plunged enthusiastically into the materials and activities of the program. They were purposeful, interested, and ready to try new experiences. Clearly enjoying themselves, they told their parents excitedly what they had done, expounded ideas to the teachers, and cooperated with the program.

Many of the D children were characteristically passive in spite of being in motion most of the time. As the teachers expressed it:

> Most of their time was spent wandering about doing nothing, aimlessly, lethargically and yet sometimes impulsively moving from place to place.
>
> It was difficult to interest or arouse them or give them pleasure. They moved toy automobiles; in the doll corner there was some hint of play but it was repetitive and stereotyped—feeding the dolls and moving dishes about. They picked up books, flipped the pages and put them down, picked up toys, let them drop, and continued wandering, usually finding something else to touch.
>
> We felt as though we were talking to the walls—there was a dull expression on so many faces, no aliveness or alertness. Sometimes we felt that we were speaking a foreign language to them.
>
> We visited Joseph when he was sick. He didn't move in the bed.
>
> If we don't persistently arouse some of them, nothing happens. They constantly need pushing.

Relations to People

To the extent that it is possible to generalize, it was characteristic of the P children that they were friendly, open, and outgoing. They talked a great deal to the teachers, expressed their feelings, and told stories about home. Very aware of the teacher's presence or lack of presence, they were uneasy when she was not close by; they showed their affection for her, seeking attention and approval. They were also very aware of the other children, made efforts to play near them, even though they were too young for protracted play together. Fairly soon after the beginning of the programs, they began to play in groups of two or three or more. They jockeyed for positions of leadership; formed friendship groups—in-groups and out-groups; and fought over possessions.

Again generalizing, many of the D children were withdrawn, shy, and suspicious of others. Their speech was markedly limited; they did not address the teacher and often did not answer her when she addressed them. They spoke to each other long before they began to speak to her. When they had no choice but to call the teacher, they pulled at her skirt without speaking. They did not appeal to her for help, but would give up when faced with difficulties, never thinking of turning to her.

When the teacher showed interest in them or gave them help, they at first seemed impassive and unresponsive. They did not seem to feel that the nursery was there for them but that it belonged to the teacher and said "your nursery," "your book," in contrast to the P's who immediately said "our."

Some D children seemed to be "loners" in the nursery. When one child tried to play with another, he frequently received no response. They did not fight much, but, on the other hand, most of them did not play together. When group play began, it was often in pairs. In contrast to the P's, they rarely fought over possessions, usually just giving up their claim.

The change in their relations to the teacher was gradual but dramatic. As she proved herself over and over again as a person to be trusted, they began to cluster near her and even became sticky and clingy. When she sat down, they gathered around her, wanting the physical contact; they even followed her to the toilet. They were very anxious to be liked by her and to please her. They wanted her to sit by them as they worked, and needed her encouragement or they would leave what they were doing. Some of the children tried to attract her attention in negative ways that were clearly designed to bring her to them, as, for example, open disobedience.

Some of the teachers' comments were:

They have become demanding and want to be spoiled.
Sometimes they don't need any help but ask for it in order to get attention.
They have begun to shout for me across the room.
When they finally do begin to relate to someone, they form a very close attachment.

This phase, although protracted, later passed as the D children became truly independent and sure of the adults and of their own capabilities.

The P's, on the other hand, had begun their relationship with the teacher by clearly indicating that they needed and enjoyed her loving care. However, as they quickly became oriented to the new situation of nursery school, they began to look to the teacher for an entirely different type of attention. They wanted her to show interest in what they were doing, seeking her intellectual participation rather than her protection.

Following the clinging phase, there was also a change in attitude toward possessions among the D's. In contrast to their previous immediate surrender of a disputed toy, at a later stage, the children were observed piling all sorts of things (no matter what) into a wagon and pulling it possessively. After a further period of time, when new equipment or toys were brought into the nursery, the D children would fight furiously over possessions. It took some time until they were able to learn to take turns.

Attitudes to Themselves

The P children, for the most part (and here, too, there were many individual differences), were high-spirited, often gay, positive, and self-assertive. Though they had many misgivings and fears in the new nursery school experience, many seemed to have enough self-confidence to be ready to try new things and acquire new skills, and the others usually could be persuaded to try. They were very pleased when praised and showed their work proudly.

Many of the D children, on the other hand, were unenthusiastic, and there seemed to be a sad quality about many of them. When confronted with a new task, they appeared afraid to tackle it. They were unsure of themselves and would shrug their shoulders in refusal or give up as soon as they met with the first difficulty. They tended to drift to the small, structured materials where they could sit at tables and feel less conspicuous, rather than building with blocks, doing carpentry, or anything that seemed to require more self-assertion. When they did begin to build, their buildings tended to be small, in contrast to the characteristically expansive buildings of the P group.

The D children frequently showed no pride in their work, and the teacher's praise did not appear to produce the same effect that it did on the P children. Saddest of all was that it never entered their minds to make demands, as if they did not feel that they deserved special attention. They seemed to have so little sense of worth or importance, so little awareness of themselves as unique individuals, that many of them even were unable to recognize their own photographs, let alone feel care and concern for their bodies and their appearance.

Language

The differences between the groups in their use of language were striking. Most of the P's seemed to babble much of the time, making contacts with teacher and children, suggesting ideas, relating experiences, giving instructions, asking questions, and reacting to everything that occurred. Their language was often surprisingly rich and expressive. They used concepts of space and distance and names of places, despite their considerable confusion on these subjects. For the most part, they spoke in short sentences, lisped and spoke unclearly, made grammatical errors, and created words when they did not know the correct ones, but they all verbalized and were easily understood.

The D's used speech in a much more constricted manner. When they spoke, they used isolated words and seemed unable to construct a whole sentence. The higher-spirited children would hum nonsense syllables as they worked or played—lalalo, trr-trr, and so forth. Their vocabulary was very often limited; they did not know the names of things, and rarely used connective words, such as *and, but, if,* or relative words, such as *above, low, tall, around,* or *into.* Their lack of information was sometimes surprising; they did not know the names of animals, colors, or clothing, could not name the parts of their bodies, and did not even know the word for helicopter, although helicopters passed overhead frequently. (The P children knew not only the word but also the implication that probably more wounded were being brought to a nearby hospital.)

Many D children were unaccustomed to listening. They found difficulty in concentrating for more than five minutes when being told something, sat with blank expressions on their faces, and then began to fidget and get up. They were unable to listen to a whole story. Many were unable to follow directions that were given to an entire group; when each child was given directions individually, with ample demonstration of what was meant, the directions were more often understood. Many of them spoke very unclearly and could not be understood by their teachers; their pronunciation was poor, and they used incorrect grammar. Several of the children did not speak at all in the nursery, either to other children or to adults.

Modes of Thinking

It was characteristic of the P children that they were interested in knowing things and in discovering new information. They were curious about animals, about people and how they behave, about natural processes, about work processes, and machinery—in short, about almost everything with which they came into contact. They were fascinated by the everyday things around them—automobiles, electric switches, water faucets, garbage collection, buying and selling. They looked at, examined, and when possible took things apart, tried them out, and asked questions. They listened with interest when they were given information by an adult. Some were able to describe what they observed and to notice differences and similarities, and they were capable of classifying items with similar characteristics into groups. Many also looked for the "whys" and "hows" of occurrences. They were full of ideas, in general and in their play, and showed much initiative in carrying them out.

In contrast, the D's often seemed to perceive the world around them as if in a fog. Nothing seemed to have any order, system, or clarity. Things had no names and were not remembered even though they had happened half an hour earlier. They were perceived vaguely with no apparent notice of any detail or distinctive features. Unable to discriminate the various aspects of what was happening when taken to the next-door biological museum where they saw insects, small animals, and snakes, one of the children asked "Why were there so many donkeys?" (It would seem that donkey was his generic term for animal.)

They seemed confused in their sense of time, place, and order. It was very difficult for them to grasp that the nursery day followed a definite schedule—that one activity followed another regularly—or to remember that each piece of equipment in the nursery had a special place. They had particular difficulties in sitting at the tables for meals and frequently jumped up and went off.

Most frustrating to the teachers was what seemed to be their lack of interest, enthusiasm, and curiosity. They seemed to let things happen without trying to find out what had happened or why. The teachers complained:

> On trips they saw nothing and did not seem to know how to look. We would stop at a tree and I had to force them to look upward to see what the top of the tree looked like. No passing bird interested them and even a train going by very close to them in the field aroused no interest. They didn't even look at it.

They seemed to accept things that happened as if some magical force brought them about, and they did not think to question or even to examine how anything worked.

They showed little initiative and rarely seemed to produce any ideas for play. The teachers found that they themselves had to introduce every new idea and had to excite them into playing. For instance, the D's would hold a driving wheel and "drive," whereas the P's would hold a driving wheel and "drive" to a specific place and remember to need gasoline on the way.

Impulsivity vs. Ability to Tolerate Frustration and Delayed Gratification

Both groups of three-year-olds had much difficulty in tolerating not getting what they wanted when they wanted it. Both groups had to learn about taking turns and sharing. They had to learn that sometimes it pays off to wait a little longer, to work a little harder, and then to get a better reward.

However, the D group, in spite of their usual apathy, at times would react with surprising impulsivity. They would suddenly run away from or destroy something they were making if it were not going well; some would suddenly run home. At the beginning, the D children frequently exhibited scenes of impulsive behavior, such as throwing themselves on the floor and kicking and screaming when they had to accept restrictions. The P children, on the whole, were more controlled and more tolerant of reality restrictions.

Painting and Music

The D children responded immediately to the music and rhythms, the colors and painting. They were more spontaneous, original, and free than were the P's and expressed greater delight when the music teacher appeared. Their paintings had far more originality and free use of color than those of the P's; their feeling for rhythm was delightful.

Parents

It was interesting that when we asked the teachers to talk about the differences between the groups of children, they usually began by mentioning the parents. The first thing that struck them was the difference in how the two groups of mothers reacted to the teachers and to the adjustment period.

The P mothers were concerned about their children's adjustment to the nursery. They stayed with them or arranged that a relative or maid stay. They understood that the children were going through a difficult transitional period, were concerned when they cried, and were interested in what they were doing. They tried to cooperate with the teachers and their suggestions and shared information with the teachers about their children's behavior at home.

Most of the D mothers seemed unaware that their children were undergoing adjustment problems and showed little interest in how the children were reacting. Many did not come to the nursery when they were invited, and they seemed indifferent to what their children were doing. In many cases, the D mothers delivered the children to the nursery and immediately set out for home. If the child protested, they would reassure the teacher "He'll get used to it, he'll get used to it," and had no patience with the children's protests. A few lied both to the teachers and the children as to their time of return, promising to be back in a few minutes and returning at the end of the day. Furthermore, they gave no pertinent information to the teachers about their children or their home.

HYPOTHESES CONCERNING ORIGINS OF THE DEFICIT

Since the children in both groups were within the normal intelligence range, we asked ourselves what particular aspects in their home backgrounds might have caused such great differences in their emotional development—their behavior with people, their feelings about themselves, their use of language, and their mode of thinking.[3] We felt that is was necessary to make some hypotheses about the precipitating causes of these differences in order to define for ourselves the specific deficits of the D group. On the basis of the deficits in the home situations, we hoped to be able to plan if and how we could compensate for them in the nursery school setting.

The first outstanding difference between the two groups was the apparently different quality of the mother-child relationship. The consistent acceptance, understanding, communication, deep concern, and protection that is associated with "good mothering" appeared often to be deficient or to have a different quality in the D group. Having provided the children with their physical needs, there were many mothers in this group who did not seem to be aware of the need to be on constant guard to protect the child's health and safety; these mothers also appeared unaware of the importance of their role in the child's emotional development and happiness. They did not realize that playing with and talking to the child, being concerned when he was upset, and expressing consistent affection, understanding, love, and praise were as essential to his development as food and shelter. They often seemed unaware of the relationship between emotional well-being and behavior.

Of course, the D mothers felt and demonstrated much affection for their children, hugged and kissed them, called them pet names, and told them they were "good." It was when the children were annoying, fretful, and demanding that the mothers did not seem to realize that they had to consider the cause of such behavior and to act accordingly. They felt justified and "educational" when they told the children to "shut up," when they punished them or sent them from the room for their "bad" behavior. They appeared to be unaware that it was important for the child always to feel accepted and understood, even when he was behaving badly. It was not that the D mother loved her child less than the P mother loved hers,

[3]In contrast to many other countries, there was usually not a marked disparity in the economic levels of the two groups. Israel's wage and tax structure tend to create an egalitarian economy where, except for a small group at each extreme of the population, the range of incomes is not very wide. In our school population, there was a small well-established group, but many of our P parents were students and just entering professions, generally overburdened with economic worries, still paying for their homes, their furniture, and so forth. On the other hand, although several of the D families were concerned primarily with subsistence, many of our D parents were on a fairly good economic level, some of them better off financially than many of our P parents.

In addition, the problem to which cultural deprivation is often attributed, that of broken families and the absent father, was not a factor in our D group. With one exception, the families were all whole. Among the P groups there were only two instances of divorced parents.

but she frequently seemed unaware of the nature of the child's needs. Many of these mothers, therefore, did not succeed in conveying to the child the basic feeling that he was someone very special and important, or that she loved and understood *him* and *his own* specific individual qualities.

In the large families, there was a tendency to group all the children together and to fail to underline each child's individuality. Often, in fact, the child did not have his own bed or even a permanent place in a specific bed. (The house may have had a large, well-furnished living room, but there was rarely more than one small bedroom for as many as seven or more children.)

In addition, many of the mothers seemed to have a basically passive attitude to life and a lack of faith in their own ability to change things. Their feeling that they had no control over their fate extended to their attitude to mothering. They did not see *themselves* as responsible for their children's behavior—they might complain and worry about them but did not seem to see the connection between their own relationship with the child and the child's subsequent behavior. When the child became seriously ill or was hurt as a result of neglect, the mother was upset at the ill fortune that had occurred but did not blame herself for not having prevented it. The mothers felt angry but helpless when their children played with dangerous objects or out in the streets in traffic. This passivity extended to their feelings about the neighborhood: "The neighbors are all bad, so how can I bring up good children in such a neighborhood?" The D mothers seemed to have a general tendency to blame external forces and often had a hostile attitude to the neighbors.

They felt they had adequately performed their mother role by providing a home and food, some clothing, and some discipline. Our D mothers were burdened with very large families and a constant feeling that they could not cope with their heavy, never-ending load of work. Many felt obliged to devote enormous energies to keeping the house clean, a value that was very highly regarded, and they often had to keep the children out of the house to preserve its cleanliness. Some of the D mothers had to go out to work, and a few had to cope with poverty and illness. Yet in spite of these burdens, what appeared to underlie their seemingly shallow relationship with their children was their personal experience with their own mothers, who had manifested similar attitudes. Having themselves experienced feelings of rejection and hostility in their relations with their mothers, they were unable to formulate different behavior toward their own children. It often seemed that they themselves needed personally to live through a different kind of relationship—an experience of being understood, respected, and cared for—before they could learn to communicate with their own children in a more accepting way.

It was our hypothesis that this deficiency in consistent concern and care inhibited the D child from developing a feeling of basic trust in adults. Since he did not look to them for protection, he had to learn too early to fend for himself. He was emotionally not yet ready for such premature independence and thus was torn between his strong needs for dependency, love, and protection and the demands of adjusting to the real world he lived in. He was cautious and suspicious of people, and he seemed wary of closer relationships, possibly because of his fear that they would be inconsistent and disappointing.

It was our assumption that since the D child was not accustomed to much encouragement, praise, nor approval, but rather was often shouted at, beaten, blamed, accused, and restrained from doing what he wanted, he had developed a feeling of inadequacy and inferiority. He felt himself unworthy, and had little faith in his capabilities; he did not see himself as a unique individual with his own praiseworthy qualities, hence his lowered self-esteem, confused self-identity, and lack of belief in his own capacity to achieve something.

Where there are optimum understanding and accepting and guiding love transactions between parent and child, the child learns to control certain behavior in order to please his parents. Our D children, never having had the advantage of such a relationship, had not learned to defer gratification of their immediate desires in the certain knowledge that their parents could be trusted to arrange things. We assumed that this was the cause of their impulsive behavior and low frustration tolerance.

In the more severe cases, the children were frequently exposed to an atmosphere of demoralization. They were witness to lack of solidarity between their mothers and fathers and sometimes severe marital disharmony, with mothers being beaten and parents shouting and cursing; they were exposed to scenes of neighbors fighting and police involvement, to violent behavior and juvenile delinquency; some of the children were themselves severely beaten and roundly cursed. All of this seemed to be the background for these children's deeply rooted suspiciousness and lack of trust.

The second outstanding difference between the two groups was in the area of intellectual development. In many of the D families there was a marked absence of a teaching adult in the child's early life. Here, too, many of the mothers did not see that they had a role to play as the teacher of their children. They did not behave as the bridge or translator of the outside world to the world of the child. They did not try to clarify, explain, or straighten out his confused thinking.

In contrast to the P mothers, who used language as the chief means of communication with their children, there was limited language communication in the D homes. Much of the language exchange consisted of the mother's giving orders or expressing disapproval. She had little time for or interest in listening to the children or playing with them, nor did she try to explain events or take the children on outings in order to point out interesting things. Unlike the P mothers, the D mothers did not accompany their activities with words, keeping up a running patter with the child, nor did they teach the names of things as they were introduced. Stories were seldom told and books were almost never read.

In general, conversation in the home was very limited and was restricted largely to the concrete events of daily living. Many of the D mothers themselves had limited vocabularies and weak knowledge and use of Hebrew, and they were sometimes quite inarticulate. They had no books in the house and rarely read, and in many cases there was so little discussion among the adults that the children did not hear much real conversation. To the extent that language was taught, it was designed to teach the children to repeat certain words or to answer questions for show. If an explanation was given to the child, it was final and "full stop," in contrast to the answer in the P home which was usually given in such a way as to encourage more questions.

The D parents saw the children's natural curiosity as a nuisance— "he gets into everything," "he takes things apart," "he pesters me with questions." They saw their major educational role as teaching the child to obey and to conform to the rules of the home.

Nor did the D mothers view the play of children as an important process in their development. Hence they did not encourage it by buying toys or playing with their children, and only occasionally did they show the children that they understood and enjoyed what they were playing. It did not occur to them to express in words what the children were playing ("The dolly is hungry and you are feeding her"), or to join the child in his play. The purchase of toys was near the bottom of their list of priorities, which was headed by such items as buying a television set, a washing machine, fancy furnishings, clothing, and other status symbols.

It was our hypothesis that the children's lack of early experience in talking, listening, and being listened to; in being stimulated to notice things; in playing and expressing feelings and experiences in play; and asking for and receiving explanations, was the background for the verbal deficiencies of many of the D children and for their inability to perceive and delineate things clearly. We assumed that the active repression of the children's tendencies to explore, investigate, and ask questions was a contributing cause of apparent apathy and lack of curiosity.

Another important deficit seemed to stem from the less organized mode of living of some of the D families. There was no regular mealtime (in some families there was never a joint family meal). Bedtimes, waking times, and other routines of family living were also very irregular. We assumed that because life was irregular, the children did not develop a sense of order, of time, or of one thing following another in organized pattern.

They expected anything to happen at any moment and thus did not develop an understanding or expectation of natural laws and sequences. This lack of order led to difficulties in systematic thinking and would lead to difficulties in logical thinking based on the premise that one thing follows another. There could also be no incentive for scientific curiosity if the children believed that things happen with no seeming explanation or logic. (Also, in some cases, another stumbling block in the D children's development was the atmosphere of magical thinking and superstition by which they were surrounded.) The parents' lack of faith in their ability to control their own destiny, their feelings of helplessness in the face of events and phenomena, their own deficit in cause-and-effect thinking, and their superstitious fears all left their marks on the children's mode of thinking.

CURRICULUM IMPLICATIONS FOR THE COMPENSATORY PROGRAM

On the basis of the foregoing hypotheses concerning the causes of the deficits of the D children, we then planned our nursery program in the hope that a new corrective experience in living—within the nursery school setting—would compensate for some of these emotional and intellectual lacks. Since we believed that the culturally deprived child frequently has been deprived emotionally as well as intellectually, it seemed clear to us that if we were to relate only to his poor language development and scant store of information, we would not be dealing with the roots of the problem.

The emotional and intellectual development of a child appears to be so completely interdependent that it seemed fruitless to relate to one aspect without the other. The child who has had few gratifying relationships with people; who has not been given the feeling that he is a valued person, appreciated as an individual in his own right; and who has not developed basic trust in others or belief in himself, often does not seem to develop much interest in the people and things around him—" . . . it is through the active relationship with people, it is through being known and felt and understood as a person that the child's basic curiosity and interest in the world begins to flower and develop."[4] Even more so would this seem to be true of the child who is concerned about his own self-preservation and who is involved in premature attempts at independence. He often has little available additional energy with which to look around at the world and learn new things, unless they impinge directly on him.

[4]Barbara Biber, *The Impact of Deprivation on Young Children* (New York, N. Y.: Bureau of Child Development and Parent Education, University of the State of New York, [n. d.]).

On the other hand, the child who is limited in ability to express himself and is confused by events around him cannot develop self-confidence or a belief in his ability to tackle problems and to learn. It seems that the child's personality and emotional development affect his ability to learn, and his ability to learn affects his healthy personality development— the two are integrally connected. In many cases one cannot help a child to develop rich language, logical thinking, scientific curiosity, and initiative without at the same time being concerned with the child's development of basic trust and healthy relationships with people, his ability to control impulses, and his enhanced self-esteem and true independence. Psychoanalytic theory has even proposed that abstract and symbolic thinking are dependent upon the development of ability to tolerate delayed gratification and to inhibit impulsive behavior.

The program we planned, therefore, tried to bear in mind the various aspects of the child's emotional and intellectual development. It was based on the "assumption . . . that these children will not . . . be effective learners in any *meaningful* way, unless we can help them build a kind of emotional strength along with specific skills."[5] The curriculum was designed to deal with the following areas:

Establishing a Meaningful and Satisfying Teacher-Child Relationship

The accepting and caring atmosphere in the nursery and the teacher's warm, understanding way of relating to and communicating with each child individually were designed to expose the child to a corrective experience in being accepted, protected, and valued. The teacher tried to become for the child the gratifying and supporting, yet controlling, adult who could give him a new experience in how people could care for, understand, and behave toward each other.

The teacher tried to find ways of establishing contact with each child, of showing him that she cared what happened to *him* and that she understood *his* feelings. At first she tried to be alert to sense and gratify his needs, sometimes almost before he was aware of them himself, and thus to become indispensable to him. When he was ready for it and allowed her to, she showed him affection and established friendly physical contact. By compensating in this way for his past experiences and by listening to him and trying to understand him, a deep relationship was established. His distrust and suspiciousness began to dissolve, as he gradually learned how it felt to be cared for and to care for others. The teacher became an

---

[5]Barbara Biber and Patricia Minuchin, *A Child Development Approach to Language in the Pre-School Disadvantaged Child* (New York: Bank Street Publications, 1967).

important figure to him, and it became worthwhile to him to do things to please her.

Through establishing a one-to-one relationship with each child, the teacher was able to respond to each as an individual and not just as another member of her group. In these contacts, she also tried to give him a clearer feeling of who he was, to make him aware of his likes and dislikes and of what was special about him. In order to do this she had to acquire a certain amount of background knowledge about each child and his family.

The teachers tried to be aware of and sensitive to the emotional conflicts that most nursery-age children face. They showed the children that they accepted them as they were with their fears, anger, and outbursts; they helped them to deal with and control these conflicts in their relations with adults and with other children. Through these experiences, the children learned more socially acceptable behaviors.

Clarifying Confused Ways of Experiencing Events and Things

By examining, pointing out, and dramatizing each object and event with the children, the teacher tried to shake off some of their vagueness and to help them to fully feel an experience, to become alert observers of what was happening around them. The children were stimulated to sharpen their senses to become more aware of shapes, colors, sensations, and sounds; to name things; to see differences and similarities; and to classify objects with similar characteristics. No item or event was taken for granted—everything in the immediate surroundings that impinged on the child's experience was thoroughly examined. The children discovered that to observe was to learn, and they enjoyed the process of exercising their sense perceptions.

Stimulating Acquisition of Information Through a Variety of Experiences and Materials

The equipment and variety of materials in the nursery were designed to provide the children with opportunities to become familiar with the physical facts of the world as well as to develop their own bodily skills. Through their use of climbing, balancing, pulling, and pushing equipment, and their manipulation of such materials as blocks, clay, and paints, the children developed concepts of size, weight, texture, numbers and so forth. They did not need much additional formal teaching in these areas when they had had actual experiences with real things. In addition, trips around the neighborhood and the city and related discussions, pictures, and books broadened the children's world and exposed them to additional information and concepts.

Arousing Curiosity and Readiness to Inquire, Investigate, and Experiment

The teacher was aware that her role was more than just to teach facts and introduce the child to knowledge; it included asking arousing questions and indicating ways of obtaining information. She raised or encouraged questions such as "I wonder why this block building keeps falling?"; "Where does the sand in this sand truck come from?"; "How does the carpenter do his work?"; and encouraged the children to find out through trying, questioning, exploring, and looking for answers in books and pictures. She encouraged them to discover for themselves many physical facts and laws, to sharpen their own observations, and later to look for the whys and hows of events and processes. She did not always answer questions directly but rather, when possible, guided the child in trying to find the answer himself.

When she asked a question, the teacher was careful not to give the children the feeling that she was waiting for only one "correct" answer. Rather, she showed them that she appreciated their spontaneous and original replies and that she enjoyed the way they were thinking, even if they reached the wrong conclusions. She often waited until, in their own way, the children arrived at deeper understanding; thus, they developed a belief in their own thinking ability and did not feel pressured to produce a standard, accepted answer. In other words, the teachers used the "discovery method" and the "discussion method" wherever the children were capable of responding to it, rather than the technique of direct teaching of correct facts.

The goal was to develop in each child a method of thinking based on questioning, investigation, and implicit understanding of the principle of cause and effect, rather than one based on passive and submissive acceptance and belief in magic and mysterious processes. However, the teacher did not stop at the discovery stage but later helped the children to express their findings, to integrate them, and to verbalize them in their own unique ways of expression in play, art work, simple discussions, and creative writing.

Encouraging Dramatic Play as the Means of Absorbing Knowledge and Learning

If given an opportunity, the nursery-age child freely expresses his experiences, feelings, wishes, and thinking primarily in his dramatic play. With great pleasure in his make-believe world, he expresses the ideas and emotions that he has experienced in the real world. Playing is the essence of the learning process for young children—it is the natural way they have devised for learning and it is the foundation upon which they build their ability to think. They relive their experiences and solve problems in their play and, in this way, digest and integrate their understanding of the world around them. They are stimulated by their play to use language, to learn how to get along with other children, to learn to control their impulses, to try out their ideas, and to express their feelings. They play the roles of the grown-ups who are their heroes and they also play the role of the baby they would sometimes like to be. They review the information they are being exposed to in the real world and play it over and over again until the knowledge becomes an integral part of them. Play is the young child's work and his school.

Play is also the manner in which children learn to think in symbols. It is not real life; it is "make-believe," "as-if," and it later becomes the foundation for the ability to understand the concept of symbols involved in reading, mathematics, and abstract thinking.

In our program, play was the chief tool in the teaching and learning process. The children created the play spontaneously. The role of the teacher was to provide the materials for the play—ample time, the dolls and domestic equipment, blocks, toy automobiles, dress-up clothes, crates, sand, water, clay, paints, and so forth. She also was there to provide the encouragement and the interested attention; to stimulate the play when it lagged by adding a piece of equipment or a question, or sometimes even by playing a role herself; to observe where there was confusion in thinking as revealed by the play; and to choose carefully an opportunity to clarify confusions through either stimulating a discussion or planning a trip.

It is difficult to conceive a successful program for nursery children that does not fully recognize and give ample time for play. A young child still needs to orient himself in his immediate world and to distinguish between fantasy and reality, between magic and non-magic. He must be given many opportunities to investigate the immediate world around him and to digest and integrate his findings in intensive and repeated play experiences before he is really ready to absorb and organize more complicated information in the wider world. By having many opportunities to create his own fantasy and make-believe play, he then learns to distinguish between fantasy and reality.

Developing the Intellectual Ability to See Relationships

"Seeing relationships," in the sense that Lucy Sprague Mitchell[6] has made famous in her important contributions to educational thinking, is

[6]Lucy Sprague Mitchell: *Our Children and Our Schools* (New York: Simon & Schuster, 1950).

the integration of knowledge, the end goal of the thinking process. It is not sufficient for the child to understand the purpose of a store; he needs to be helped to understand the store in its relation to where the products come from, the role of the money transaction, how and why things are weighed, and so forth. It is not sufficient for him only to observe and play bus (which is of dramatic interest to him); he needs to be led to see the relationship between the bus and roads, gasoline, haulage, and transportation.

In this area too, dramatic play plus group discussion and planning are the tools that seem to be most effective. The teacher's goal was to stimulate the children to observe things and to begin to see and express in their play the relationships between the various bits of information that they were absorbing.

Developing a Sense of Order, Space, and Time

In order to promote the development of a sense of order, space, and time, equipment was kept in clear and specified places, the schedule of the day was definite and consistent, and organization and routine were an integral part of everyday living at the nursery. The knowledge gained from such routine, that it is possible to plan and to expect one thing to follow another, was an important foundation for the evolution of logical thinking that followed.

The teachers underlined and stressed the routines of the day, and the children slowly learned that they were to sit at the table at snack time and not to jump up at will. They played games of putting things away in their proper places, and classifying them into colors, shapes, functions, as well as sizes, and amounts, games of lotto and arranging picture stories according to their sequence in time. These activities were designed to heighten the sense of order and of meaning in their everyday life.

Encouraging Creative Expression in the Arts and Music

The goal was to help the children develop a sense of their own ability and the freedom to express themselves in the plastic arts and in music. We wanted to encourage the heightened self-esteem and feeling of strength that a child feels when he produces a work of his own creation. In order to avoid stereotyped productions, the teacher stressed her appreciation and acceptance of *every child's individual expression*—there was no one *right* way to do anything, and everyone's way was accepted and valued. In music the teacher tried to intensify the ability to perceive rhythms, tones, and moods. She admired and encouraged the children's own creative movements and songs. In the arts a variety of materials was offered and the children were taught to be aware of colors, forms, and moods.

Using Supplementary Structured Learning Material

In contrast to many programs for culturally deprived children that are built largely on planned lessons and structured learning materials, our program used the structured lesson and equipment as valuable additional and supplementary material. They were used to *underline* the basic program of actual experiences with people and things and of active assimilation of information through play, creative expression, and discussion. The program evolved as a balance between structured and unstructured learning opportunities, the balance being flexible and dependent on the children's needs and responses.

Because of their deficits, we were aware that some of the D children were not always able to take full advantage of the opportunities for active investigation and discussion. They often needed additional help and direct teaching in order to be ready to use and absorb their experiences. The structured teaching lessons, therefore, were exercises and reviews of things they had met with in their actual life and play. In addition to the review of information and concepts that had arisen in play, trips, and discussions, planned teaching lessons helped the children learn specific concepts and words like, *wide, under, light, darkness, transparent, colors, numbers, many, few,* etc. Didactic materials like lottos, puzzles, form-boards, workbooks, stories in sequences, boxes of various items classified according to shapes and colors, and classification games were also used as needed. These lessons were rarely presented to the whole group. As the teacher assessed the children's needs, she worked with individual children and occasionally with small groups. Actual teaching, of course, was taking place at every moment in informal teacher-child interactions.

In addition to the constant stimulation of logical, cause-and-effect thinking through questions like "why," "how," and "what if," there were planned lessons in logical thinking based on the work of Carl Bereiter[7] and Marion Blank.[8]

The children were given tasks to perform and complete and were taught specific skills like cutting and pasting and use of art materials and carpentry. These structured tasks served a very important function in offering the children an opportunity to experience the feeling of accomplish-

---

[7]Carl Bereiter and Siegfried Engelman, *Teaching Disadvantaged Children in the Pre-School* (Englewood Cliffs, N. J.: Prentice-Hall, Inc., 1966).
[8]Marion Blank and Frances Solomon, "A Tutorial Language Program to Develop Abstract Thinking in Socially Disadvantaged Pre-School Children," *Child Development*, 34, No. 2 (1968).

ment and satisfaction in completing a specific job. In order to finish a piece of work they had to persevere, to restrain their impulsive behavior, and to plan and think. The didactic materials and the art materials were especially useful in developing these traits.

Stimulating Language Usage and Enlarging Vocabulary

It is not accidental that discussion of the important area of language development was left for last. In effect, all the previous areas of curriculum that have been described above are important aspects of the language program, designed to develop in the children the *art of communication through words*.

The language enrichment program sometimes began nonverbally simply through the development of a warm relationship between the teacher and child and a wordless exchange of interest and respect. The development of the need for and pleasure in communication with other people was the first goal of our language program.

The teachers kept up a constant stream of conversation. They accompanied every action with words, encouraged the children to talk and listened carefully to what they had to say, read and told stories, and looked at and talked about pictures in books. But it was the children's actual varied experiences and stimulations in the everyday life of the nursery that were the base of the language enrichment program. Their heightened awareness of things around them was the foundation for the development of richer language usage and clearer thinking.

In addition there were direct language teaching lessons, which can be classified into the following categories:

1. Lessons on specific words and concepts.
2. Stimulations to observe, discriminate, and talk about fine shadings of sounds, sights, smells, touch, and tastes.
3. Games designed to stimulate the children to describe and to classify objects.
4. Discussions and reading of books appropriate for the level of language development of the children.
5. Play with language, rhymes, rhythms, humor, and puns.
6. Creation of original stories, poems, and dictations by the children to the teacher.

The language development program was not designed primarily and exclusively to correct the specific deficits of the D children, but rather to meet the needs of all the children for stimulation and experiences that would widen their horizons. It viewed the disadvantaged children as *"chil-*

dren whose original drives, curiosity and capacities are the same as all children's, but whose development has been hampered by life circumstances."[9] Hence they were especially in need of the enriching program planned for all children in a good nursery with a provision for additional attention and structured training in order to help them profit more fully from the learning opportunities.

[9]Barbara Biber and Marjorie B. Franklin, "The Relevance of Developmental and Psychodynamic Concepts to the Education of the Preschool Child," *Journal of the American Academy of Child Psychiatry*, 6, No. 11 (1967).

2

The First Days

SEPARATION FROM HOME AND FAMILY

For all the charms that going to nursery school holds for the young child, under the best of circumstances he looks upon his first step into the world as a mixed blessing. During his first few dependent years, his home and his family had been the source of whatever sense of security and trust he had acquired. Let us assume that all has gone well in his life, he is physically healthy, his life circumstances have not been unusually deprived or anxiety-provoking, and relations between him and his mother have been satisfying to each of them. In such a case, he probably has developed a feeling that he is a pretty good fellow, that the world is a pretty good place, and that he can safely begin to investigate and make his place in it. Even so, his first step out into the world, away from the warm, protecting atmosphere of home is necessarily tentative and exploratory, and sometimes it seems preferable that one hand still hold onto mother for a while.

But what if life circumstances have not been so kind, and he has been exposed to neglect or lack of sufficient protective care; has been silenced, teased, and beaten; has seen violence, cruelty, superstition, and fears; has had a non-satisfying relationship with his mother, or any combination of such circumstances? The chances are great that he is wary and suspicious and that he has not developed confidence in himself or in the people around him.

He lives with the feeling that bad or dangerous things may happen to him at any moment and that people are not to be trusted. He has not developed a belief in his own worth or capabilities. Thus he often steps out into the world with full protective armour to keep himself intact, guarding carefully against any new experience as a probable danger bet-

27

ter to be avoided. He may seem to leave his mother with apparent uncon-
cern (because long ago he has learned that it has not helped him much
to make demands of her), but he nevertheless sees this new school environment as holding far greater perils than the familiar dangers and dis-
appointments that he had learned to cope with. He may behave as though
the transition to the nursery is an everyday occurrence and say goodbye
to his mother casually or not seem to notice when she leaves. On the other
hand, sometimes he is so involved in protecting himself that he has little
energy left for concentration on the fascinating possibilities of the new materials, or on the stories read by the teacher. Sometimes he does not seem
even to notice the teacher herself.

So, under both the best and the worst of circumstances, the first days
away from home are very important and meaningful, yet difficult for the
young child.

The child who has had a good beginning experience in life still worries: "Will mother come to take me home?" "Who will help me if I have
to go to the toilet?" "Will I be taken care of?" "Will they like me?" "Will
somebody protect me if the kids take away my toy?" Compounded with
his own anxieties are the anxieties of his mother, of which he is well
aware: "Will my child be as bright, as capable as the other children?"
"Have I been a good mother and will he be a credit to me?" "Will he
like the teacher better than he likes me?" "Will he miss me as much as
I will miss him?"

The child who has had an experience of neglect and deprivation
may have some of the same worries as the protected child, in addition
to his overwhelming fear of new experiences. Also, it may seem to him
that mother is not very interested in what is likely to happen to him, that
she will not protect him if things go wrong; what's more, she may have
warned him of the dire things that will happen to him if he does not behave well in school. With this background of possible difficulties in mind,
we tried to plan the children's introduction to the nursery in a way that
would allay anxieties as much as possible. We decided to make a gradual
transition rather than to plunge the child into the new way of life from
one morning to the next.

After the child had been registered and about a week before school
was to begin, the teacher made a short home visit to meet him. This also
gave her an opportunity to meet his mother in her own home. The focus
of the visit, however, was for the teacher to become acquainted with the
child; she chatted and played with him for a short while and invited him
to visit her at the school with his mother. A time was set for this visit
on the days that the teacher was involved in preparing the classroom for
the coming year. There was some equipment out for the child to play
with, and the teacher took him on a short tour of the nursery. When pos-

sible, the mother and/or child helped the teacher in her preparations—painting some furniture, arranging crayons, etc. The gradual acquaintance-ship with the teacher and with the actual nursery building and equipment was designed to remove much of the fear of the unknown. It probably would have been even better if the child had been more specifically pre-pared for the school visit and if the teacher had explicitly told the child that there would not be other children present but that the visit was meant for him to acquaint himself with the nursery. (Some expressed disappoint-ment when they saw there were no other children.)

On the last evening before the actual beginning of the school year, a parents' meeting was called. (Such a meeting would have been pref-erable several days before the opening of school.) Here, too, the basic purpose of the visit was to allay the anxieties of the parents for whom a first separation from their child was going to be difficult. It was also de-signed to make all the parents aware of the meaning of this big step in the child's life and to prepare them for his possible reactions. We antici-pated that the parent's meeting would be an opportunity for the parents of the privileged children to talk out some of their own feelings about their child's entry into nursery school, as well as to prepare them for the babyish behavior that might subsequently appear. We expected that such a discussion would lighten the atmosphere and remove some of the ten-sions around the first days. At the same time, it was hoped that the par-ents of the deprived children would be made aware that even though they might not show it, their children might feel threatened. Our goal was to alert the parents to their own child and to what he was feeling. Mothers were requested to be prepared to spend several days, or possibly weeks, in the nursery until the child was ready for independent participation.

The first two weeks of the nursery school were planned as a gradual introduction to the full program. For the first three days the children were divided into four groups and each group was invited to come at a different hour. In this way, we were able to maintain a relaxed atmosphere, without the noise and excitement of many children and parents milling about. The teacher was able to make contact with each child, introduce him to the equipment, and get to know something of his personality. At the end of this one-hour visit, usually with their mothers in the immedi-ate vicinity, the children were dismissed when their interest was at its height, and thus they were anxious to return. After three to five days, two of the groups were invited simultaneously for a two-hour period, the other two groups coming for the next two hours. (Technically, this was often difficult to implement because the D parents tended to arrive whenever it was convenient for them.) Each of the two groups continued meeting for about a week until the teacher felt that most of the children were ready for the full group and the full program of activities (although a much more restricted and narrow one than we knew the children would be capable of later).

In the first group discussions and also in private talks with the children, the teachers encouraged them to talk of how they felt about going to nursery school and remaining without their mothers. The teacher mentioned some of the anxieties children sometimes feel but at the same time buoyed up their pride at being grown up enough to go to nursery. Together they sang songs about "being big" and "going to school."

Some very sharp differences in the adjustment of the D and P groups were immediately apparent. On the whole, the P children had much more difficulty in allowing their mothers to leave, with tears and clinging not an unusual pattern. In each group, at least one-third of the mothers had to stay for a week or two, although two-thirds of the children were independent after a few days. While they were adjusting toward independence, many of them were already actively playing, some of them in groups, making contacts with the teacher and telling her about their experiences, participating in games and routines and listening to stories read or told by the teacher. After the mothers left, the children talked a great deal about their mothers and when the teacher felt that a child became anxious, she suggested that he telephone his mother on the toy phone. In most cases an active "conversation" took place and the child seemed relaxed afterward.

The D's, on the other hand, seemed to make a smooth adjustment. After four days, and in most cases much sooner, no mother was present. In many cases, already on the second day, brothers and sisters, rather than the mothers brought the children to the nursery. Although there were a few cases of violent protest[1] and running home alone (the returning home phenomenon occurred only in the D group and only with children who had been accustomed to spend much time on the streets), most of the children seemed to be unconcerned about not being at home.

In some cases the D children began to exhibit separation problems several weeks after they had "adjusted" to the nursery. In the few cases where they did talk about home, they talked about their fathers rather than their mothers. In the three groups where the D and P children were integrated, the D children also used the "telephone" to "call" home, but this use of the telephone was imitative of the P's and not really meaningful to them. In contrast to the D's in the homogeneous group, the D's in the integrated groups requested their mothers to stay for a longer period

---

[1] It was interesting that the children who did allow themselves to protest were completely uncontrollable, throwing themselves on the ground and beating their heads, in contrast to the P's who cried but without such extreme manifestations.

of time. This, too, seemed to be an element of imitation both for the children and the mothers.

The characteristic behavior of the mothers was equally different. P mothers, for the most part, were prepared to stay at the nursery during the adjustment period (if there were working mothers, an arrangement was made for the maid, the father, or grandmother to stay with the child). Most of the P mothers gave the impression of being ready and interested and seemed aware of what their children were going through. In a number of cases, they found great difficulties in leaving their children. Sometimes they remained for a longer period than they needed to, and here it was the mother who needed help with her own emotional problems of separation from her child.

Most of the D mothers, however, had no patience for their children's separation problems. Somewhere the communication between the mothers and teachers had broken down, and though the teachers tried to convey the reasons for a gradual separation process, it apparently had not really "reached" these mothers. In the cases where the mothers were "good girls" and remained because the teachers had requested them to, they sat in the anteroom and gossiped, hardly noticing the children or their activities and, after a short while, they began to complain that they were wasting time.

In evaluating the problems that arose in the separation process, we came to the conclusion that perhaps instead of the group meeting, it would have been more advisable to have had an individual talk with each mother at registration or during the first home visit. The purpose of such a talk would have been to discuss with her how she could prepare her child for nursery school—how to discuss it with him, how to describe concretely why he was going and what he would see and do there, and how she could encourage him to express his feelings about going to school. By seeing the mother's reaction to this suggestion, we might have been able to understand better her relations with her child. It possibly might have made some impact if we had succeeded in persuading the mother that talking things over with a child could be a delightful experience!

WHO AM I AND WHAT AM I?:
ESTABLISHMENT OF SELF-IDENTITY

MARCH 1967

Udi (P) slipped as he was running. He cried, snuggled up to the teacher who came to help, examined his knee carefully for a nonexistent scratch, and demanded bandage and plaster.

SEPTEMBER 1967

Chaim (D) fell off the swing and banged his head, which immediately became swollen. He didn't utter a cry, seemed unconcerned, kept a bland expression on his face, and did not respond to the teacher's efforts to comfort him.

Such very different responses to bodily injury were typical of the
differences in the two groups. We felt that great progress had been made
when the D children began to cry and demand attention for their injuries.

Each child's photograph was hung on his individual clothes cubby. The
children were delighted to examine their pictures and identify each child.
Many of the D children recognized everybody's picture except their own.
With a blank expression on their faces, they said they didn't know who it
was.

P children, for the most part, reacted with enthusiasm to most of the
equipment. They tried everything, were usually proud of their achievements,
called the teacher to see, and were pleased when their work was put up
for display with their name on it. D children were frequently reluctant to
try the materials, sometimes shrugging their shoulders as if to say "I don't
know how." When they did begin to work, they tended to give up on en-
countering the slightest difficulty, such as the collapse of their block building, or a puzzle piece that didn't fit in easily. Sometimes they would comment disparagingly on something they had made: "It stinks."

At first glance the above anecdotes seem to be unrelated, yet they
all seem to tell us something about how the children look at themselves—
the P's with high self-esteem and a feeling of importance, and the D's frequently with a sense of unworthiness and failure.

One of the saddest phenomena we encountered among the D children was what seemed to be their low opinion of themselves, their low
expectations for themselves, their minimal demands for attention and
care. They seemed to melt into the walls while the P's clamored for attention, expressed ideas, and tried things out. This low self-esteem extended even to a lack of attention to their own bodies, to their appearance,
their clothing, and their injuries. They did not even know the names of
the parts of their bodies or what their physical capacities were.

As had been pointed out previously, many of the D children had not
been accustomed to careful, consistent concern for their physical and emotional needs. There were times that there was inconsistency in their physical care as well as in emotional and intellectual areas. Often they were
deprived of the sense of personal importance a child gets when it matters
to somebody that he knows or learns or experiences something new. Yet,
at other times, when their parents were in the mood, the children were
smothered with love and kisses, dressed in expensive clothes for holidays
and parties, made a fuss of and shown off. This inconsistent attitude on

the part of their parents caused much confusion in the children's self-esteem and self-identity.

A child develops his positive or negative feelings about himself—what kind of a person he is, whether he feels himself likable, worthwhile, beautiful, intelligent, or not—as he sees how the important people in his life feel about him. If they view him as clever, beautiful, charming, he tends to accept this opinion; unfortunately, if they view him otherwise, he will react accordingly. A feeling of self-esteem (a healthy ego) is the basis for the development of other good qualities, such as the ability to enjoy, to be curious and inquiring, to be creative, sensitive, understanding of people, and so forth. We expected that as the child began to feel himself more important and more accepted as a person, his body, which is such an essential part of him and his own special individuality, would become more precious to him and that what happened to him and to his body would begin to matter much more.

So, our work as teachers was cut out for us. We had to help each child to develop a more vital and meaningful idea of his own identity and his own self-worth. We had to encourage the child's confidence in himself and in what he produced.

First of all, of course, we hoped that the intense individual care, thought, and attention lavished on each child would serve as a corrective therapeutic experience. We also hoped that the children would see themselves and their importance reflected back to them through their teacher's positive attitude toward them. In addition, specific games, techniques, and programs were initiated in order to make up for the cognitive deficit that the emotional deprivation had caused. These included the following:

1. The morning arrival was a very important event. The teacher greeted each child warmly by name as he arrived and this meeting was used as the first one-to-one contact of the day. It was then that the teacher talked with the child about his clothing, the weather, or some event that the child had experienced. Stories from home were encouraged and discussed. The teacher tried to make him feel that it was *he* who was being welcomed.

2. Each child's clothes cubby, towel hook, and individual shelf for his work were identified by his photograph and his name. This gave him a sense of possession; for some it was their first experience of sole ownership. This sense of ownership also helped them to understand that other people also are individuals and also have their own possessions. Discussions and examinations of the photographs were part of the program content.

3. At the beginning of the year, roll call was a ceremony. The teacher called each child by name, and he had a choice of running, jumping, tiptoeing, etc., to the teacher; she would then bestow a big hug and

greeting to the accompaniment of smiles on the part of the children looking on. (It was interesting to see how all the children seemed to get an additional, vicarious pleasure as they saw each child receive his greeting.)

4. An essential part of the equipment were two mirrors—a long one and a half one. The children spent much time looking at themselves, dressing up, and examining themselves again. They compared how much they could see of themselves in the long mirror and in the half mirror; experiments were made to see what happens when two children look together. Discussions on differences in appearance took place; each child was measured in front of the mirror.

5. Attention to appearance was fostered. One of the ceremonies in the small group meeting that preceded going home was for each child to examine his hands and clothing to see if they were clean, and to arrange his clothes, tuck in his shirt, smooth his hair, and generally examine his appearance.

6. In order to establish individual identity, songs and games using each child's name were used frequently at the beginning. Since we also wanted to develop the children's ability to perceive other children as individuals and to recognize that they too had unique qualities, some of the games using children's names included careful scrutiny of a child, noticing differences and individual characteristics in clothes, voice, walk, and mannerisms. These characteristics had to be put into words and remembered in order to play the game. Such games included: *Tick,. tock, who am I?,* in which one child hid his head in the teacher's lap. Another child then tapped him on the back and said, "Tick, tock, who am I?" The first child had to guess the second child's name by recognizing his voice even though he whispered or tried to disguise it. Another typical game was *Tell about me.* Here, one child stood in the middle of the circle, and each of the other children described something about him. "Eli has brown shoes," "Eli is tall," "Eli has shiny eyes," etc. Individual needs and special abilities of the children were verbalized by the teacher. "Moshe needs to sit on my lap today; he is sad." "Yaakov makes lovely drawings and Danny has good ideas in building." In addition, games with the names of the parents of each child were played in order to give the children a sense of belonging to a family unit.

7. Birthdays were exploited as an excellent means of helping the children develop a sense of identity and of individual importance. A wreath of flowers was made by the children for the birthday child and much was made of measuring the size of his head and fitting the wreath to his individual requirements. The family of the birthday child was invited to the birthday celebration, and the mother was asked to bring snapshots of the child at various stages of his development. With the teacher's help, she also prepared stories of specific episodes in his life which she told to the children. The birthday child was dressed up for the occasion

and there was much scrutiny and discussion of his beautiful appearance and clothes.

8. A "book" on each child was compiled with the help of the children. It was called "Danny Knows," or "Ilana Knows," etc. On the front cover of the book—which was sometimes decorated by the child in finger-paint—was the child's photograph. Each book contained samples of his work including drawings, collages, and stories which he dictated, as well as his fingerprints, anecdotes about interesting things that he had done at the nursery, and photographs of him at various activities. The teachers frequently made additions to each child's book. The children loved their own books, looked at them often and exchanged them with each other.

9. We used several methods designed to help the child become more aware of his body, its various parts, and the way they function. We began in the rhythms period. Each child was asked to feel his head and its round-ness, then to feel another child's head. The teacher also felt each child's head in a loving gesture. From there, they moved to limbs, ears, eyes, nose, neck, mouth, tongue, stomach, buttocks; they then went on to ac-tivate muscles—opening and closing of hands, stretching of limbs, jump-ing on one foot, then on two feet. All this was accompanied by songs, gestures, and rhythmic music.

Picture books on the body and its parts were compiled, consisting of pictures of children and adults, as well as of illustrations of eyes, ears, hands, etc. The children were given cut-out pictures of various parts of the body and asked to arrange them on a flannel board to make a picture of a person. Group and individual discussions took place around this ac-tivity and similar discussions arose in the doll corner as the children ex-amined the dolls carefully.

10. At a later stage, the teacher tried to reenforce the children's in-dividuality and self-esteem by giving them many opportunities to make their own decisions and choices.

In these small and subtle ways,[2] we tried to strengthen the child's perception of himself as a unique and independent being, as a person who was worthy and capable of mastering skills and learning, as a person who could be liked and who was capable of liking others.

SPELLING OUT AND RECALL: DISCRIMINATION AND DIFFERENTIATION

As mentioned above, one of the things that stood out about the D children was the vague and confused way they seemed to perceive things. To them,

[2]The section in Chapter 3 on "The Role of the Teacher in Emotional Devel-opment" discusses in more detail some of the methods and approaches used to encourage self-identity and self-esteem.

all fruits were "oranges;" they seemed unaware of the differences between animals; they called each of the teachers by the same name. After
what appeared to be a vivid experience they would recall nothing of what
had happened; they seemed unable to recall anything of what they had
seen in the grocery store where they had just gone to buy lollipops.

Perhaps the sharpest example of this followed the Succot holiday.
Only a small portion of the P children had had a succa at home, but
apparently all the children had visited a succa.[3] After the holiday, the P
children came back to the nursery full of their experiences in a succa,
telling the teachers all about it—what it looked like, how it was decorated,
what they ate, how the food was served. The D children *all* had had
a succa at home, yet they could recall very little of what it looked like,
or what they had seen and done during the holiday—it all seemed to
have melted into a vague and unremembered past. We asked ourselves
why the D children seemed to be living in a confused cloud, and the answers seemed to point to the atmosphere at home of inadequate meaningful communication and the absence of a teaching, stimulating adult.

What could we do to overcome this, to free the children and help
them to observe more vividly, to become more aware, and to learn? As
a first step, we felt that offering them a safe, secure, and satisfying daily
experience would free them to start noticing some of the fascinating things
going on around them and they would be encouraged to try new things
without fear. At the same time, the teacher would have to serve as the
bridge between the child and the world. She would literally introduce
him to his immediate surroundings. She would have to dramatically arouse
him from his apathy, and help him become conscious of and interested
in things around him. It seemed to us that our first job with the children
was to arouse them to consciously examine the specific and unique details
of the familiar things in their lives.

At the beginning we did not sufficiently recognize the urgent need
for examining each detail of an object or an experience, and it was only
after the sharp example of the children's reaction to the "succa" that we
began to give this aspect of the work greater attention. It was then, too,
that we realized that much of this work would have to be done on an
individual basis. We realized that we could take nothing for granted, that
it would be necessary, for example, to examine every single item and
routine in the nursery. We would need to name it, look at it, feel it, talk
about its uses, size, shape, color, etc., in order to help the children to
observe and become aware of the everyday things around them. Our attention included such varied and routine subjects as the clothes the chil-

---

[3] An outdoor booth made of tree branches, symbolic of Israel's period in the
wilderness, used for family gatherings and meals during the eight days of the
festival.

dren wore; the names and specific characteristics of the teachers and children; the blocks, paints, books, faucet, toilet, stove, windows, doors, kitchen equipment, and the regular schedule of the nursery day.

This ongoing work was done mostly with individual children (so that we could be sure that no child would miss it), sometimes with small groups, and only occasionally with the whole group. The teachers tried constantly to remember that this was a basic part of their job. They tried to keep everything as simple as possible. Equipment was kept to a minimum at the beginning so that everything could be thoroughly examined and understood. A one-time examination was not enough, it needed to be repeated and repeated. There were frequent reviews and opportunities for the children to recall what they had done and learned. The work of the teachers in developing awareness of details of each experience and ability to recall continued throughout the two years and became progressively more complex.

The following examples move from the simple to the complex:

After Succot and after much discussion of their succa experience, the children built succot of blocks, clay, plasticene, match boxes, etc. Outdoors, they built succot with crates and played in them, and in this way relived the experience.

We played a game: "What is there in the nursery that is also at home?" First answer: "Nothing." Little by little the chlidren thought of windows, doors, floors, tables, chairs, dishes, food, etc.

A child was working with clay and started to model a table but ran into difficulty. The teacher and the child examined a table thoroughly—they observed its shape, its surface, how many legs it had—and then went back to this examination frequently as problems in the modeling arose.

Or . . . two girls were building a house with blocks and made a window. Teacher asked what does a window have? Together they went to the window, examined it, and discovered it had glass and curtains. The teacher gave them translucent paper and cloth, and they completed their window.

At a much later stage, we were able to move from recall of simple things to larger experiences. The children were asked to "close your eyes and think about what you did this morning." After each day's play, the group discussed thoroughly what had happened that day. After each trip, the details of the outing were talked about and dramatized, and stories about their experiences were dictated by the children and read back to them on various occasions.

JANUARY 1969: Discussion on Trip to Railroad Station

Teacher: Let's write about our trip.

Chaim (D): We rode on the train.

Reuben (P): We saw clocks that tell you when the train starts.

Uri (P): I heard the engine driver tell the teacher that there is no driving wheel, there are just gears.

Aliza (D): I saw cars, many cars.

Amnon (P): We bought lollipops.

Reuben (P): We saw the emblem of Israel Railroads.

Uri (P): The ticket agent sold us a ticket.

Aliza (D): The gentleman from the train told how to make the motor start and stop.

Ruth (D): The man who told the train to go, put on the signal light.

Teacher: He is called the starter.

Edna (D): One train came from someplace else and an Arab lady got off, all dressed up.

Ruth (D): She had two children.

Dafna (P): Also Ronnie's aunt got off the train.

Ron (P): We saw steps for old people who can't get up the high steps.

Eli (P): The car that was first was the last to leave.

Aliza (D): When a grandmother wants to go up, you need the steps.

Gabriel (P): There were soldiers and they guarded the train. They guarded so there wouldn't be thieves.

Ilan (P): That there wouldn't be bombs.

Ron (P): We saw a soldier make a telephone call, and also a girl.

Naomi (P): When we were there, a boy said he would kill us but I said he wouldn't because there are soldiers there to guard us.

Reuben (P): The soldiers wore khaki clothes.

ESTABLISHMENT OF ROUTINES AND SENSE OF ORDER

We found that, at the beginning, many of the D children had difficulty not only in recalling what had happened in the past, but seemed to have little ability to anticipate future events. Many of them were not accustomed to think "after this, comes that." We considered the consciousness of regularity to be a very important and basic ingredient for later ability to think logically "if this . . . then that." For this reason, we made very few variations in the daily schedule at the beginning and few changes in the placement of equipment. We wanted to instill a sense of sequence and of planning, and we found that the order and predictability of the schedule and the nursery setting also served to give the children a feeling of security.

A constantly recurring problem in the first year was what seemed to be inability of some the children to understand that there was a framework to the schedule and to the life in the nursery, that they could not do what they liked when they wanted. At first they could not grasp that things had a special place and had to be put back there—some would wander around picking up things and dropping them on the floor, creating a general confusion. They had to be taught work habits and that equipment had special uses. Much time was spent in the establishment of routines—washing of hands, toileting, sitting at the table. Mealtimes especially were difficult; it took a long time for the children to grasp the idea that one sits at the table; that there could be pleasant, quiet conversation; that one does not jump up or shout; that mealtimes are a pleasant, restful part of the day. At routine times, as with washing and toileting, the children needed very clear and organized supervision, with a teacher always present. One of the games that we played was built on reviewing the schedule of the day and forecasting what would come next. By frequently asking them to recall what they had seen or felt or done, we were forcing the children to *think* about what they did and to begin to expect and plan what would happen next.

The daily schedule at the very beginning was:

8:00 MORNING GREETING

This was regarded by the teachers as one of the most important events of the day. She greeted and conversed with each child and helped him to find his cubby.

8:15 HOUSEKEEPING: Chores and Care of Animals and Plants

The animals were introduced very gradually so that there was much time for observing and becoming familiar with each animal and his habits. In the course of time, there were white mice, birds, guinea pigs, a porcupine, fish, and chicks.

8:30 FREE PLAY

There was ample time for becoming familiar with the materials. for motoric activities with the equipment such as moving big loads of blocks, wheeling wagons, toy automobiles, and trucks, handling the dolls, dishes, pots, etc. Art materials, water play, and carpentry were gradually introduced. Some beginnings of group play began to emerge.

Books also were popular. Small groups sat with the teacher, looking at a book, learning how to handle it, talking about the pictures, and reading it.

9:15 CLEANUP

Learning to cooperate in cleaning up was a gradual process. At the beginning, cleanup time was utilized for exercises in classification and for teaching order and organization.

9:35 GROUP MEETING

The daily group meeting consisted of a selection of the following activities: (1) discussion for the purpose of introduction of each material, showing how it could be used and what its properties were; (2)review of small events that had taken place (the garbage truck coming, the rain, etc.); (3) games for establishment of self-identification and familiarity with the body and body parts (see page 31); (4) language games (see page 157ff.); (5) circle dances to establish the feeling of a group, and rhythms and rhythmic games for muscular recall of experiences and events (see page 182); (6) discussions of common feelings—separation from parents, going to nursery, birth of siblings (see pages 52–54).

Where possible, the group was divided into two for the meeting; it was found that the children were more easily reached and involved when they were in smaller groups.

9:50 TOILETING AND WASHING UP

These routines were highly organized and supervised. This also was a time for conversation and talk about the schedule and what was about to happen.

10:00 SNACK

The children were seated at two large tables with a teacher at each table. Conversation was encouraged and included jokes, language games, and discussion of foods, (see page 151).

10:20 OUTDOORS

When possible, some of the outdoor equipment was removed from the storeroom and set up before the children went out. They went out as an organized group with the teacher and their activities were carefully supervised. There was much motor activity and the beginning of dramatic play.

We also held ten to fifteen minute sessions with individual children indoors during the outdoor period. The teacher tried to develop a meaningful relationship with the child as well as to improve his language facility; they discussed occurrences of the day in order to reinforce the child's awareness of experiences.

11:20 QUIET TIME

During quiet time, art materials, and didactic materials (puzzles, games, science and language games) were available; in addition, we had music and rhythms several times a week in this time slot.

11:45 STORIES and DISCUSSION

(With the group divided into two)

12:00 FAREWELLS

Each child receives an individual farewell.

3

The Educational Setting

THE ROLE OF THE TEACHER IN EMOTIONAL DEVELOPMENT[1]

The pleasant emotional climate in a good nursery is the medium in which the teacher nurtures mental health and well functioning personality development. The consistently warm atmosphere that the good teacher generates is designed to give the child a positive experience outside of his home. For the deprived child, it can serve as a corrective emotional experience. The goal of the good teacher is to make the nursery so highly gratifying that learning becomes a satisfying and pleasant occupation.

However, good teaching is so much of an art and a personal expression that there can be no recipe prescribing how to be a "good" teacher. On the contrary, such prescriptions would inhibit the expression of the teacher's own unique personality which is such a valuable asset in the teaching process. Nevertheless, if we define our ultimate goals in the education of our children and try to match our teaching methods to these goals, we find that certain basic principles emerge.

Let us determine, therefore, what our goals are in educating children to function well in a democratic, science-oriented society. A truly demo-

[1]This chapter deals with the emotional requirements of young children, and it relates to the normal needs of all children. However, the special sensitivities and vulnerabilities of disadvantaged children would lead one to believe that they are in particular need of the emotional climate described in this section. Because the D children often manifested a deviation and an arrest in their emotional development, they needed special support and intimate one-to-one relationships with the teacher in order to overcome their lowered self-esteem, lack of confidence, confused sense of identity, and suspiciousness. Some of the approaches that were developed in order to achieve these goals have been described in the first two chapters. They will be further elaborated in a later section of this chapter and in the section on Individual Work, page 169.

cratic society is based on a fundamental respect for each individual and his freedom to express himself in his own unique way, provided that he does not disturb his neighbor. A science-oriented society thrives on a freedom to investigate, to deviate from and avoid the stereotype, and to create new ideas, processes, and products. The goals, therefore, of developing the unique potential and the individuality of each child and of fostering the scientific mode of thinking would lead us to believe that the child ideally should be exposed both at home and at school to an atmosphere which will nurture his:

physical health;

sense of security and basic trust;

confidence in himself as a competent, worthy, and unique individual, with faith in his ability to cope;

initiative;

capacity to have satisfying relations with people, to be accepted and accepting, and to be ready to love;

freedom from fears and guilts which may inhibit and disturb him;

growing ability to channel his impulses and tolerate frustrations;

freedom to think independently, to explore the real world and not necessarily be bound by what has been accepted by others.

These goals are all deeply interrelated since emotional growth, intellectual curiosity, and learning seem to be dependent upon each other. If we should succeed in helping our children to come closer to achieving these goals, we will have made an important contribution toward a world less beset by fears, hostilities, and rigidity.

Not only are these goals at work in the teacher's personal relationship with the children, but also they are implicit in her teaching methods and in the general atmosphere she creates in her group. She does not foster initiative and freedom to think originally if she is inflexible and demands one "correct" answer nor if she sticks rigidly to the specific information she wants to present and allows no first-hand investigation or straying from the subject to an allied question which has spontaneously arisen. She does not develop a sense of self-worth if she is hostile or punishing. She cannot expect that, in an authoritarian atmosphere, she can encourage creativity and individual personality development.

The teacher, also, always should be aware that children learn more quickly and readily when teacher and child have a good relationship, when they like and respect each other, and when they feel allied in their goal of teaching and learning. The teacher's attitude to the child is the basic factor in the quality of this relationship. She tries to be sympathetic and understanding, to convey to the child that she does not judge him to be weak when he needs help, that she does not reject him when he shows fear and hostile feelings. If, in addition, the teacher can succeed in replacing his feelings of failure with pleasure in what he *can* do and in his ability to handle difficulties, she is strengthening his belief in himself and his trust in others. She is helping to free him to use his energies for learning, exploring his interests, and developing his own potentialities.

Having defined these goals, we must examine how to translate them into educational principles and practice. There are certain basic principles of mental health on which we can build an "education for individuality."[2] The following is a presentation of some of those principles which we tried to define and to apply in the education of the three- to five-year old children in our nursery.

Atmosphere of Acceptance

The warm atmosphere of acceptance and mutual respect is an essential element in an educational setting which wishes to foster mental health and growth. As human beings, we are very sensitive to what other people think about us, and our perception of these attitudes influences our behavior. Since the young child is still in the process of developing his sense of himself and tends to evaluate himself as he perceives how others view him, he is especially in need of being made to feel liked and important and to feel protected both from outside dangers and from his own outbursts which frighten him. An atmosphere of acceptance and protection can be expressed in many ways in the life at nursery school.

Acceptance that Children are Children and not Adults. This is so axiomatic that it is amusing to have to state it and yet, too often, we as educators and parents tend to forget that children take a long time to grow up and that we cannot expect "instant" adult behavior. At times, they are noisy and overactive by adult standards; they are selfish and egocentric; they are overdependent and demanding; they are unreasonably independent and defiant; they are not in sufficient control of their emotions and cry and fight too easily; and when they do make large steps toward more mature behavior, they disappoint us by regressing and becoming babyish. We know all this and yet we frequently have to remember that the process of growing up is a very long one, marked by characteristic ups and downs, and that we as educators have to be careful not to make unreasonable, impatient demands for maturity.

[2]Barbara Biber and Patricia Minuchin, "Educating for Individuality: A Reexamination," Paper presented at the American Orthopsychiatric Association meeting, March 1967.

Acceptance of Individual Differences and Encouragement of Individuality. If there were any "golden rule" for good teaching it would be that the good teacher sees each child as a separate human being with his own special characteristics and personality and that she is ready to accept and respond to each child, at his particular level of development. The teacher truly respects the differences in the children, does not label a child as "stupid," "aggressive," "bad," or "good," nor does she demand too much from the better-functioning child. Instead, she constantly seeks ways to help each child to function better beginning where he is and not where the teacher imagines he should be.

As each child is encouraged to be himself and his special qualities are developed and appreciated, and as his particular interests and needs are recognized, he begins to develop a sense of his own identity and worth. Frequently, this experience of consideration and respect toward him then inspires him to be able to show consideration and respect to other children.

Some of the specific techniques for fostering the sense of individuality and self-worth have been discussed in the section "Who Am I and What Am I?," page 33. The teacher tries at all times to reinforce the successes of each child rather than to point out his failures. She tries to notice and to praise the smallest gains and thus inspire further ones, and she appreciates accomplishments and encourages where encouragement is needed. In addition, the teacher remembers to use the technique of addressing children by their own names and assigning them to responsible jobs in order to augment their sense of importance.

The following examples of comments by a teacher illustrate the ways which she transmitted her encouraging approach and her enjoyment of each child's specific qualities:

> You really know how to throw a ball far, Uri!
> You learned how to do this puzzle very quickly, Eli.
> Ehud had a very good idea today in the block building.
> Look at Sari's picture, she made such beautiful colors.

She also encouraged gains in social maturity and responsibility:

> Mazal, you shared the doll's clothes today with Sarah in such a grown-up way.
> Malka really knows how to wait patiently for her turn.
> Ruthie was in charge of cleaning the doll corner today and look what a beautiful job she did.

She helped a child overcome discouragement or difficulty:

> Never mind, Uri, that your clay table fell apart. You will learn how to make it firmer next time.

Come on, Moshe, you can climb this tree. I will help you if you need me.
I know it's hard to let Mother go home, but I think you can.

And, she showed the children that she appreciated their individual differences:

How wonderful you all are! Every one of you dances in your own way to this record.
How nice that Eli has blond hair and Yoram has black hair.

The teacher's job is a demanding one. She must give individual attention and praise and yet must be careful not to let the other children feel neglected. At times, in spite of much discouragement, she must continue to believe in a child and his ability to overcome his difficulties. Above all, she herself must have the maturity to feel honest respect and appreciation for each child. If she "follows the rules" but feels inward disapproval or indifference, the child will be quick to perceive it. She must not smile or show affection when she is seething or disgusted. At such times, the teacher can be helped by discussing with others her own personal reactions, trying to understand from her own life experiences why she reacts in a particular way to a certain child. At other times, she develops greater insight and tolerance of the child's behavior when she learns more about him and his life experience.

It is to be hoped that if the teacher succeeds in developing in the child a sense of security and belief in himself, this self-confidence can become part of his personality and he will be less prone to feelings of unworthiness, fear, and hostility later in life.

Acceptance of Conflicting Emotions and Hostile Behavior.   When we deal with children we are sometimes delighted and sometimes frustrated by the extremes of their emotions. They express joy, disappointment, anger, and love, with no restraints and with their whole body and being. Their needs are strongly felt: "I *need* it!" is said with the utter conviction that nothing else in the world could satisfy.

It takes time and much experience in living before these strong emotions become modified and controlled. Hopefully, such control develops as the child matures. The understanding teacher helps his pupil to greater control, yet at the same time avoids giving him the feeling that he is "bad" when his intense emotions erupt in outbursts. She helps him to feel that he is wanted and loved even if some of his behavior is unacceptable. The teacher tries to reduce the child's guilt feelings by expressing them in words and pointing out that everyone has similar feelings sometimes. She shows the child that she is confident that little by little he will learn to control his strong negative feelings and expressions, but that his present

"I am angry!"

behavior is inappropriate. The teacher prevents and controls the child's destructive behavior and thus reduces his anxiety at his outbursts.

> I know how angry you are that he threw your block building down; it would make anybody angry, but you may not hit him.
>
> Picking up a child with a temper tantrum, she carries him to a quiet corner and says calmly, "You are very angry at me because I couldn't let you keep the wagon all morning. I know how much you wanted it. In a little while you'll feel better." She stays with him and comforts him or she comes back in a few minutes to see if she can interest him in something going on.
>
> Eli kept interfering with Danny and Ron who were building together and refused to let him join them. The teacher sat down with Eli and they built a tall building together. Then they tacked a large sign with his name onto the building.

The teacher has to set up necessary rules and limits:

> Say it in words, not in blows.
>
> Wait for your turn; everyone will have a turn.
>
> Tell her what you want instead of crying.
>
> In our nursery we don't let children hurt each other.
>
> In our nursery we don't let children throw stones.

The teacher expresses the child's feeling in words:

> You are upset because Mommy hasn't come yet. Every child gets worried and upset when Mommy is late. She'll come soon; maybe the bus didn't come on time.
>
> She addresses a crying child: You are crying because Mazal doesn't want you to be the daddy, but she already asked Uri to be the daddy. Would you like to be the daddy in Ruthie's house?
>
> You are very angry at me because I stopped you from going out now. We could talk about it; you don't need to throw the blocks if you are angry.

Children become very frightened when they express their anger and frustration by attacking the teacher or the parent:

> Teacher, as she firmly holds the child's arms: "I wouldn't let you hit me because you will feel very sorry later."

The teacher shows the child there are other ways of handling a situation—more socially acceptable ways!

> Without moralizing or accusing, she stops a child from grabbing a pail from another child, saying, "Uri is using that now. Here's another pail for you and then you can both play together."
>
> In addition she provides constructive activities—carpentry, ball playing, climbing—that channelize some of the aggressive energy. These muscular activities sometimes free the passive or restricted child, who fears his own aggressive feelings, to become more assertive and to stand up for his rights.

In each episode of unacceptable behavior, the teacher tries to handle the situation in the light of what she knows of the particular child and his background, his present level of functioning, his present needs and ability to tolerate frustration.

> Ron and Avi had both made an unholy alliance for rebellious behavior and breaking rules. Ron who was the spoiled child of overpermissive parents, needed firm control and setting of limits. Avi, who had a background of very rigid parents and punitive discipline, needed encouragement for his attempts at independence and rebellious behavior. (The life of a teacher is not an easy one and here the teacher had to relate to each of the children according to his individual needs.)
>
> Hannah was outstandingly passive, almost nonparticipating and spoke very little (and this little exclusively to children, never to adults). At the slightest frustration, she threw herself on the ground, shrieked and banged her head. Any movement on her part towards more active participation was greatly encouraged by the teachers.
>
> From the observer's records: Hannah has suddenly begun to grab things for herself. She pulls a wheel away from Yossi, she grabs a box from Jonah. When some of the boys come to his aid, and take the box away from her,

she throws herself on the floor and cries. Teacher finds her on the floor, covered with muddy tears and running nose. She picks her up, washes her, comforts her and tells her that "children don't like it when you take their things away by force. You can tell them that you also want it." Teacher gives her a candy.

Later when some of the children are preparing the 10 o'clock snack, Hannah pushes Sarah off her seat and tries to sit there even though there is an empty chair nearby. Sarah succeeds in pushing her off and Hannah throws herself on the floor and cries. Teacher picks her up and seats her on the empty chair explaining, "Here is an empty chair. Sarah has a chair and you have a chair. Here is a piece of bread for you and one for Sarah." Hannah calms down.

(The teacher recognized how important it was that Hannah had begun to demand things for herself and realized that she must encourage this and at the same time gently teach her a more acceptable way of getting her share.)

Encouraging Expression and Resolution of Fears, Conflicts, and Guilts (Ventilation, Catharsis, and Sublimation)

Without our being aware of it, all of us are influenced by the irrational fears, guilt, ideas, and conflicts of our childhood, which remain with us through life and determine and sometimes disturb the way we function. As adults, these fears, conflicts, and childish misconceptions are often deeply repressed and influence behavior without our being conscious of the motivations. They can influence the way anger is expressed or strongly repressed; they can influence tendencies toward overdependence or independence, behavior to partners in marriage, to one's children, etc. In other words, these unconscious feelings are an important factor in making us the kind of people we are and in the way we behave and feel. These hidden thoughts are difficult to root out and often it is only when a painful attempt is made to uncover them and examine them realistically and rationally that one is able to relieve some of the heavy feelings of fear, guilt, and anger and consequently to modify our behavior. Until we succeed in bringing these ideas to our conscious awareness and examine them to decide whether they are logical or not, we frequently cannot change our sometimes irrational and self-destructive behavior. In childhood, these ideas, fears, guilts, and misconceptions are still in the process of formation and are not yet deeply repressed. When we succeed in helping the child to become aware of his feelings and ideas and to express them, they often become less intense, misconceptions can be clarified, and the child is relieved.

Young children's tensions and concerns are often caused by their feelings of weakness and dependency, their sense of guilt and fear. They seek independence and yet they are drawn to childish dependency; sometimes they fear rejection and abandonment; they fear aggression—their own and other's; they are guilty about their hostile feelings; they are disturbed by their conflicting feelings of love and hate to their parents and their brothers and sisters; they fear wild animals and supernatural beings; they fear darkness, doctors, barbers, loud noises and so on.

By helping children express their feelings, the teacher usually can deal with these revelations casually, and continue to show the child her respect and acceptance. In this way, she frequently succeeds in modifying or even eliminating the guilt and negative feelings and behavior. At the same time that she is encouraging the children to express their feelings and fantasies, the teacher is also helping the children to know the real world and to learn facts; in this way she is helping the children to distinguish between irrational and rational fears, illogical and logical ideas. This introduction of reality and rational thinking helps to dispel children's fears and to establish confidence in their ability to cope with their feelings. As the child is stimulated to know and face reality, the chances are he will be less involved with fantasy and fears.

> Reuben (P) was a bright, constructive, and cooperative child but he was very frightened of animals. He screamed and was fearful every time he saw goats in the nearby field. The teacher encouraged him to talk about his fears and led a group discussion with the children about their fear of animals. She told them she too had been afraid of dogs when she was little and the children told about their private fears.
>
> She also had a talk with his parents about what was happening at home and as an outcome it was decided that father would spend more time with him alone, doing "men things."
>
> In the nursery, the children had turns holding the hamster on their lap each day as his cage was cleaned. They would pat it and talk about its behavior. Reuben was revolted at first but after a while brought himself to touch it gingerly. At a later stage he fought for the privilege of holding it every day and finally he was allowed to take it home for the holidays. His mother, who was also squeamish about animals, couldn't believe it when he became completely freed of all the fears of dogs and other animals. When school closed, Reuben insisted on bringing the hamster home as a gift.

Very often, the children themselves find their own natural outlets for expressing many of their feelings and fantasies through their play, their stories, and their paintings. The sensitive teacher notes what the child is expressing, and often it is sufficient just to let him play it out and work it out by himself.

> Amnon (P), for almost a whole month, painted a frightening figure "in the dark" and talked openly about his fears until they gradually abated.
>
> Danny (P), for a long time, tended to build cages for lions, tigers, etc., or built tanks for "shooting." After awhile, with some encouragement from

the teacher, the cages became a zoo and his interests moved on to what real animals eat in the zoo. From the tanks and "shooting" he moved to building tents, army PX, etc.

Sometimes the children try to "work through" in their stories and play some of the frightening, confusing experiences and violent adult speech they have been exposed to in reality.

Chanting as she jumped and danced, Dafna (D), a well-functioning child who played and spoke freely from the beginning was recorded by the teacher:
>The man is sleeping in the train
>And he rides and rides
>Big, big
>He rode on the train
>Hay, vay, vay, vay
>Ki, ki, ki, ki
>The beard climbed onto the old man
>And he didn't feel it
>And he ran, ran, ran
>He saw his son killed
>His son!
>He saw the gun and killed him
>And said
>Don't cry!

From a fragment of a discussion in the sandbox (homogeneous D group):

Yael: Your mother should burn up!

Ruthie: Your mother should get buried!

Yael: Die!

Ruthie: No!

Yael: Why do you talk to me? You deserve it! Die!

Ruthie: (No answer)

Yael: Your father should die!

Ruthie: Your father should kill you!

Yael: Don't talk to me.

Ruthie: I will so!

(Yael has been shouting out with much pleasure and smiles, using her arms to emphasize what she is saying and Ruthie seems quite indifferent. Throughout this interchange they are playing together, pouring sand from pail to pail and exhanging pails with each other.)

When she thinks she understands and feels capable of doing so, the teacher can help the child by expressing his feelings in words and showing him that she really grasps the hidden meanings of his fantasies. Of

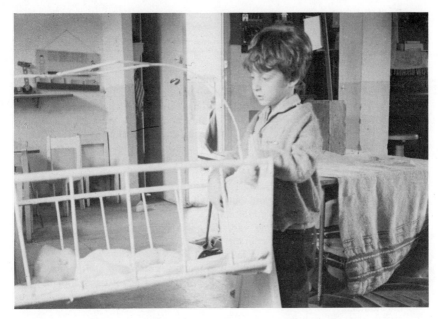

"How do I feel about this baby?"

course, the teacher must be very careful and sparing in the use of interpretations and may only express them when she has reason to be sure of her ground.

Ruth (D), four years old, is very demanding of attention, irritable, aggressive, unhappy and unable to bear anyone else receiving attention. She is obsessed with thoughts of her infant brother, talks about him constantly.

From the teacher's diary: Ruth ate a great deal at the 10 o'clock snack and said "Now I'll be fat and have a little Benny (infant brother) in my stomach and there'll be two Bennies."

Teacher: You also want to be a mommy and have your own Benny. When you grow up, you'll also be a mommy.

The next day:

Ruth (working with clay and making a "birthday cake"): Today we're making a birthday.

Teacher: For whom?

Ruth: Benny (continues working and singing). Today is Benny's birthday. (Turns to teacher.) I go to school.

Teacher: Yes, soon you will be six years old and you'll go to school.

Ruth: And after that I'll be bigger and Benny will go to school.

Teacher: You'll always be bigger than Benny.

Ruth makes a birthday cake and decorates it with six candles which she counts, proud of her ability to count.

Dorit (P): So he's bigger than you.
Ruth: No, he's four and I'm . . . six.
Ronnie (D): It's not true.
Ruth: My brother is three.

This discussion was painful for Ruth and she reverted to her attention-getting devices, complaining to the teacher about an imaginary stain on her dress and whiningly asking for help with the clay.

Teacher explains the properties of clay and how to work with it so the candles won't fall off and in the course of the discussion remarks: "Sometimes children feel bad that it takes so long to grow up. But you're getting bigger and bigger till you'll be big enough to be a mommy. Today you even learned how to work with clay.

Judy's father has been in and out of jail. In this incident Judy can express her fears of her father if only indirectly.
Judy: My father came home very dirty, his hair was very dirty. He came from his dirty work. He works in his house.
Teacher: What work does your father do?
Judy (apparently not to the point): We found a dog in the storeroom. Daddy found it. We found another dog. We found a lot, a lot of dogs and they ate me. And we went on a ship and the fish ate me and they took me out of his stomach.
Teacher: I guess that was frightening, when father came home so dirty. Maybe he was tired and angry too and it was frightening like sometimes we're frightened of dogs.

Sometimes the teacher has to be more active in order to stimulate the children to talk about the things that trouble them and be alert to respond when they do express their troubles. This ventilation and expression of feelings makes for good mental health, and in addition, the teacher is better able to see the child's point of view and have better insight into his feelings and the meaning he has derived from his experiences. Once having encouraged the child by giving him the permission to express the feelings that trouble him, the teacher then tries to relieve his sense of guilt by showing him that his feelings are not unique, that he is not a bad boy because he feels that way, but that everybody has feelings like that some time. It is then possible to examine his feelings, to talk about reality and to think about alternative ways of behavior which might be more successful and socially acceptable. It is to be hoped that this will lead the child eventually to channel his energy in creative, positive, satisfying activities and behavior.

JANUARY 1968: Heterogeneous Group
In the discussion period, the teacher asked a leading question on how the children felt when they had to remain in nursery without mother. The children responded by talking with great enthusiasm and relief about how they had cried and what teacher had done to help them. They realized they all

A chat with Mommy.

had similar fears and feelings and they needn't feel ashamed of them. At the same time the teacher stimulated their pride at being big enough now to be on their own in nursery and enumerated all the new things they were learning.

MARCH 1969: Heterogeneous Group

The children had played barber, obviously with much inner satisfaction, but the teacher felt that although they were overcoming their fears of the barber through reenacting their experience, there was still something to be gained by talking about it and here is an excerpt from the discussion:

Edna (D): Children don't know what the barber will do.

Ron (P): They're afraid of scissors.

Aliza (P): I'm afraid of the machine.

Dorit (P): The white apron looks like a doctor. Once when I was little I cried a lot when I went to the barber.

Daphne (P): Today Aliza was my baby and we went to the "barber."

Ruth (D): I was the "barber." I cut Aliza's hair.

Edna (D): I also want to be a "barber."

Teacher: (Reads the children a poem about the barber.)

Sometimes children express very hostile feelings and they are frightened by them.

Naomi's (P) parents went on a trip to the Sinai Desert for five days and Naomi's grandparents came to stay with the children. Naomi is especially attached to her parents, frequently plays the doctor role because her parents are doctors.

On arrival at nursery school Naomi said to the teacher: "My parents are ka-ka. When they come back, I'll throw them into the toilet and flush them down." Teacher recognized her feeling of being very angry at having been left and encouraged her to talk about it. She said, "I'm very glad you told me how you feel and that we could talk about it." They went on to talk about her parents' trip, why it is not allowed to take children along and what arrangements had been made at home.

Later in the day, the teacher initiated a discussion with the children about how they feel when their parents go away. Some of the children expressed anger and fear and others talked about the presents they receive when their parents come home. The teacher led the discussion to the things they can do by themselves when mother is away and how pleased she will be when she comes home and sees how they've grown.

Sometimes children are afraid of expressing their hostile feelings or fears in words, as if expressing them will make them happen. It is sometimes easier to behave badly and be punished in a predictable way than to run the risk of the unknown punishment for expression of angry feelings or deep fears. In those cases it helps when the teacher verbalizes these feelings for the child and in this way relieves his feelings.

To a child who was having difficulty recovering from the trauma of having gotten "lost" when in town with his mother, Teacher said, "When I was little and got lost I thought that mother didn't want to find me because she was angry at me."

"Some children are afraid that if they learn how to dress themselves, mommy won't ever take care of them anymore."

Up to this point we have discussed how the children themselves express their feelings and fears spontaneously in play and talk and how the teacher can encourage these expressions in order to prevent the develop-

"I want to be a baby."

ment of tensions, bottled-up fears, and anxieties. There are some subjects, however, which seem to the child (and often to the adult) to be surrounded with prohibitions and secrecy and which are often avoided in "polite" conversation. Yet often these are the very subjects which are especially emotion-laden and guilt-ridden and may cause havoc to healthy personality development. If these subjects are avoided, the child may begin to feel that he should be ashamed of his curiosity and emotions or that there is a guilty mystery about certain subjects; the feelings he cannot express become repressed and may later appear in uncomfortable symptoms.

For adults, too, there are topics which we find difficult to talk about to children. Because we were brought up to repress certain matters, we have our own inhibitions, conflicting feelings, fears, and shame. Often subjects like sex, death, and feelings of hatred and hostility to parents arouse too much feeling in us and we lend a hand to ignoring these problems. However, if we are aware of the dangers to the child in conspiring to repress his feelings and fears and to keep them hidden, and if we are at all times aware that it is our job to bring feelings to expression and to face them, we can find it within ourselves to create ways to keep these areas open with the children. Our object is to bring the feelings around these subjects to consciousness, to put them into words, and usually we find that when they are seen in the light of reality they are not so black. One of the techniques that can be used is open group discussion. Such a group discussion has just been described in the story of Naomi who is angry at her parents for going away on a trip. Similar discussions with the children on jealousy of younger siblings is described in the section on "Areas of Interest—Babies," page 124.

Death is usually one of the taboo subjects with young children, yet they are constantly being exposed to the word as well as the threat and fact of death. They are more ready to accept the facts of life and death than we think. When these subjects are talked about matter-of-factly, without tension or hesitance, the children, too, assume a direct and matter-of-fact attitude. Though this is difficult for some of us (and it is also necessary to avoid upsetting any religious teachings or beliefs that the children may express), it is important that children should understand that the life cycle consists of birth and death as natural phenomena.

Many teachers are troubled when a pet animal in the nursery dies and they try to hide the fact from the children. Instead of whisking away the animal and maintaining secrecy she might allow the children who are interested to examine it, and she could answer their questions openly and honestly. "When it is dead, it doesn't move or breathe or sleep. It doesn't feel anything, so it doesn't hurt." A group discussion on what happened, with the opportunity to air feelings of sadness and possibly to ask further questions about who dies—mostly old and very sick—can even be followed up by a burial of the dead animal.

Sexual curiosity is a phenomenon which frequently appears in the nursery—children peek into the bathroom, undress for exhibition purposes, are interested in examining each other's genitals. When they do this, they are usually furtive and secretive, feel guilty and excited and generally only succeed in becoming more confused and guilty. This behavior can be diverted by having open discussions where the children can raise the questions and discuss the feelings aroused. Such a discussion could begin with the teacher's remark, "Some children have been very interested in peeking in the bathroom and looking at each other's peepee, I guess there's something you don't understand and are trying to find out." After such a remark by the teacher there is usually an embarrassed titter but as she opens the subject further and encourages the children to talk about the differences in boys and girls, about differences in size and body apertures, there is usually a notable reduction in embarrassment as well as in furtive exploratory behavior. The children have learned that they have a right to be interested in their body, even though there are limitations in how they may behave.

When animals are born in the nursery, there is an excellent opportunity for a group discussion in which children can raise questions like "where did they come from?" "where do children come from?" "why are there so many animals born at once?" etc.

A similar discussion can take place when there is an epidemic of "dirty talk" which sometimes happens. Here, too, the teacher might lead a group discussion, starting with "I've been hearing a lot of talk about wee-wee, duty. Do you like smelling duty?" No answer. "Some children do, lots of them." A child asks, "Are there children who touch their duty?" Another asks whether "some children taste it." The teacher leads the group to go on to talk about how some babies like to play with their feces and even smear it on the walls and on themselves. She then leads the children to talk about why babies do this—they haven't much else to do lying all day in their beds, and they are proud of these things they make. They then go on to talk about all the things they, the big children, can make— paintings, clay objects, block buildings, etc. They can be proud of their good, more grown-up products. The dirty talk usually peters out after such discussions and the children apply themselves more enthusiastically to their work.[3]

One of the pleasant by-products of such group discussions of common feelings and worries is the closeness and understanding that develops among the children. They seem to become more affectionate toward each

[3]Augusta Alpert, "Education as Therapy." *Psychoanalytic Quarterly.*

other, they begin to show sympathy and understanding for the feelings of others, and they learn to comfort each other.

> Chana (D) was sitting in the doll cradle looking very much the "baby." Ruthie (D) came over and began to rock her and croon comfortingly: "Mother went away, mother went away."
>
> Ron (P) watched Yair (P) working with the clay but he himself was undecided whether to touch the messy stuff. Yair said to him encouragingly, "It's not duty; don't be afraid, it's clay."

Special Needs of Deprived Children

It cannot be repeated often enough that the most important factor in nurturing the D children's basic trust, sense of identity, and increased self-esteem was the one-to-one relationship and the warm interest which developed between the teacher and each individual child.

The children all remembered with gratitude and warmth the teacher's first home visit and referred to it frequently. She continued the individual relationship in short, but intimate, one-to-one talks and exchanges at every opportunity throughout the day, in addition to allocating a specific period for individual work with each child. This individual relationship was maintained throughout the two-year program. After several months, however, the teacher was also able to relate to all the children as a group, and they too were progressively more able to have joint activities.

In order to overcome the children's suspiciousness of the teacher and to reduce their often superhuman efforts to achieve premature independence, the teacher found herself responding to them in unorthodox ways. She tried to guard against the child's "being lost" even for one minute; she made efforts to show him that she was always aware of his needs and ready to help; she developed intense sensitivity in order to acquire this awareness and to be for him a dependable, consistent, good mother figure. In spite of the fact that each child wanted her for himself exclusively, they learned to respect and enjoy vicariously the warm attention she was giving to another child. This too developed their trust in her as a consistent giving person.

At the beginning of the work, the teachers found that they needed to relate to the children as if their emotional level was much lower than their chronological age. Our three-year-old D children seemed to respond best to the games and humor of one-and-a-half-year-old children. The teachers became aware that they were picking up and carrying the children a great deal (after some relationship had been developed); they played peek-a-boo; they encouraged them through frequent distribution of candy, food, and little presents. They roused their attention through the songs and dances that are usually appropriate for younger children. They found

Teacher is comforting.

that it was necessary to present things very dramatically; even when telling a story they had to be especially dramatic, raising and lowering their voices in order to hold the children's attention.

The children needed lavish praise and encouragement. At first this praise had to be bestowed for microscopic achievements, and even though the children seemed not to respond at the beginning, the teachers continued with their praise and their attention. Later, as the children made more evident gains and would produce a good building or a good painting or an original dance movement, the teachers showed much enthusiasm and would call the other children to come and look.

After the first year, the teachers found themselves responding to the D children at their proper chronological age levels, but throughout the relationship, they remained aware of the children's hungry need for encouragement, warmth, and recognition.

Goals for Greater Maturity

Up to this point, the basic principles of mental health which underlie the good teacher's relationship with children have been discussed. However, the teacher does not stop at accepting the child at his present emotional level but rather is constantly aiming for higher and higher goals in his emotional maturation and capacity for social behavior.

Striving toward Independence.   The teacher is constantly encouraging and underlining the child's efforts to achieve independence. She enjoys each child's individual growth and recognizes that each will go along at differing rates of progress. In one case she shows Jonah how pleased she is that he could stay in nursery without his mother, and at the next moment she is enthusiastic that Yoram could care for the animals so responsibly, all by himself. However, she recognizes that with the spurts toward independence there are frequent pulls to dependency and babyishness. She knows that she must recognize this legitimate need without shaming the child. Sometimes she even encourages it by "babying" a child who is suffering from the birth of a new baby in the home and provides opportunities in the doll corner for him to play out his need to be a baby. At the same time, she points up the advantages of growing up.

Developing Capacity for Sympathy and Cooperation. It is a slow process to move from the utter egocentricity of a young child to becoming a social animal with capacity for consideration and real concern for others. The teacher knows this and yet is constantly holding up this goal to the children as something to be valued. She teaches these values and moral codes first of all by her own behavior and example. When she shows how pleased she is by each child's unique qualities (and she includes the weaker children), the children too learn to value and accept each other. When the teacher joins them in discussing feelings common to all, the children develop sympathy and affection for each other.

The teacher also explicitly teaches mutual help and concern for each other. She emphasizes that they are a group and that as a group they must work together and be friendly, that it matters what happens to each one. She asks "Who is missing today?" "Who can visit him?" "What gift could we make for him?" On trips they learn that they must help each other. When climbing, the teacher will say, "Help her, you are stronger," or "The tall ones walk behind to watch the smaller ones," or "We wait for each other." They play circle games and dances which help to reinforce the feeling of being one group.

Socially-Acceptable Behavior. Learning to share, taking turns, playing the role of both leader and follower, learning to bear responsibility, to delay immediate gratification, learning persistence, orderliness, and how to get along with others are all consciously taught in a nursery setting. The children are taught that "other people also want things." The teacher's awareness of this and her repeated statements about it—"Uri also wants a turn," "Ehud needs that now"—help the children become aware of it. Responsibility is presented as an important value when the children are assigned specific jobs regularly—setting the tables, cleaning up, care of the animals. A person who carries out his job is highly praised, as is the child who shows persistence at a job.

Some children have more difficulty than others in learning how to get along with other children and often the teacher can help.

Eli (P), an extremely bright child, bursting with ideas, could make no satisfactory relationships. He was very aloof and "superior," showed the children that he "knows it all," would hit and bite at the slightest frustration and actually was usually nonproductive in spite of his abilities. The teacher praised his abilities but showed him that he must learn to be more tolerant of others or else nobody would want to play with him.

She discussed the problem with his mother who announced proudly that she too doesn't make friends with "everybody" and talked of what a superior family they are. The teacher succeeded in convincing her that Eli would be much happier and more productive if he had friends and the mother began inviting children from the group who lived in the neighborhood to play with Eli in the afternoon.

At nursery the teacher was very firm with him. In order to deflect him from spending his time making fun of other children, she gave him responsible leadership jobs that involved other children—"see who needs the drums, and who needs the castanets," "distribute the books," "you and Reuben count how many cups we need at this table." She praised his cooperative behavior rather than his intellectual achievements and slowly Eli began to enjoy his more positive role. He was then freer to use his good ideas and to join and lead others in play. By the end of the year, he still needed much help and guidance in his relationships but he had made considerable progress.

Self-Control and Discipline. The question of how to set limits and achieve socially accepted behavior troubles many teachers. It seems clear that discipline which is achieved by threats, shame and punishments will lower a child's self-esteem and reduce his readiness to use his own initiative and capabilities. The goal is not to have the teacher impose the discipline from above but rather to inspire the child towards self-discipline and self-control. It is when he identifies with the teacher whom he loves and admires, that the child begins to identify with her expectations of him. He himself then wishes to achieve discipline and self-control and tries to accept the reasonableness of the teacher's restrictions. She gives him rational reasons for her rules, and tries to be flexible enough to modify them in order to meet the individual needs of each child.

Whatever rules the teacher sets must be stated clearly, consistently, and with conviction so as to avoid confusions. With an affectionate gesture, she communicates to the child that she understands his feelings and yet must set limits—so she freely gives a comforting pat or hug, holds a disturbing child in her lap, or sometimes picks up and takes out a child and stays with him till he regains control. Then again, she expects a child to pick up the beads he has thrown down in anger, but she also offers to help him.

Essential Aids to Teacher's Understanding of Individual Children

Parents. It goes without saying that in order to really understand any young child's behavior it is necessary to know his parents and also to see the child through their eyes. The teacher must know about various aspects of his past experiences and behavior, how his parents feel about him, his eating and sleeping habits, his toilet training, his brothers and sisters and how they behave with each other, the atmosphere of the home, how he reacts to discipline, and so forth.

Our teachers tried to convey to each mother that they were working together on a joint project for the child's good, and that in order to succeed they would have to keep in contact with each other and exchange information as well as make plans for the child. A plan needed to be made by both teacher and parents because without the parents' cooperation it was not likely to succeed. This was more difficult to achieve with some of the D parents but attempts in this direction were always made.

When a mother sensed that the teacher really liked and was interested in her child, it helped her too to see her child as an individual and as a worthwhile person. The teacher would tell the mother about some special skill or achievement of her child and would show her own pleasure in his qualities. At the same time she would praise the mother for a special way she had handled her child or taught him some skill. This mark of interest often aroused the parents to begin to see and to value their child more and to recognize his own special needs and abilities.

Sometimes the teachers sensed that parents were dissatisfied with their children because they showed immature behavior and they tried to educate the parents about normal behavior for children of this age level. This information was conveyed in individual meetings between parent and teacher, in discussions at parent group meetings, and also by having the parents observe in the nursery to see how children of this age level function.

Home visits by the teacher were invaluable in establishing closer parent-teacher relationships and in helping the teacher to understand better the child and his environment.[4]

Teachers' Observations, Notes, and Reports. Teachers are usually delightfully surprised at the amount of knowledge and understanding they have gained about a child when they read short records that they themselves have written of individual children. Such notes could take the form of a running record of his behavior for ten minutes, jotting down an anec-

---

[4]More detailed description of work with parents is given in Chapter 5.

dote at the end of the day, or a more detailed summary of one full day of his activity in the nursery. When the teacher makes an effort to observe a particular child, she suddenly acquires insights into his behavior that she rarely gets when she sees him as part of the larger group. She discovers how he makes his contacts with other children, spends his time, carries out his ideas in play or work, and expresses himself. By analyzing her detailed notes, she is more able to make a hypothesis of why he is behaving the way he is.

Our teachers usually kept a pad of paper and pencil in their pockets and when there were a few free minutes, they would record observations of a particular child—both his behavior and what he seemed to be feeling. At the end of the day, in addition to their recording of the group's activities, they would try to write a summary of a particular child whom they had chosen to observe specifically that day. One set of teachers found it was helpful to tack up a notice to themselves with the child's name in order to remind themselves that this was the child under observation that day. With the help of the insights from the records, the teachers felt more able to plan for the individual child and to assess his rate of progress.

Making a summary and assessment of an individual child after a period of time is another aid to the teacher in organizing thinking and planning for the child. Such a summary would include a description of the child, his physical development and abilities, his relationship to both children and adults, his feeling about himself. It should also include an assessment of his intellectual development—language, perception, concept formation, memory, attention span, as well as character traits such as dependency, ability to tolerate frustration, negativism, and aggressiveness. It is helpful when the summary ends with an evaluation of the strengths and difficulties of the child, the plan that was made to help him, what the outcome of the plan was, and recommendations for future planning.

EDUCATIONAL PHILOSOPHY

Curiosity—The Basis of Learning

Every child is born "with a tremendous urge to find out about things."[5] He wants to explore the physical world surrounding him; he wants to taste things, feel them, move them, starting with his own body, progressing through the pots and pans in the kitchen to complicated as-

[5]Lucy Sprague Mitchell, *Our Children and Our Schools* (New York: Simon & Schuster, 1950).

pects of automobiles, airplanes, electricity, and moving onto everything else within his experience.

Curiosity is the child's greatest asset in the development of his learning and thinking; it is when he has an inner urge to find out something or to do something that he does his most eager learning. Barbara Biber and Patricia Minuchin have said, "Learning is optimal when it takes shape as an independent pursuit by an actively involved child."[6]

A child's natural learning process begins with examining the things about him through the use of his senses and muscles. Through much trial and error and repetition, he eventually arrives at conclusions and makes generalizations. He makes mud pies hundreds of times, thereby learning the principle that you can make them only from wet, and not from dry, sand. Sometimes his conclusions are wrong, as when he induces that the milk bottles in the milk truck come from the grocery store because that is where his mother gets the milk. These conclusions have to be reexamined and retested in the light of reality.

However, he makes these discoveries and uses these reasoning processes only when he is dealing with matters that are real and important to *him*, and related to something significant in his own life experience. When he is given more and more opportunities to satisfy his curiosity, to sense and explore the things about him, and to gather more information, he establishes the foundation upon which he can develop concepts. At a later stage, he develops the ability to "see the relationship" between relevant pieces of information. It is in the more complex process of concept formation that aid and guidance by the teacher is needed.

Curiosity, with which every child is endowed at birth, is the basis of scientific thinking and needs to be nurtured and encouraged. It can easily be stifled by numerous or punitive restrictions, or by inadequate stimulation. Many of our culturally deprived children had their natural wish to explore suppressed by limitations in the home environment, and they came to the nursery with passive, accepting, and magical modes of thinking. Their curiosity seemed to have been inhibited. It we could free them from the restrictions that dampened their natural curiosity, if we could encourage and arouse it, their energies would again be directed toward the absorbing task of satisfying their need to explore the world. The mode of thinking that involves searching for the "why" and the "how" is basically different from the approach of culturally-deprived children who accept things as they are or who seem to believe in mysterious forces that cause things to happen. Therefore, they are especially in need of the experience in examination, investigation, and discovery.

[6]Biber and Minuchin, "Educating for Individuality."

Self-Motivated Learning versus Passive Learning. The child who *wants* to investigate something will learn far more from his experience than the child who is passively taught something that educators have decided is good for him. Research has shown that a child who climbs a tree because he wants to get to the top gets far more valuable exercise and muscle development than the one who does routine gym exercises. Similarly, mechanical word drill will never take the place of the self-motivated use of language when an excited child has something important to tell.

The child shows us clearly the directions of his interests and questions. The teacher or the parent then can encourage his attempts to investigate; can stimulate him to widen his area of interest and to question further; and can enable him to clarify his thinking through provision of materials, pictures, books, discussions, and trips for further investigation. But the initial interest and direction usually must come from the child, to achieve maximal learning.

A discovery approach to learning does not obviate the need for review, repetition, and drill, which is a necessary ingredient in the learning process. Disadvantaged children, especially, need structured exercises as well as repeated opportunities to recall past experiences and concepts that they have gathered in their free explorations in order to digest their newly acquired knowledge more fully. In working with the disadvantaged child it is sometimes necessary to change the proportion of time allotted in the curriculum for activities initiated by the children in order to provide more opportunity for review and drill. Nevertheless, in planning a program for disadvantaged children, the basic way in which children naturally go about learning must be borne in mind.

"Learning by Doing." Researchers and thinkers in education and learning theory such as John Dewey, Lucy Sprague Mitchell, and Jerome Bruner have all stressed one other important principle in the learning process. John Dewey has put it very succinctly: "learning by doing" and Lucy Sprague Mitchell has described "the inner urge to do something about it"[7] when we are truly learning. We have only really learned something when we have *used* what we learned, when we have actually tried it out or combined the new piece of information with a fact already known to us, or when we suddenly discover that it fits in with another area which is of deep interest to us.

Let us stop at this point and think about our own educations. What are the areas that we have forgotten or remember only vaguely and what things have we really learned and always remember and use? In each case, we will find that what we remember is in some area where we had to do

---

[7]Mitchell, *Our Children and Our Schools.*

some investigation on our own, where we had to organize information and present it in some form. Perhaps there was a project in school that became a living experience since we presented a play or wrote a story or prepared a chart or built a model, or perhaps we needed to teach it to others or do some other kind of group or individual activity with it.

——— The learning process is not one-way. It is made up of both *intake* and *outgo*[8]—children absorb and digest what they have experienced and observed (their intake) by *doing something active* about it (their outgo). They express their knowledge, ideas, and feelings through their play and their use of materials and thus make their knowledge an integral part of themselves.

Applications to Curriculum Planning

In translating these learning principles to curriculum planning on the nursery level, we found it necessary to expose the child to many real experiences and then to provide him with ample equipment and opportunities to try out and act out all the vast pieces of information that he constantly was absorbing. The teacher did less direct frontal teaching but saw herself more as a prodder and stimulator to more exploration and more active use of the information and knowledge constantly being acquired. She did less teaching of words and concepts and more presentation of opportunities and challenges to discover.

Play as the Cornerstone of the Learning Process. What is the young child's "outgo" in the learning process? How does he absorb and assimilate his learning experiences? It is through playing, through the active use of his body, that he does his research, his learning, and his digesting of knowledge. As he pokes his fingers into the clay or picks up the blocks, he learns through his own senses what is soft, what is hard, what is long, what is small, and so forth. As he plays that he is the driver, he is thinking about an automobile, what it feels like when it rides, and what makes it run; as his play centers on an airplane, airfield, and observation tower, he is absorbing and digesting his fascinating trip to the airfield. "It looks like play but it is thinking, too." He is reviewing his experiences and expressing them in his own special symbolic language—play.

Only at a later stage does he prefer to use words as a way of expressing his thoughts. He is gradually building his vocabulary through his explorations and through his play. The adult can and often should accompany his explorations with a "bombardment of words," but these words are an accompaniment and not a substitute for his actual experiences.

[8]Lucy Sprague Mitchell, "Ages & Stages," *Child Study*, February 1938.

In planning our curriculum we made provision for the children's spontaneous play as the cornerstone of our program. We did not see play as "busy work" but as the form in which pre-school work and learning take place. We provided the time and the raw materials for play. We knew that the children's choice of what they would play would reflect the interesting and exciting events in their daily lives and in their inner lives. We decided that the teacher's major teaching role was *with the play*.

The teachers understood that the child engaged in dramatic play is rehearsing and examining his information about the real world and in his fantasy play also was identifying with the various roles of heroes and villains and drawing out his own private feelings. In presenting the children with first-hand experiences and information, the teacher helped them to recognize what was real and what was fantasy. Frequent trips into the neighborhood to encourage interest in and understanding of the fascinating everyday elements of daily living were an essential part of the curriculum. The trips served as stimuli and material for enhancing and clarifying the play. The teachers used the group discussions as well as discussions with individual children to verbalize what had happened in the play and to clarify the ideas that had been enacted. These discussion periods also were used to plan what new elements could be added to make the play richer and more satisfying.

In this way, the play became more and more of a learning experience. As it became more complicated and purposeful, higher and higher elements of the thinking process were called for. The children moved slowly from simple manipulation and exploration of the materials to more detailed examination of the real life situations for the purpose of having richer play experiences. Finally they were able to achieve the expression of more and more involved ideas in their play and discussions.

Other Aspects of the Curriculum.   Other channels for the children's "outgo" were creative art work, carpentry, cooking, music, and dancing. Phenomena in nature were examined as they were encountered, as were other "science" experiences.

Structured Learning Experience.   The principles and practices that have been described up to this point apply to all young children and their basic needs. We felt that it is the right of every child to have such an educational environment and that culturally deprived children should not miss this vital, satisfying, and stimulating experience, their obvious cognitive defects notwithstanding. However, it was clear that they needed additional help and teaching to enable them to use their experience; they needed extra exercises to improve their ability to perceive what was happening around them. Above all, they needed many and varied stimulations to use language.

The problem required much sensitivity, and it was not easy to determine the proper balance in programming for each individual child. When and how much did he need opportunities for his own exploration and play and when was it preferable to give him more drill in perception and verbal expression? In spite of long-term planning for each child, we constantly had to make instantaneous decisions. Many questions frequently arose on this issue. Do you always correct his errors in pronunciation and grammar, or is it sufficient sometimes to appreciate his readiness to express himself and to wait with the more structured drill for another opportunity? Does this child need additional exercises in classification and categorization when he has been excellent in arranging the blocks according to size and shape and the cups according to colors? At what point after his own repeated experiences with blocks and with water play and carpentry, do you actually teach him to classify height, weight, volume, etc?

Only occasionally did we use the structured learning experience as a frontal teaching exercise for the whole group. For the most part, we designed the exercises for work with individual children in separate sessions and occasionally we arranged a small group who needed help on a specific cognitive problem.

We were very eclectic in our choice of structured learning experiences—we used some of the work sheets of Nizza Naftali,[9] and techniques based on the work of Carl Bereiter,[10] Susan Gray[11] and Marion Blank.[12] These were in addition to the many games that we devised in the process of the work, as well as form boards and lottos that were available.

In summary, our curriculum approach was based on a few fundamental points of view about young children's development and the thinking process, as well as certain outlooks on cultural deprivation:

1. Young children learn through their own experiences and activities which are sparked by their natural curiosity and wish to find out.

2. Children's sense of identity and self-esteem is based on the way they perceive the attitudes of their parents and teachers to them. Their sense of worth is enhanced as they experience that they too "can do" and that what they do is important and respected.

3. Free play, in which children spontaneously and repeatedly relive their experiences symbolically serves as an important medium for children's learning and developing deeper understanding of the world about them.

[9]Nizza Naftali, *Work Sheets*, Israel Ministry of Education, 1969.
[10]Carl Bereiter and Siegfried Engelman, *Teaching Disadvantaged Children in the Pre-School* (Englewood Cliffs, N. J.: Prentice-Hall, Inc., 1966).
[11]Susan Gray, Rupert A. Klaus, James O. Miller, and Bettye J. Forrester, *Before First Grade* (New York; Teachers College Press, Columbia University, 1966).
[12]Marion Blank and Frances Solomon, "A Tutorial Language Program to Develop Abstract Thinking in Socially Disadvantaged Pre-School Children," *Child Development*, 34, No. 2 (1968).

The culturally disadvantaged child needs additional help to:

1. restore his curiosity and ability to perceive clearly,
2. learn to express himself in words and in symbolic play,
3. develop a sense of basic trust and self-esteem.

ROLE OF THE TEACHER IN INTELLECTUAL DEVELOPMENT

The attempt to arrive at a clear definition and understanding of the role of the teacher in stimulating intellectual development was one of the most difficult aspects of our work. We sat together and thrashed it out at long seminars before we began the actual work with the children; we continued to think about it and enlarge on it at weekly meetings of the staff and at weekly supervisory meetings with individual teachers; and we further revised and redefined it as problems arose in the day-to-day work.

One thing was clear—a teacher's job is to teach. She must be aware at all times that she is there to promote learning and thinking. The difficulty was that our joint beliefs in how children learn led us inevitably to see the teacher's role as a very flexible one, one that could not be defined in exact rules and recipes as to what a teacher should be doing at a particular time, in a particular situation.

As stated above, we were all deeply convinced that children learn best when they are driven by their own natural curiosity and desire to know. We believed that the children had to be exposed to many experiences; to be stimulated to perceive, examine and understand what they were seeing and doing; and to be free to express what they were learning through active and spontaneous play. We realized that without active stimulation, interest, and encouragement by the teacher, the play might have a tendency to become static. We were convinced that the teacher can play an important role in arousing questioning, and yet on the other hand, has a tendency inadvertently to stifle explorations in the interests of order and organization in the classroom.

This was our guideline, but the problem was how to translate it into concrete action. When and how do you set up the conditions for spontaneous exploration and play, and at what point does the teacher step in to stimulate further, to question, to add information? What about the children who do not seem to want to play or know how to play? What about the children who do not talk or who talk very little? What about those who move impulsively from one piece of equipment to another but do not seem to relate to any of it? What about the children who seem glued to the tables in stereotyped and repetitive activities? How does the teacher make

herself more aware of an opportunity for arousing curiosity and for seeing when a learning situation is at hand? At what point should she be
ready to move with the children into a new and unexpected field? When
does the teacher's stepping in inhibit the child's fantasy? These and many
more questions were being raised constantly. In most cases, the answer
was a qualitative one—it depended on the individual child, on the circumstances, and on the teacher's own ability to be flexible without feeling
torn and strained. It became increasingly clear that in many cases there
could be no formula and that the teacher would have to rely on her own
instantaneous decision.

In practice, we saw that the teacher's role in intellectual stimulation
had enormously wide scope. It extended from merely *setting up the scene*,
providing the materials and letting the children go on from there, to actually *getting into the play* as one of its participants. It ranged from *noticing* that a child was observing, questioning, or examining something
and encouraging this investigation, to pushing and *arousing* a child to
see or hear or smell. It included *talking constantly* to an inarticulate child
and being ready to listen and understand his garbled talk, to *stimulating
children to express themselves* in creative writing and expression. It varied
from *actual structured exercises* and games in classification, discrimination, language usage, and expression, to exposing the children to real life
activities which required these thinking processes (like putting away blocks
according to size and shape). It ran from *actual exercises in logic* to constant *stimulation of logical thinking* through questions like "What happened here?" or "How do you know?" or "What would happen if . . . ?"
The teacher sometimes *casually provided a material* that would encourage
a play experience to expand into a related area, and at the other extreme
she sometimes *planned a detailed project* that would encompass a whole
segment of a life experience, like "our neighborhood," which included
houses, stores, schools, synagogues, electricity, water, etc. In each instance
the deciding issues were: Where is the child in his present development
and what are his particular needs?

The teacher saw her role as a stimulator to independent thinking,
more than as a disseminator of information; as one who goads to greater
awareness and use of the senses, to greater feeling of confidence and independence, rather than as a disciplinarian who must see to it that the
children learn to accept a set program.

The following episodes are designed to illustrate some of the varied
roles of the teacher as she attempted to stimulate play and thinking, as
she strove to underline the cognitive aspects in the play activities and in
the use of the materials.

The following episodes are taken from the daily records of the observer or from the teacher's diaries. It is interesting to note the dates

in order to obtain a clearer picture of the children's development over the two-year period from September 1967 (when the children were three years old) to June 1969.

Teacher Sets the Scene: Arrangement of Equipment and Adding of Materials When Needed

DECEMBER 1967: Homogeneous Group D

A pleasant, warm day. The children are scattered around the yard playing with wagons, self-made slides and tire swings. Teacher decides that something besides the motor activity should be introduced into the outdoor play. She demonstratively arranges blankets over the open side of three large crates which she places side by side to resemble rooms with doors. This is enough of a hint for Adena who organizes the play. Five children leave the running about and become a family that lives in the house. There is much argument about assigning of roles—all the boys want to be father— and teacher suggests that there be two families. The play continues as the two families begin to feud and call in the police.

DECEMBER 1967: Heterogeneous Group

The doll corner play has become static. The girls sit with the dolls, occasionally carry them about and feed them.

Teacher decides to give the play a push by placing medicine bottles and cotton in the doll corner. The children find it in the morning and immediately the play develops around the illness of the dolls. Noa (P) becomes the doctor, Ronit (D) is the nurse, and the babies are brought to the health clinic.

MARCH 1969: Heterogeneous Group

For two days, the girls have been playing hairdresser. They sit in front of the mirror, comb each other's hair, and occasionally put on some rollers. Teacher makes a hair dryer by attaching wires to a basket which she fixes to a hook in such a way that the dryer can then be raised and lowered. The girls immediately begin wetting their hair, putting on curlers, and using "spray." Discussions on the temperature of the water, on costs and payments for the hairdresser continue for several days.

Teacher Demonstrates How to Play

NOVEMBER 1967: Heterogeneous Group

The D children have not yet really begun building with blocks, although they have been observing how the P children are building.

Teacher decides that the time has come for them to build their own buildings. She sits down on the floor and begins building by herself quietly. Immediately Shlomo (D), Jonah (D), and Ruth (D) sit down beside her. Wordlessly they each take several blocks of various sizes and begin building—imitating the teacher's structure. Shlomo continues the teacher's building as she stops. Jonah is concentrating intensely and adds a slanting roof to his building. He brings a car over and drives it around the building. Ruth continues building until her structure reaches a height of one meter. She is very careful and exact in her choice of blocks and enjoys the stability of the building. Later she takes it apart very carefully block by block and not in the usual pattern of kicking it down.

Teacher Takes a Role in the Play and Makes Direct Suggestions

NOVEMBER 1967: Homogeneous Group D

The children play with dough and Dafna says to the teacher, "Here is an egg." Aliza and Gila imitate what she made and they also make eggs. Dafna wanders about the room with the egg in her hand shouting "Eggs, eggs." There are no buyers. Teacher buys an egg from Dafna but still there are no buyers. Teacher suggests to her to make a store and sell the eggs there. Dafna and Aliza use the empty blocks shelves for the "store" and deposit their eggs there. Teacher takes a shopping bag and goes to the store and buys eggs, and asks if they have other products. This brings Shmuel who sits down on a chair near them and sells "pittot" (Oriental bread). Danny joins him and also sells pittot. This begins a rash of salesmen. Yaakov seats himself near a wagon full of blocks and shouts, "Watermelons." Shlomo takes dough and places lumps on the floor. To teacher's question, he answers, "They are cakes." Teacher suggests making a nice shape for the cakes and hands him a long, flat block as a tray. He shapes the cakes, places them on the blocks, takes more blocks and manufactures more cakes. He covers this all with a shirt. When teacher asks why, he says, "So no flies will come."

Teacher is a playmate.

The play attracts more children, but everyone wants to sell. Teacher divides the children into buyers and sellers. The noise and hawking make the sound of a marketplace. Children shout their wares and the buyers buy happily. [The teacher's very active intervention succeeded at this stage in activating the more advanced of the children who were able to use her suggestions. But it was still too early to have much carry-over without active teacher supervision.]

Teacher Stimulates and Encourages Curiosity and Exploration

JANUARY 1968: Heterogeneous Group

Yoav (P) keeps disappearing into the bathroom, playing with turning on the faucet, filling the sink with water, letting it drain out. Teacher comes in to find him and entice him back to the playroom, but senses his deep involvement and interest in what he is doing. Together they examine what happens when you turn the faucet on, what happens when you pull out the stopper. They both watch these processes fascinated. Teacher throws out the questions: "I wonder how the water gets there," "I wonder where it goes," and makes a mental note to go back to this when the occasion arises, perhaps with Yoav alone, perhaps with a group who would also be interested, perhaps when they build a house. Perhaps at water play she will bring a faucet and water pipe and see whether this subject will interest more children.

OCTOBER 1969: Heterogeneous Group

Uri (P) and Ron (P) are wheeling a wagon, hit the threshold, and get stuck. This happens several times as they run about with the wagon. Teacher (her mind and eyes on the clay table) goes over and lifts it each time over the threshold. Finally on the fourth time around she sits down next to them and wonders why it gets stuck. They examine the threshold and the wheels. She asks: "What can we do?" Ron lifts the front wheels, pulls, and lifts the back wheels. Both children are delighted as they come back to the threshold each time in their rounds and handle the wagon themselves.

SEPTEMBER 1967: Heterogeneous Group

The water box is being filled for the first time. The teacher attaches a hose to the faucet and the other end to the water box. She turns on the water, and the children are delighted as the water comes in. [We ask ourselves, was this a lost opportunity? Should we have examined how it works and had the children take turns in opening and shutting the tap, or was it sufficient that they were having a first experience in water play?]

DECEMBER 1967: Heterogeneous Group

Udi (P) is building a complicated structure with blocks (his favorite occupation). He places a long block on the floor and stands a block on the floor at either end. He takes another long block and tries to put it across the top of the two standing blocks. As he places it on one end, the other end falls down. He tries repeatedly, each time failing, of course. Teacher watches this, notes it carefully, and lets him go on with his repeated attempts. [She decides that he is well enough motivated and has sufficient belief in himself to keep trying until he hits upon the solution.]

DECEMBER 1967: Heterogeneous Group

Sara (D) is finally building a "house." The blocks keep falling and she is about to leave it. Teacher sits down with her and they build together. [Sara needs the satisfaction of a finished product and the closeness with the teacher, as well as a satisfactory experience with a new material.]

Teacher Stimulates Through Questions

MAY 1968: Heterogeneous Group

Edna (P) and Dalia (P) are playing in the doll corner for a long time in the repetitive play of putting the baby to bed and feeding her. They change mother and baby roles frequently. When Edna is the mother, she brings the bed over to the stove, puts Dalia into the bed, and prepares food to feed her. Dalia is not ready to remain in the bed, stands up on it, and "cooks" at the stove.

Teacher (to Dalia): How does your mother cook at home? What does she stand on?

Dalia (getting the hint): In our house the bed isn't in the kitchen.

Teacher: Where is it?

Edna: In the bedroom.

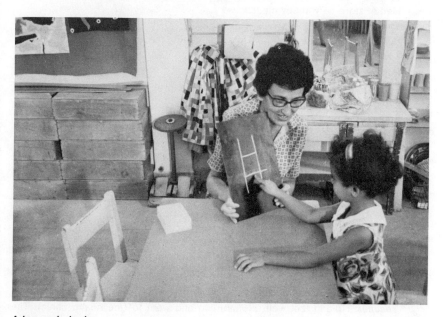

A lesson in logic.

Both girls push the bed into the "bedroom" and busy themselves re-arranging the house and the furniture, adding decorations.

MAY 1968: Heterogeneous Group

Ilan (P), Shlomi (D), and Yoav (P) are pushing cars back and forth from room to room making a lot of noise. Teacher comes over and begins questioning where they are going, where is the road, etc. The children discuss it and decide that they are driving to the garage and that they need a road. They begin to build a road and a garage. When the road is finished they are faced with the problem of the height of the road above the floor (the height of the block) and how the car can get off the road. Teacher sits down with them as they think about it together. Uri (P), who is standing at the side watching, brings a ramp block and solves the problem. The children are excited with the slanting ramp and drive happily.

The next problem that arises is how to get into the garage which has been built without a door. It is decided that a door is needed. Teacher helps the children to plan how to make it. They go over to the entrance door of the nursery and examine it carefully, especially the hinge. The children go back, choose one of the blocks to be a door, and attach it to the garage using adhesive plaster as a hinge. They also add a handle made of plasticene.

SEPTEMBER 1968: Heterogeneous Group

The children are playing in the "doctor's corner." They are mostly concentrating on the medicine bottles and the salves.

Teacher: Let me see what you have there. It looks like a store. In what kind of store do you buy medicines?

Yoav (P): In a pharmacy.

Ron (P): There's a man there who gives out the medicines.

Teacher: What do you call him?

Ron (P): A pharmacist.

Yoav (P): My mother is a pharmacist. She prepares medicines and salves and gives them out to people.

Teacher: How does the pharmacist know what medicine to give to people?

Ron (P): The doctor examines and writes a note.

Edna (D): He gives syrup.

Ronit (D): Salve.

Ron (P): Medicine.

Teacher: What else do we need here in the doctor's corner?

Ron (P): We need an office for the doctor. Let's build it.

Yoav (P): (Immediately brings a telephone. There is a division of jobs—a doctor, a nurse, a clerk, a pharmacist.)

Naomi (D): The nurse gives injections and medicines.

Aliza (D): And salves.

Ron (P): The doctor examines.

Teacher: I didn't feel well this morning and went to (the health clinic). The clerk gave me number I in the queue.

Aliza (D): Goes in first.

There is much activity in preparation of queue numbers.

Teacher Alerts to Comparisons

DECEMBER 1968: Heterogeneous Group

Children are planning a trip to the railroad station. They will go there by bus. Teacher leads a discussion on the similarities and the differences between a bus and a train. This discussion was repeated after the trip when many details were added.

The discussion held before the trip led to the following dictation by the children:

A bus has wheels; a train has wheels.

A bus has a motor; a train has an engine.

A bus carries people; a train carries people.

But a train has many cars, and a bus has one car.

But a train rides on tracks, and a bus rides on the road.

Similar discussions took place when they compared children and hamsters, dough and plasticene, plasticene and clay, houses and tents, plastic and iron (they heated each of them).

Teacher Uses Trip to Stimulate Discussion and Play

OCTOBER 1968: Heterogeneous Group

The active airplane play led to a need for a trip to the airport. The purpose of the trip was to observe real airplanes, an airport, taking off and landing, the waiting room and control tower. This was clearly planned in several discussions preceding the trip.

At the airport we succeeded in seeing and experiencing all we had set out to do except for the control tower, which we were not able to see in operation. We had set too many goals and we felt that the excitement of the children and the many areas we wished to observe impeded real absorption. Nevertheless it was a very meaningful experience for the children.

As soon as we returned, Danny (P), Eli (P), and Reuben (P) (who had originally begun the airplane play) sat down with the blocks to reconstruct what they had seen. They built a runway and a control tower. At lunch time there was a lively discussion about the trip. The children asked many questions and were deeply interested. Danny, Eli, and Reuben were the most active in the discussion. The others listened with seeming interest, but Annette (D) said to teacher; "You know today we went to the airport."

[This again brought home to the teacher the gap in the two groups and how much the D group needed extra help. No doubt Annette had been very stimulated by the trip and wanted also to participate in the discussion, but the experience was still a confused jumble to her. Her remark was a signal to the teacher that she would have to work with Annette individually in order to help her absorb and organize what she had seen. They would have to go over and recall all the events and scenes of the trip. They would have to look at books and pictures, watch how the children were reenacting the experience in their play and then they would talk about it.]

Teacher Asks Leading Questions to Stimulate Thinking and Richer Language Usage at Discussion Time

It is a hot day. Teacher asks, "How do you know it is hot today?" Children answer, "My face is hot," "I am tired," "I feel thirsty," "perspiration," "I want to sleep."

The children are running outdoors. When they sit down, teacher asks, "What does your body feel when you run?" Children talk of being out of breath, feeling hot, sensing their heart pumping.

Similar questions are: "How do you feel when you come in from the rain?" "How did you know that it is a ball without seeing it?"

Teacher Uses Everyday Events for Learning Purposes

DECEMBER 1967: Homogeneous D Group

The teacher comes to school with a can of kerosene. She arouses a discussion on this by asking why one buys kerosene, and where. She fills the kerosene stove with the help of the children. They talk of the smell and the feel of the kerosene. She lights the stove while they carefully observe and then they sit near it and talk about the heat the stove is giving off.

[No worker (plumber, carpenter, electrician) who came to perform some service was ignored, and each was used as a primary source of learning. The children were asked to think about why he had to come; they observed his work and were encouraged to ask many questions and examine his tools. Delivery wagons and garbage trucks became objects of interest for the children and the teacher.]

Teacher Uses Discussion as Means of Deepening Understanding

MARCH 1969: Homogeneous D Group

Yoav, Edna, Danny, and Jonah built a bus and drove it. As they got off the bus at their stop, they wanted the driver to give them their money back. Jonah, the driver, refused saying, "No, you already had a ride on the bus." There was an argument, and they turned to me complaining that Jonah took their money and won't return it. I decided to leave a full discussion of this for the discussion period:

Teacher: This morning Yoav, Danny, and Edna were riding in Jonah's bus. They paid money to Jonah and when they got off they wanted the money back. Jonah didn't want to give it back because he said they had already had a ride for the money. What do you think about that? When you get on a bus with mother what happens?

Danny: Mommy gives the driver money when she gets on the bus.

Teacher: And what does the driver give Mommy?

Yoav: Money and a ticket.

Teacher: Yes, Mommy gets a ticket that she paid for the bus and sometimes she gets change if she gives too much money. Does Mommy get money when she gets off?

Yossi (very definitely): No, she already rode for the money.

Teacher Is Persistent When Necessary

DECEMBER 1967: Homogeneous D Group

Nissim, who spends much time sitting and doing nothing, looking lost and frightened, picks up a ball from the floor. He rolls the ball a bit in his hands and examines the pictures on it. He yawns but continues to look at the ball. He raises his head a bit and looks in the direction of the door, holding the ball very indifferently, begins to examine the ball again and makes some minute rhythmic motions with his head and the ball.

Teacher approaches with a broad smile. In a subtle way Nissim seems to react to the smile. She leans down to him: "Would you like to come out with me to play ball?" She reaches her hands out toward the ball. Nissim lets go and the ball falls to the floor.

Teacher (smilingly): Here, you throw the ball. Catch it quickly before it rolls away!

He makes no move. She bends down, picks up the ball and throws it gently to him.

Teacher: Here, catch. (The ball touches him gently, he smiles but doesn't catch it, yet continues to watch the path of the ball.)

Teacher picks it up, throws it to him again and says: "Maybe you should stand up and then you'll be able to catch the ball." He smiles weakly but still doesn't try to get the ball. Teacher assists him gently to stand up. He looks down rather than looking directly at the teacher. Teacher rolls the ball to him, then walks to it, bends, picks it up, holds it in her hands and says to Nissim, "Throw it to my arms and not on the floor." She raises her arms, gets ready to throw it, but bends down and hands it to Nissim. This time it remains in his arms while he remains standing and smiling. She says, "Throw it, throw it to my arms, not on the floor." She actually takes the ball from him and hands it back but he at least holds on to it when he gets it. An infinitesimal gain, but a long step for Nissim.

MARCH 1969: Homogeneous D Group

Yossi has persisted, in spite of our efforts, in wandering about lazily and purposelessly. He has always refused to cooperate in the clean-up period. The only activity in which he has shown some interest is in playing auto. In a stereotyped way he would set up a driver's wheel on one of the wooden fences used to protect the block area, pull up a chair, sit down, and "drive," making automobile noises. This activity would continue a good part of the day.

I decided to use forceful methods to spur him into activity. I told him not to use the fence for his car but instead suggested that he build a car "like we saw on the trip." In spite of my suggestions, he persisted in ignoring what I had said and again built his usual car. It took a week of persistent attention, insistence, and encouragement before he began to build a car out of blocks at all.

Today he built a car with a seat, a complicated front window, and extra seats for passengers. He supplied himself with cigarettes and matches, placed near the driver's seat, put on glasses, and began to drive, taking on passengers.

At the same time that I encouraged his building, I was also very insistent in demanding that he pick up blocks during clean-up time.

. . . today was a high point in his progress. He seemed to be such a hard-core problem over such a long period in his unreadiness for concentrated and protracted play. Today, what stood out especially was his pleasure in his building, in his own activity, and his very thorough participation at clean-up time.

Teacher Assists When Necessary

SEPTEMBER 1969: Heterogeneous Group

Uri (P) sat at the table making a derrick out of wooden screws and bolts. He was running into difficulties and came to me saying, "My derrick doesn't work and it makes me mad." Since he had been working in a very concentrated way, I felt he needed some help and encouragement. I sat down with him and said, "Let's think together what we could do so that the derrick won't collapse." He suggested, "Let's add a wheel." We added it and I brought a book with a picture of a derrick. After examining the picture he said: "We need rope." He added the rope and by then four other children (two D and two P children) had gathered to participate in the work. They handed us screws, asked questions, and gave advice.

In the discussion period we talked about Uri's derrick and his problems in building it. We all examined the picture of the derrick and talked about how the problem was solved. We went on to discuss the function of a derrick and decided to talk about it again tomorrow.

Teacher Picks Up a Cue and Expands on a Theme

FEBRUARY 1969: Heterogeneous Group

Each of three children builds his own house. Each house has cellophane windows "so that there will be light in the house," says Oded (P).

The teacher joins them to discuss the problem of light in the house. Yoav (P) says, "At night it is dark." Teacher: "How do we see at night?" Natan (P): "We need electricity." Eli (D): "You need a light switch to have electricity."

In the group discussion, Jonah (D) tells that he had built a garage.

Teacher (continuing the earlier discussion): How can you see in the garage at night?

Ruth (D): You open all the windows and all the doors so the light can come in.

Teacher: And if it is dark outside?

Gabriel (P): In the street there are street lamps but in the house you need electricity.

Yoav (D): The electricity comes from the power station. (Opposite the nursery is an electric power station which services the area.)

Yaakov (P): The electricity comes from there.

The teacher leaves the problem to percolate.

The next day, in the early morning planning period, Yoav (P) and Eli (D) say they want to build together and need an electric wire to connect their house to the power station. The teacher takes a small group out to look at the power station—to see how the electric line goes from it to the nursery. They see that the electric line disappears into the walls. They come to the conclusion that the line is in the walls. They also notice that there are lines going to other houses too. At a later stage of the morning, Oded (P) and Ilan (P) build a building so filled with electric wires that they decide that it will be the powerhouse itself. The lines go out to all the buildings—to Zvi's (P) house, to Jonah's (D) garage (at his request), to the "military headquarters," and to Naomi's (D) house. Each house that had an electric wire also had an electric switch.

Oded (P) and Ilan (P) add a large electric switch and other electric poles to their power station. There is an electric grid going all over the nursery. They then add a large cardboard pole and gleefully announce, "This is the television of the power station." (The teacher decides to leave this confused thinking for a later date.)

The next day a series of buildings are again built and the electric grid becomes even more complicated. The children dictate signs (which the teacher makes for them) saying, "Electric Power Station—Don't Come Near," "Danger—Electricity—Don't Climb."

The group decides to go again the next day to the power station. They examine the heavy poles and ask, "Where is the electricity?" They decide it goes from the big wheels in the power station into the wires. Gabriel (P) asks "What's in the building?" Oded says, "There is a big battery with electricty."

The next day the teacher brings batteries, bulbs, and electric wires, and the children experiment with connecting the wires to the batteries and the bulbs. They find that the bulb lights when you connect two wires to the battery. Some batteries don't make the bulb work. Yair (D) says "It is used up, it's old, it has no power anymore.' They conclude that perhaps if a battery is old, it doesn't work.

At the end of the year when the model of the "neighborhood" was built, the children remembered to attach electric wires to the houses.

Teacher Questions Her Role

JANUARY 1968: Heterogenous Group (from the teacher's diary)

The children are not always pleased at our readiness to help them when they build. Perhaps we don't always sense the correct moment. When we don't seem to get a positive response, we usually decide that the child still needs opportunities to experiment with the material at his own pace. We offer help but we don't impose it.

Today we felt the children's need to build as high as they could. The children called the building the Supermarket building, but actually it could have been called anything else, because they ignored the Supermarket on the main floor. When I asked about the Supermarket, they ignored my question, concentrating only on making the building wider and taller.

Sometimes the children only partially use some of our suggestions and help.

Uri (P) built an automobile and when I brought the basket of "junk items" he chose only odds and ends accessory items, two cardboard cones which he covered with jar tops and called headlights. He used other odds and ends as decoration, and I felt that I should not question what they were for because he seemed to enjoy the decorations for themselves.

I did try to clarify the purpose of the headlights. I asked, "How does a driver see the road at night?" Uri couldn't answer. I asked, "How do you see a car from far away at night?" Ron (P) said, "You see lights." A light came into Uri's eyes.

Of course, the teachers did not rise to every opportunity which presented itself. For every time that the teacher stepped in and succeeded in stimulating further thinking and creativity, at least a hundred other opportunities were missed. Partially this was because the teachers needed much more experience in understanding their role and therefore did not recognize an opening when it presented itself, and partially because a teacher could not possibly divide herself sufficiently to meet every need that arose. At best, she chose where she felt she was most needed.

There were also many sins of commission as well as omission. Sometimes the teachers were much too quick in stepping in when the children needed more experimentation, more fantasy play, more flights of imagination, and were unready yet to examine the real life situation.

At other times, the teacher jumped in without finding out what the situation was all about—she heard noise and what seemed to be disorder—and "reorganized" the children without realizing she had just broken up a "wedding party" with some wonderful play and dancing.

In their eagerness to advance the children's play and introduce information, the teachers were often too quick in giving a full answer instead of helping the child to think through the problem with the aid of questions. Even when they brought in materials and equipment, the teachers were often too ready to prepare a fully ready gadget, rather than to wait for the children's ideas on how to make them. On the other hand, the teacher's imaginative originality often stimulated the children to look for original solutions by themselves. For example, the fact that in one of the groups the children designed an elevator for their building by themselves may very well have been influenced by seeing the principle by which the teachers had arranged the hair dryer.

The preceding examples and those that follow tend to present an ideal situation. Every one of the examples are taken from the notes of the observers or the teachers on actual situations. However, they were the bright flashes among many mundane moments when teaching was less stimulating. As the teachers became more experienced in this mode of work, and as the children became more and more responsive, the number of missed opportunities began to diminish.

Of necessity, the examples in this chapter tend to show the teacher in a very active role. However, it cannot be stressed enough that much of the children's day-to-day activity was spontaneous and independent, needing very little teacher stimulation and assistance.

EQUIPMENT AND ARRANGEMENT OF THE NURSERY

Having agreed that play, exploration, and encouragement of imagination were to be the media of our work, the arrangement of the nursery and choice of equipment followed naturally.

Arrangement of Furniture

We tried to leave as much open space as possible to make the blocks and the dramatic play corners accessible, convenient, and tempting. The blocks and the accessories for block play—cars, colored blocks, etc.— were on long, low, open shelves in the most commanding spot of the room. Next to them was the housekeeping corner, placed in such a way that the block play and the housekeeping play could intermingle conveniently. By the second year, the space for the housekeeping corner was cut down since a larger proportion of the children were drawn to the block play and this needed even more space.

Since the emphasis in our program was to be on active dramatic play, we kept structured didactic work at tables to a minimum during the free play period. We tried to avoid the use of the didactic materials as an escape into mechanical repetitive motions (so many of the D children chose such activities in order to avoid impingement of a more dynamic program). We grouped a few tables in the corner so that the didactic play materials and table work would not be the central focus of activity. Next to the tables were the didactic materials on shelves, and usually some art material was laid out each morning. The remainder of the tables and chairs were placed along the walls and brought out for "snack time" and for "quiet time," when didactic materials were used in a selected, supervised way.

There were several inviting areas in the room. The eventual goal was for the children to choose independently the activities that would be meaningful and absorbing to them. Each area was designed in such a way that a minimum of teacher intervention was needed so that the

teacher's time could be used more profitably than as a distributor of supplies. The arrangements encouraged independent behavior on the part of
the children and freed the teacher to give the children the special attention that only she could contribute.

>The *easels* and *paints* were set up so that the children were able to supply
>themselves with paper, paints, brushes, aprons, water, and drying rack. A
>minimum of teacher's help was needed.
>
>The *book corner* was arranged attractively, with a convenient table and
>chairs and a tempting display of the books.
>
>The *music corner*, after the children were well acquainted with the in-
>struments, was made very accessible, and drums made by the children,
>phonograph and records, and instruments were available to be used as
>wished.
>
>The *carpentry table* was kept in an anteroom so that the noise would not
>overwhelm the playroom. However, since we felt that carpentry needed
>much teacher attention, we tried whenever the weather permitted to have
>the carpentry outdoors during the outdoor play period.
>
>The *science and nature corner* had frequent additions and changes. Each
>nursery kept a number of animals (not all at the same time)—hamsters,
>white mice, birds and fish—as well as collections of rocks, insects, leaves,
>and growing things of all kinds. There was a very large magnifying glass;
>a thermometer; colored plastic transparencies; scales and measuring in-
>struments of all types; batteries; pumps; pulleys; funnels; and picture books
>of animals, birds, and fish; as well as frequently changed pictures on the
>wall of the science corner.
>
>On the *walls* all around the nursery were arrangements for hanging the col-
>lection of each child's paintings with his name clearly marked above. *Bul-
>letin boards* were hung low enough for the children to be able to see what
>was on display.

Since our budget for equipment was very low, we decided to econ-
omize on furniture rather than on educational equipment. We repaired
and renovated discarded, broken tables and chairs, which we painted
brightly; we used a shelf and simple hooks for cubbies; and we acquired
some discarded office cabinets with small drawers to provide individual
drawers for each child. Straw mats which were spread on the floor and
used for group meetings, stories, and rhythms were very valuable but in-
expensive. Sitting on the straw mats gave a feeling of informality and intimacy.

The Blocks

The bulk of our equipment money was spent on blocks, since we felt
that this would be our basic tool. We provided four sets of unit blocks

for each nursery (about 400 blocks for 25 children) and two sets of hollow blocks which were used primarily outdoors. After a very short time, the teachers found that the number of blocks, which at first seemed to be enormous, was insufficient and whenever possible we bought more. The teachers estimated that we needed at least twice as many blocks as originally bought to enable the children to carry out their ideas.

The blocks were arranged on low shelves in cubbies designed according to the block sizes. They were kept carefully arranged according to shape. Since there was an insufficient number of blocks, the teachers added such supplementary items as wooden and cardboard boxes, and large flat pieces of plywood to be used as roofs.

On the block shelves were also miniature toys—cars, airplanes, boats, dolls, tables, dishes, variously sized pieces of cloth, small pieces of rugs, mosaic tiles, small colored blocks, and miniature people made of wood, of pipe cleaners, of cardboard, and of wire. The miniature people were dressed as men (fathers), women (mothers), children, and various adult workers—nurses, doctors, workmen, teachers. The accessories to the block play were added and removed according to the areas of interest of the children, with new accessories occasionally stimulating a new subject of play. A low "garage" with a corrugated roof to house automobile parts and tools was added to the block corner toward the end of the first year.

Housekeeping Corner

The domestic corner was kept as simple as possible, with no elaborate stoves, refrigerators, kitchen cabinets, or sinks. There were shelves where normal-sized pots, dishes, and kitchen implements were kept, as well as a basin where dishes could actually be washed. On other shelves, dolls, doll clothes, and many pieces of cloth were arranged. There was a corner, with a mirror, for dress-up clothes, and there was a bed large enough for the children to lie on. The stove was a crate with four burners painted on. Sometimes real food, such as carrots or crackers, was introduced to stimulate the play. The housekeeping corner included two telephones, brooms, an ironing board and iron. The attempt was to keep everything very simple so that imagination and symbolic play would be at a maximum, and so that the children would have to use their imaginations. We tried to provide only the basic raw materials and avoided all elaborate household equipment and doll accessories.

When the need arose, a hairdressing shop with curlers and mirrors, a barber shop, or a doctor's office was arranged, with just enough equipment to stimulate the play.

Didactic and Table-Play Materials

The didactic play equipment was frequently changed. The teacher presented the child with the piece of equipment she felt he needed for experience or drill. As much as possible, she tried to avoid letting the child engage in stereotyped activity with a piece of didactic equipment like bead stringing, pegs, or some puzzle too easy for him. The didactic equipment included puzzles, sequence stories, picture lottos of all sorts, large domino games, number games, mosaics, construction toys, and interlocking wheels. There were "feely" boxes of variously textured materials—fur, smooth and rough materials; boxes of various objects of one color—a box of orange items, a box of red items; and boxes of various types of shapes that could be classified. In addition, crayons, paper, scissors, and plasticene were easily accessible. We tried to arrange that the games and puzzles would be well-supervised at first, and in the course of time the children learned to organize and conduct them by themselves. A teacher always tried to keep an eye on the use of didactic material to help the children to use it correctly and to avoid mindless, repetitive use of the same materials.

Creative Art Work

We tried to give the children as large a variety of experiences as possible with many materials. We used paints, clay, dough, finger paints, leaves, stones, and bits of wood and plastic. The art materials served as a means both for exploration and for expression in design and color. Some children needed more time for simple experimentation of the materials; others began to use the materials more for expression and making designs.

Carpentry

The carpentry equipment consisted of a sturdy workbench, vises, hammers, nails of all sizes with flat heads, a cross-cut saw, small wooden wheels, dowels, glue, and a full supply of soft wood in various shapes. The wood was acquired by collecting scraps at carpentry shops.

Water Play

Very large plastic tubs on a stand were used for the water play. Measuring cups of all sizes, sprinkling cans, containers, kerosene pumps, lengths of hose, sieves, ladles, plastic bottles, sponges, drinking straws, soap of different types—liquid, powder, cake—pieces of wood that would float, all served to stimulate much exploration and discovery as well as to satisfy the children's natural affinity for play with water. The children learned to roll up their sleeves and to wear rubber aprons for the water play. For the most part, the water play was outdoors, but in the first year of work, it also was introduced indoors, using warm water.

Cooking

Cooking was a much-loved activity. A small stove, pots, and cooking equipment were readily available, as were boxes of jello, pudding, and various foods to make soups, salads, chips, omelettes, juice, and cakes. The goal was for the children to work independently, with the teacher keeping a watchful eye from the distance. We would have liked the cooking materials to be set up in the housekeeping corner, but the teachers felt uneasy about the hot stove, and usually the cooking took place in the kitchen, with the teacher present.

Odds and Ends

The teachers and the children were very diligent and resourceful in collecting all sorts of odds and ends which were used creatively in the dramatic play as well as in the art work. Automobile parts, crates and boxes, wheels, old clocks, dishes and pots, radios, blankets, rug samples, fabric samples, bottle tops, colored papers, bits of plastic, mosaic tiles, scrap paper of all textures, old tires, old license plates, lead pipes, electric wires and switches, old locks, were collected from homes, workshops, and factories. The teachers were constantly on the lookout for new ideas and possibilities.

Outdoor Equipment

The outdoor period was a vital and integral part of the curriculum, where supervised and purposeful activities were stimulated. Here, too, the equipment was designed largely to encourage dramatic play. The play was more real in that the children used larger equipment—hollow blocks and crates—and got into the "house" or "auto" with their own bodies, in contrast to the indoor play which was more intentionally symbolic through the use of small unit blocks and miniature, representative human figures.

The outdoor equipment centered around very large crates and packing cases. These large crates were sanded down and attractively painted. They were large enough for several children to get into or to climb on. They could be closed off by blankets covering the opening, or by large sheets of plywood or boards. The crates immediately became cozy places to hide in, houses, stores, autos, fire engines, spaceships, airplanes. Accessories to the crates consisted of large boards, large hollow blocks, ladders, pulleys, ropes, hoses, dolls, trucks, wagons, wheelbarrows, and tree trunks cut in various sizes.

Sawhorses and long boards were used to make slides, seesaws, and ingenious arrangements for climbing and balancing exercises. At first the teachers made the enticing arrangements and later the children themselves became original designers of equipment.

We tried wherever possible to avoid hanging regular swings and took down the swings in those schools where they had been provided by the municipality. We found that many of the children used this means to avoid activity. Furthermore, it required too much teacher attention and supervision. We would occasionally hang tires on which several children could swing together.

Although we considered climbing to be a very important activity for young children, we were unable to provide good climbing equipment because of budgetary limitations. Where there were trees, we tried to nail on helping steps to enable the children to climb. We could not afford to build tree houses, and we missed them because they are such a wonderful stimulus to imaginative play.

In one of the schools there was an abandoned automobile in the yard. The other nurseries were located in such inaccessible areas that the cost of hauling automobiles was prohibitive, even though we found that we could get abandoned automobiles at no cost. In addition, the yard contained a sandbox with appropriate sand toys, measuring instruments, and watering cans. A garden was cultivated in those nurseries where there was no danger that the neighbors would destroy it. Whenever weather permitted it, carpentry, water play, and art materials were brought outdoors. A shed for storing the outdoor equipment was arranged in each nursery. We also designed a very large platform on wheels, on which the outdoor equipment could be piled and brought out easily from the shed to the yard.

DAILY SCHEDULE OF THE SECOND YEAR

We experimented considerably before we arrived at a daily schedule that best fit our needs, and it underwent several changes during the two-year period. The changes were due both to our own experimentation (how much "quiet time," how much individual work, one group or two groups for stories, etc.), and the changing needs of the children. The schedule we set for the second year of our program (when the children were four years old) was as follows:

8:00   ARRIVALS

Individual greeting and conversation with each child. Care of animals and plants and housekeeping tasks.

8:20   INFORMAL GROUP MEETING

While standing, a quick review of plans for the play and choices of roles and areas.

8:25   FREE PLAY

Block play, doll play, and art materials. Use of art materials and carpentry to make supplementary props for the dramatic play.

9:30   TOUR OF THE PLAY AREA

Individual children explain to everyone what they have done and receive the children's criticisms and suggestions.

9:40   CLEAN UP

All children participate; each child chooses a specific task.

9:50   GROUP MEETING

Discussion of a topic that had come up in the play, occasionally with the addition of an appropriate story or information supplied by the teacher. Planning the play for the next day. Sometimes language games, records, rhythmic movements. Free discussion on some common group experience or topics raised by the children.

10:05   TOILETING AND WASHING UP

Supervised by teacher.

10:15   SNACK

Emphasis on conversation, word games, jokes. The group is divided at two long tables, with a teacher at each table.

10:30   OUTDOORS

Children go out as a group with teacher always present. Where possible, the outdoor equipment is partially set up before the children go out. Emphasis on dramatic play with all available equipment.

A garden tended by the children, when possible. (We saw to it that only one group was out in the yard at a time. In the school which had to share a schoolyard, we changed the schedule and used the yard first thing in the morning for the first year in order to avoid two groups together. The second year, the arrangement was reversed.)

Ten to fifteen minute sessions indoors with individual children. This time was used for stimulating the use of language, didactic games and exercises. Some of the concepts and information occupying the group at the time were reviewed and worked on for clarification where necessary.

11:30 QUIET TIME

Didactic materials, art materials, science materials, language games, writing, and dictation of stories or music and rhythms.

11:50 GROUP MEETINGS

Group divided in two for story, songs, talk.

12:00 FAREWELLS

Each child receives an individual farewell.

This program was varied once a week by a planned trip with the group. (Sometimes the group was divided in half, and each of these smaller groups went on the trip at a different time.) Small supplementary trips were also made where a point of information needed clarification. Birthday parties were kept to a minimum of time and wherever possible were fitted into the snack time.

4

Curriculum

DRAMATIC PLAY

The play of the D children, when it appeared at all in the first month of work, was dull and sporadic. It consisted largely of holding objects such as dolls, cars, and driving wheels, while, presumably, some internal fantasy with these objects was taking place. Occasionally, the objects would stimulate the children to some short-lived activity such as making automobile noises, wrapping the doll in a blanket, arranging the dishes, and piling some blocks. There seemed to be fleeting concentration and much moving from one piece of equipment to another.

The following are a few excerpts of play taken from the observer's records of the homogeneous D group during the first months of work:

SEPTEMBER 1967
Shmuel and Jonah fill the sandpail with water, wander around the yard and shout, "Water, who wants water?" No one responds.

OCTOBER 1967
Dafna, Aliza, and Gila bring chairs and dolls to the packing case outdoors. Dafna suggests, "Let's put chairs. We'll make a birthday party."

They make the preparations, no word is said and no birthday follows. Shmuel, David, and Reuben join them, sit down, and no further action develops.

SEPTEMBER 1967
Nissim moves about looking disoriented (he was found late in the morning standing outside the door of the nursery and was brought in by the teacher). He seems to be only vaguely aware of what the children are doing. Teacher leads him over to the little cars, but he makes no move. Teacher hands him

a small car which he holds tightly. He goes out to the anteroom. He sits down on the floor, leaning on a wall, still clutching the car. He falls asleep.

Much of the play was sheer motoric activity.

SEPTEMBER 1967
The boys all have driving wheels, run about the room, or sit on a block holding a driving wheel. No further action or talk.

SEPTEMBER 1967
Most of the activity in the yard consists of pulling wagons or dragging an empty wheelbarrow back and forth.

SEPTEMBER 1967
Fifteen minutes of jumping from the steps—no words.

Some excerpts from the description of a morning's play period:

DECEMBER 1967
Aliza plays alone all morning in the doll corner with one doll, feeding and talking to her.
   Gila takes possession of the new doll and holds on to it all day, both indoors and outdoors, snack period included.
   Hannah holds a small pot and sits near Shmuel in his "car" (a few blocks and a driving wheel). Shumel is eating the roll Hannah brought from home— apparently they have made some arrangement about this. When Hannah sees that Shmuel is about to finish the roll she makes a wordless exchange with him, giving him the pot and taking what is left of the roll.
   Jonah leads Dudi, David, and Reuben and they help him to stand the large crates up on end and pile boards, ladders, and hollow blocks on them. They decorate the pile with small colored blocks and with this they finish their play.

The following excerpt from the teacher's diary describing one morning's play (during the "Our Neighborhood" project) shows how the play in the homogeneous group looked after two years.

MAY 1969
As the children arrived, we reminded them of yesterday's plan for today. Yesterday's discussion had dealt with the subject of where the goods in the grocery come from, and the children had decided that they would add "factories" to today's block scheme.
   Aliza, David and Ruthie built a "juice factory." They used a large pitcher to fill small bottles and arranged the bottles neatly.
   Naomi organized a "factory" for cigarettes and matches. Dalia and Shlomo helped her to collect all the boxes of cigarettes and matches from the scrap box and stack them.
   Anot and Naomi built "a factory" for foods that come in cardboard boxes— custards, macaroni, etc. They, too, collected all the empty boxes.

Rachel collected yogurt bottles and cans for her "factory."
Shmuel and Menashe built a grocery store.
Danny and Ari were truck drivers.
Hannah, Jonah, David, Molly, Nissim and Dalia built houses.
This preparation took half an hour. As soon as the "factories" were ready, the storekeepers went to the factories to place their orders and pay for them. They then went back to the empty grocery to wait for the arrival of the trucks. Full trucks began arriving and deposited their goods at the store. The storekeepers were kept busy carrying armfuls of goods. Shmuel worked very fast at arranging the goods and Menashe was characteristically more lackadaisical. The goods in the store were classified and arranged very quickly and at Ari's request, I made a sign "Open for Business" which was immediately put up.
The factories were emptied and the owners and workers went off to other activities. (Obviously, the children believe that a factory is a storehouse and this point needs clarification, but it seems to me to be premature to elaborate on it at this stage.)
When the grocery was opened, Mollie and Dalia came to buy cuscus (Oriental cereal) and baby soup. The cuscus was weighed on the scale. Each of the buyers (all the children came to buy) "paid" for their purchases. Cuscus and carrots were "cooked" in the houses and everybody ate.
The play was very lively and enthusiastic and continued for well over an hour.

The teacher continues her diary with a report of the discussion which followed the play:

The discussion dealt with the question of how Mommy and the family get money. Interestingly, many children said they get the money from the bank. Finally, Ari answered that "Daddy brings the money from work." We enlarged on this. We talked about the fact that Father Shmuel worked in the store today and so did Father Menashe. Where did Father Ari work? On a truck. Danny explained very clearly that he "worked as the driver of the truck which delivered goods from the factory to Shmuel's store. Shmuel paid me for bringing it."
We reached the conclusion that people who work get paid for their work. That is why Rachel, Ari, Shmuel and the others received money today.
The children were very involved in the discussion and even at age four seemed to understand the problem of earning money. "In order to earn money, you have to work," said Ari very manfully.

This is a picture of a morning's play in the heterogeneous group[1] in the second year of the program:

JANUARY 1969
Gabriel (P), Uri (P), and Amnon (P) build a garage with wide space for the tractor and narrower spaces for the little automobiles.

[1]Note the difference in the level of information between the homogeneous group and the heterogeneous group.

Amnon says, "The tractor takes care of the little cars. He is big and they are small. He is their friend."

They begin moving the little cars, but Gabriel suddenly says, "Oh, we have no gasoline."

Uri: "We have to buy it."

Teacher: "Where will you buy the gasoline?"

Amnon: "In the gas station. I'll make one immediately."

He runs to the odds and ends box and pulls out a long piece of rubber pipe while Uri hands him a large box. They both rummage, pull out a pump and a funnel, and take it all back to their block corner. They arrange the long box with a rubber pipe leading from it. Uri looks for the gas tank opening in the car so that he can fill it and Gabriel turns the car upside down to look for it. Amnon turns it back, places it on its wheels and shows Gabriel how to fill the car with gas.

Oded (P) comes over and says he has a key with which to lock the gas station. He builds a miniature gas station with tiny colored blocks next to the larger one and he finds a secret hiding place for the key in the large gas station. His colored block building inspires Gabriel and Uri to decorate their gas station with colored blocks. They begin to build a road leading out of the gas station. Each takes a car and they drive in a convoy along the road until they reach the wall and Uri announces, "This is the parking lot."

Chaim (D) who has been watching the road building and the convoy with great interest and, at the same time, building a small building on the side, announces, "I am building it." He shows them what he has built. "Here's the door." Oded (P): "It's the gate to the parking lot." They include Chaim (D) in their play.

They continue to push their cars back and forth along the road and extend the road into the next room.

Uri places two blocks on the floor with a triangular block bridging them and says, "This is Alexander Bridge." Oded and Gabriel build other types of "bridges." Uri announces, "We are going to Haifa over the Alexander Bridge."

Eli (P) joins them and says he needs a road to Tel Aviv. This immediately attracts Ron (P) who says, "Then I will build the Shalom Tower in Tel Aviv." Ron builds a tall building and adds an elevator (he has had much experience with this in his previous buildings). He places a plasticene man in the elevator, but the man falls out. Eli rushes over with his car and says, "I'll take him to the clinic," and picks up the plasticene man. He goes to the clinic where Sara and Aliza are treating their dolls. Gabriel comes running and says, "I will bandage the man in my car. I have a first-aid kit."

He fusses over the doll and then returns it to the elevator where Ron has, in the meantime, added a plasticene woman. Ron now continues moving his "people" up and down in the elevator.

Meanwhile, Uri has left the group and built a derrick of wooden nuts and bolts which he then brings to the garage.

How did this dramatic change in the quality and activity of the play take place? What was the role of the teacher? How much did the opportunity to observe other children playing serve as a reenforcing factor? To what extent was the active play in itself enriching and a stimulus to more play, more understanding, and thinking?

Progress in developing a meaningful, rich play experience was often dishearteningly slow. It often seemed that each move forward was followed by a step backward (as is so characteristic in children's growth). Because of the unevenness in the development of the children's emotional maturity, the teachers always had to be ready for and accepting of regressed periods in their behavior and also in their play.

The teacher provided guidance and stimulation, presented new information, explained things, but also understood that she did not direct the children's play. She was not "permissive" in the passive sense of the word, but on the other hand, she fully respected the natural direction the play took, and she always started from the point the children had reached at a particular moment.

The play evolved through certain basic stages, and the teacher planned her work in accordance with the particular stage at which the children were. As has been pointed out, the play was vague and generalized at first. It was enough to carry a doll and thus be a "mother," to carry a wheel and be a "car." The teacher, at this stage, worked to introduce more awareness of concrete details ("What does a car have?") in order to introduce more specific differentiation into the play situation. As the play became more detailed, she continued to stimulate the children to greater clarity in their ability to perceive what was happening around them. She introduced materials and information in order to enrich the play and stimulated them to classify objects and experiences. The teacher would encourage the children to become aware of details and would enlarge on a particular subject, such as buildings, babies, and stores, and develop it into an "area of interest" or "project." It was only after this, and very gradually, that she was able to bring the children to "see the relationships" and to indicate ways of combining various activities. The store, the house, the road they had built all began to be related to each other and part of a whole—all related, and yet separate and absorbing activities.

Independent activities were combined into cooperative projects, such as "our neighborhood" which included apartment houses, schools, stores, roads, electricity—or "transportation" which included trucks, cars, buses, roads, gas stations, trains, airplanes, and airfields. This "seeing of relationships" in their play stimulated the children to organize their thinking and their information. They had to solve actual problems that came up in the play situations, and in order to do this, they used the information that they had acquired in their trips and discussions. As they developed the ability to understand the events in their lives and in the adult world, the children developed a greater feeling of strength and knowledgeability. They then were readier to find out even more and to plan their future activities.

At the same time that the play reflected the children's attempt to understand the real world, they were also expressing their inner fears and hidden wishes. This appeared in their fantasy play which dealt with wild animals, prisoners and jailers, cowboys, and "bad men," babies, pilots, drivers, dressed-up mommies, etc.

The teacher observed all the play and tried to recognize its meaning, both to help her understanding of the emotional problems the child was groping with and also to identify his intellectual problems and information gaps. Though her goal was to help the children to clarify the difference between fantasy and reality, she respected the shifts from the real world to the fantasy world and tried to be careful not to be too hasty in leading them into an examination of reality or too demanding in expecting reality to be immediately reflected in the play.

After the fantasy was allowed full and free expression, the children seemed to be more ready to accept the limits of reality in a particular play situation. For example, "Most of the group is excitedly involved in connecting electric lines from the central 'generator' to their buildings. Gabriel goes on happily playing alone and building a fantasy Army world and Army 'headquarters' (father is on reserve duty). After playing this out, he suddenly becomes part of the group and he, too, connects electric wires to his Army 'headquarters'."

Some Methods Used to Stimulate Play

Teacher Startles Children Out of Vagueness to Purposeful Action. At the beginning the teacher sometimes had to be dramatic to startle the children, and, in effect, "cut the fog" for a moment, and then leave them to absorb as much as they were then capable of.

OCTOBER 1967: Homogeneous D Group

Again, Aliza, Annette, and Gila sit in the crate and Gila says, "It is a birthday." They continue to sit silently and dully. Teacher approaches and says enthusiastically, "I want to be at the birthday, too. Where should I sit?" The girls are galvanized into action, set up a table and chairs. Teacher asks, "Where is the birthday cake?" Gila and Annette bring plates and cups and an imaginary birthday cake is placed on the table.

Teacher Adds Materials to Stimulate Richer Play. Sometimes the simple addition of appropriate materials transforms static play into something more active, meaningful, and differentiated.

FEBRUARY 1968: Homogeneous D Group

Danny, Jonah, and Menashe are sitting on the floor, driving wheels in their hands, and are "driving." Danny says they need a bus stop. Teacher helps them to make a bus stop sign using a stick and a piece of cardboard stuck into a ball of plasticene. Danny makes another one entirely by himself. Teacher draws a chalk line on the floor indicating the road between the two bus stops. More children are attracted to the play and soon the question of money and bus tickets comes up. Teacher prepares toy money and bus tickets. The children queue up at the bus stop, give the driver money, and are given tickets. Each girl has provided herself with a baby and a pocketbook. After a short while, the play again becomes static with the children sitting dully in the "bus." Teacher raises the question of a bell for the passengers to inform the driver when to stop the bus. She attaches a rope and a bell. The play becomes enthusiastic, and toward the end all the children in the group participate.

Teacher Prompts Discussion and Asks Questions to Stimulate More Detailed Observation and Play. Each piece of equipment and material in the nursery had to be brought to the children's attention, to be observed in detail in order to dissipate their vague and unclear way of perceiving things.

JANUARY 1968: Homogeneous D Group

The children are playing more actively than before in the doll corner, but have not been dressing the dolls. Teacher gathers the children in the doll corner about her and places a doll, a dress, a blouse, and two pieces of cloth on the table. She holds up the doll which is undressed and asks, "What can we do with the clothes and the material?" They examine the doll and Ruthie says, "She's like a mommy, she has a fat tushy." Gila takes a piece of cloth and covers the doll. Dalia and Rachel then, too, take a piece of cloth and cover the doll. Teacher picks up the doll with the pieces of cloth and the cloth falls off, to the children's great amusement. They discuss what happened and agree that the doll is again undressed. Annette suggests that they put the dress on the doll and the girls work together to dress the doll. Teacher holds up the doll and the dress doesn't fall off. Teacher asks, "Why doesn't the dress fall off now?" Annette says, "Because her arms are in it." Teacher, "Yes, her arms and shoulders are holding up the dress."

Aliza excitedly says, "But she has no underpants." They look through all the doll clothes on the shelves and find no underpants. Teacher asks, "What can we do?" There is a silence. Teacher says, "Instead of underpants, we have cloth." Yael, who has a baby sister, tries to diaper the doll. Teacher introduces the verb "to diaper." Yael's diaper efforts do not succeed.

Teacher shows them how to diaper the doll, explaining the whole process. Each one then has a turn in diapering, while teacher verbalizes what they are doing.

After the doll is dressed, she asks what else can be done with the cloth

"I'm a mommy."

"I'm a baby."

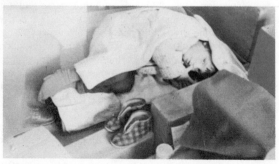

DRAMATIC ACTIVITY

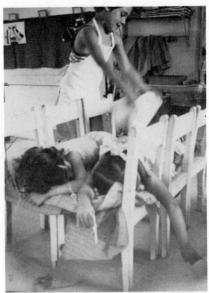

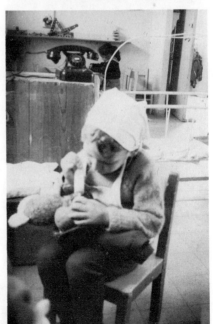

The Clinic.

DRAMATIC ACTIVITY

A wedding.

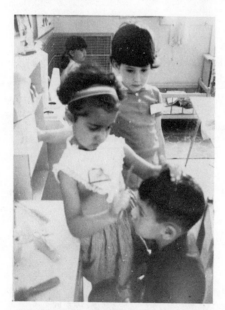

The beauty parlor.

DRAMATIC ACTIVITY

"It's fun to hide."

DRAMATIC ACTIVITY

that is left, and Gila puts the cloth on the doll's head as a head-kerchief, with teacher helping her to tie it on.

In the group discussion period that morning, teacher brings the doll's clothes cupboard to the center of the circle, and they examine all the clothes, name them, sort them, and decide what other clothes they need. The play in the doll corner from then on included dressing the doll.

Teacher Asks Questions to Define and Reactivate the Play. Sometimes, as the play is about to disintegrate, the teacher steps in with an appropriate question that helps them to define the play situation more clearly and starts it moving again.

MARCH 1969: Heterogeneous Group

A blanket is lying about and Eli (P) and Ilan (P) try to make a tent by tying it with ropes to the table. They decide to make a private tent for each of them.

As they are getting the blankets in the storeroom,

Eli: We'll make a lot of them, like a real camp.

Ilan: Two tents, one for you and one for me.

They go back to the room.

Teacher: Why did you bring so many blankets?

Eli: We're making three—one for Yossi (D), one for Ilan and one for me.

A discussion ensues as to whether soldiers sleep outdoors or in tents. Teacher says they do both. There is much activity in trying to set up the tents and difficulties in folding the blankets followed by some short-lived play of seeing "bad people" in the distance. The play begins to lag and is in danger of falling apart.

Teacher: What kind of camp is this?

Eli: A camp.

Teacher: Is it a scout camp, a fireman's camp or an army camp?

Eli: An army camp.

Teacher: How can we know that it is an army camp?

Ilan: It's written.

Teacher: Where is it written?

Eli: Ah, we need a sign.

Teacher: How else can we know that it is an army camp? What else do we need?

Ilan: Because there is a flag.

Teacher: Yes, an army camp has a flag.

They busy themselves making a flag and there is some talk of a loud-speaker system. Later, they rummage for army hats.

Teacher Develops a Familiar Subject. There were certain basic topics that cropped up repeatedly in all the groups. Domestic play, store play, and transportation play were expressions of what the children saw as dramatic in their daily lives. This was the material that they had to understand more thoroughly, to find out more about, and to play through over and over again in order to digest their experiences.

After the initial interest and sporadic play, the teacher would stimulate them gradually to understand these everyday phenomena better. She tried to add to their information and widen their areas of interest by bringing in related subjects. She used questions and discussions to arouse their *curiosity*; trips and books to help them to "study" the subject. She used their own dramatic play, paintings, and discussions to help them to *recall, reflect,* and *make connections* with what they already knew. For example, when the subject "automobiles" was expanded and studied, the enriched play that developed showed how the children were working on and digesting the new information and experiences they had acquired.

The fascination with vehicles and automobiles was evident from the beginning—anything on wheels was attractive. At first they would sit rolling a small car on their hands to see how the wheels worked. As they became more active, they dragged wagons about while making automobile sounds. The next step was to place several chairs in a row and call it a bus, each child sitting with his own driver's wheel and feeling himself the driver of the bus. Gradually, the teachers were able to help clarify and differentiate the driving experience by arousing them to see more details. Questions like "Who is the driver?" "Where are you going?" "Where is the road?" helped them to be clearer in their play. They added sidewalks, bus stops.

When this play too became static, the teachers felt that the time had come to go more deeply into the subject. The whole group was taken out for a trip to see the main road. They observed the different types of cars and trucks that rode by and they observed the road. They discussed the colors of the cars, the sizes, the speed, the names of the various types of cars.

The subject of vehicles came up in all areas of activity in the nursery. The teachers put up posters with various types of cars; the children were "fast" and "slow" cars in rhythms; the teachers brought books and stories about cars; and cars were made out of matchboxes and in carpentry. For wheels, the children used corks and bottle tops, as well as small wooden wheels. The interest in cars was reflected in their building. The children no longer were satisfied with a bus made of chairs, but began arranging blocks in a long row and calling it a bus. The teacher then stepped in with questions: "Where will the driver sit?" "What does he need?"—a wheel, a horn, a seat, a place to put his cigarettes, benches for the passengers.

The interest then moved on to trucks—what they carry, where they come from, where they go. The truck bringing sand to the nursery was investigated thoroughly and the driver was cross-examined as to where the sand came from. The children noticed that the truck had no benches for passengers. Trips were made to the grocery to watch the bread and milk trucks arrive and deliver their goods.

The question of what makes a car go was taken up. In one of the groups, the children took a ride with the teacher in her car to see how she made it go. The need for gasoline, oil, and water was discussed. A trip to a gasoline station followed. They watched the gas station attendant carefully and talked to the drivers. They were fascinated by the gasoline pump and hose, and some of them requested that their toy cars be filled. Another trip, to a garage, was taken twice to see how cars were repaired, and the children came back to the nursery laden with old, spare parts.

The play was active, and at one time or another it reviewed, re-hearsed, and incorporated all the various aspects of vehicles that had been studied. The play included building cars with seats, windows, doors, wheels, gear shifts, and license plates; buses and bus stops; garages with devices for raising the car, tools, and spare parts; roads with road signs; traffic lights and sidewalks; a gas station with fuel pump and a restaurant.

Beginning of Relationship Thinking

The teacher's goal, in the long run, was to stimulate the children to organize and integrate their information until they could see how it is all related. The hope was that having once learned the process of organization in thinking, they would then begin to apply this pattern of thinking to more complicated data.

DECEMBER 1968: Heterogeneous Group (from the teacher's diary)

(The children had recently visited the nearby filling station and also had a snack in the restaurant on the premises. In the group discussions on the function of a filling station, there had been comment on how convenient it was to stop for gasoline and have a restaurant there at the same time.)

Morning play in the following week:

Yoav (D) and Zvi (P) were building a gas station. Sarah (D) and Ora (P) drove over occasionally to get gas. Yoav said, "We have to build a restaurant," and built it. He struggled between working in the restaurant and working in the gas station. For a time he "locked" the gas station and only opened it when a car arrived.

Chaim (D) was building a house for the people "who go to work." Gabriel (P) built a garage with many rooms in which he put the toy motorcycle he had brought from home as well as other cars. He added various automobile parts from the miscellaneous box and used them to "fix" the cars.

Uri (P), Ron (P), Yoel (D), and Eli (P) were very involved in building a road which reached all parts of the room. The cars were driven over the road.

Gabriel was not ready to buy gasoline from Yoav and built his own filling station.

Ora (P) and Reuben (P) built an elaborate house fitted with rugs, furniture, curtains, and many other details. *From time to time they took a drive on the road, visited Gabriel in his garage and Yoav's restaurant.*

JANUARY 1969: Heterogeneous

Eli (P) moves two blocks together along the floor making automobile sounds (an example of regressed play in January 1969). To teacher's question, he says, "It's a chocolate truck."

Teacher: Where is the chocolate? Is it ready?

Eli: (No answer.)

Teacher (gives him small plastic blocks): This could be the chocolate. (She also hands him colored paper.)

He wraps the "chocolate" and after it is wrapped teacher asks him if he is going to deliver the chocolate.

Eli: To the store.

Teacher: What store?

Eli, Malka (P), and Amir (P) decide to build a store. They use a bench and build a building around it. They deliver the chocolate from the "factory" to the store in a small wagon. Eli calls out and hawks his wares.

At the same time, Reuben (P) and Uzi (P) are building a passenger plane. Near them David (P) is building a runway of long, flat boards. He takes a small wagon and asks the teacher for some rubber pipe to use for filling the tank of the plane with fuel. He says, "Just like in the picture." (There is a picture on the wall of a plane being fueled.)

Anat (P), playing alone, is building a small house for "babies." She adds many decorations and rugs and then *goes off to the hairdresser where Edna (P) and Simcha (D) are working.*

After they arrange her hair, they all go to the airplane which is flying to India. On the way, they stop at Eli's store to buy chocolate.

Play as Means of Expression of Feelings and Fantasies

With intense satisfaction, the children expressed their deepest feelings and private fantasies at the same time that they were reproducing their real life experiences in their play. The teachers tried to sense when logic and reality had to be introduced and when the play had to be left intact with all its illogic and immaturity. The teachers enjoyed each child's unique way of expressing himself, and since they wanted to foster this special creativity, they encouraged each child's original way of expressing both the fantasies and realities that absorbed him.

For many children the expression of feelings of frustration, fears, and inner conflicts in play served as a catharsis and freed them for further intellectual development.

Ilan (P) spent a whole week building the "tallest house in the world." As he did so he held a "cigar" in his mouth. He wanted no help from other children and was thoroughly satisfied with his activity. (We knew that Ilan was very concerned with wanting to be "big" and frustrated at waiting to be "grown-up.") Later, he applied the engineering he had learned to working with others in building the "neighborhood."

There were innumerable episodes of playing dog, in which the children were able to express their aggression in a socially acceptable way and were able to overcome their fears by playing them out.

DECEMBER 1968: Heterogeneous Group (from the teacher's diary)
On the day that Reuben's (P) mother went back to work (as a pharmacist) Reuben built a "pharmacy" and Ruth (P) (whose father is a doctor) joined him. The pharmacist was given the major role in healing the sick and (Reuben was able to play out his conflict about mother going back to work).

Often the play evolved from the children's need to identify with the adult figures around them. As they played bus driver or pilot their need to be strong and all-powerful figures was satisfied. As they became the teacher and gave instructions for rhythms or encouraged children in their clay work by making teacher-like observations, they identified with a good and giving figure.

Here is an excerpt from a moment in play which illustrates how the children used play to express their fears, bring in reality, and work out isolated pieces of knowledge all at the same time:

JANUARY 1969: Heterogeneous Group
Ehud (P), Uzi (P), and Amir (P) build a lion's cage and are the lions. Eli (P) and Dalia (P) are the lions' keepers.

Ehud: I spoke English to him. I come from England.

Dalia: The lion understands English?

Eli: He understands. He is learning English from Ehud.

Amir: Dalia doesn't come from England, she comes from abroad.

Eli: From Africa. There are lions in Africa, too, and also in England.

Uzi: In England there really, really is a queen, a king, and soldiers.

Eli: Lion, come in, come in. You can't escape here, it's Jerusalem.

Amir: Me, me, in the cage.

Dalia: What food do they eat?

Uzi: They eat tough meat!

Eli: Seeds, peanuts, chicks, and special cheese for lions.

Teacher (trying to bring some reality in): Where do you buy the meat?

Ehud: I buy it. I buy it from the guards in England. I bought it in England and came to Jerusalem.

Dalia: (distributes meat to the lions): What their name? (Each "lion" gives his his own name.)

Eli: We have three lions, nice ones. They obey us and we don't even have to punish them.

    Eli and Dalia take the teacher to visit the lion's cage and introduce her to all the lions.

Uzi (begins to roar): I'm gobbling it up!

Eli: You see, they don't devour things. Only if people want to gobble them up and annoy them, then they devour.

Problems of authority and of oral fantasies and fears are mixed with questions of reality, distances, geographical orientation, and foreign languages.

BLOCKS

The experience with children's use of blocks has testified to their importance as an aid to teaching and learning in the early years. A large set of unit blocks has become standard essential equipment for any good nursery school. Of all the materials and equipment in our nurseries, the blocks were by far the most used, the most useful, the most pleasureable, and the most effective in carrying out our program.[2] The blocks in our program seemed to encompass a whole curriculum. They served to stimulate the children to *sharper observation* and clearer *thinking*, to enable them to re-

---

[2]The writing of this section was facilitated by the use of two pamphlets issued by the Bank St. College of Education, the "Follow Through" In-Service Training Program: *Blocks as a Learning and Expressive Material*; and *Block Building—Some Practical Suggestions for Teachers* (New York: Bank St. Publications).

produce what they wanted to represent. The play around the blocks stimulated much use of *language* and active *social exchange*. They were a natural vehicle for the *expression* of the children's deep *feelings* and *fantasies*. They gave the children a quick *sense of achievement* as they viewed their real, massive productions.

In addition, we found the blocks to be ideal equipment because they can be used in so many ways—they are strong, unbreakable, and can be enjoyed by an individual child, as well as by a group of children. We used the unit blocks indoors and left the large hollow blocks for outdoor play.

The use of the blocks developed the children's muscles and coordination—as they lugged large armfuls they developed their larger muscles; as they fitted them carefully they developed their smaller muscles and their eye-hand coordination. They learned the meaning of balance and the problems relating to it; they learned, through much trial and error, that weight and balance are related. They learned, through their own repeated experiences with the blocks, basic scientific principles like the difference between inclined planes, straight surfaces, and use of pulleys.

In a very natural way, the children learned number concepts, since the blocks are all units of each other. They began to figure out how many units of one block will be needed to cover a double unit or a quadruple unit. They learned to estimate quantities, to measure, to examine shapes and sizes, and to add and subtract as they took away some blocks and added others.

Words like *high, low, around, above, under, behind, near, far*, were learned as the children experienced them in their own muscles while using the blocks. They increased their vocabularies and their language facility as they had to discuss the uses of the buildings and their ideas for play and construction.

The children were learning geography as they planned where to place their buildings in relation to each other. The simple division of a house into rooms and placement of furniture in appropriate places was a first lesson in map-making and geography. Gradually the map-making became more complicated, reaching its peak as they planned and built "our neighborhood" and constructed hills and buildings and placed them in their correct geographic position.

> If this is the street, then the nursery must be on this side and the community center on the other side and Uri's house is on the street behind the nursery.

The children were forced to do some basic thinking in order to carry out their plans. They were stimulated to gather exact information (just what is on this street, are there balconies on Ruthie's house?). They had to solve problems (how do you make a door with a hinge, how do you build steps?). They utilized the information already known to them and decided what additional information had to be sought.

Working with the blocks, the children learned to concentrate for longer periods of time, to persevere, and to wait longer and longer for the finished product as they planned more and more complicated projects. They learned how to work together in order to carry out their ideas. It was necessary to share things, to divide, to respect others' work, to help each other, to criticize, and to give advice. Through the use of many games and devices, the children began to love putting the blocks away and making order out of confusion. In this way they acquired a feeling for order and rules as well as good work habits.

But, most of all, the blocks served as the most effective tool for stimulating the children to utilize, absorb, and assimilate all the concepts, ideas, and words they had been exposed to. The blocks stimulated them to play out their experiences, to learn and use new facts and observations, to play roles and express their feelings. In addition, they had to use all the materials in the nursery and all their skills in order to build and make accessories for the buildings in their block schemes.

The development of the children's ability to build with blocks was a very gradual process. It developed with their experience as block builders and also with their own physical growth and age—a three-year-old cannot build like a four-year-old. The three-year-old lacks the skills, the information, the ability, and the desire to carry out a complicated idea, nor does he have much need or skill to work with other children. On the other hand, a four-year-old or even a five-year-old who has had no previous experience with blocks must go through the same phases and experimentations with block building as a three-year-old. He goes through these phases at a quicker pace and, with encouragement, soon reaches the high levels of achievement and complexity appropriate to his age.

Harriet Johnson, who in the 1920s wrote a pamphlet "The Art of Block Building,"[3] described the following stages in the development of the skill:

1. Making long rows of blocks or stacking them up high till they fall. This is repeated many times.
2. Making a bridge. They place two blocks with a space between them, connected by a third block.
3. Enclosures. They enclose a space usually with four blocks.
4. Building decoratively. The children try to build a building that is archi-

[3]Harriet M. Johnson, *The Art of Block Building* (New York: The John Day Co., 1933).

Piling

Decorating

**BLOCKBUILDING DEVELOPS
IN STAGES**

Building block houses.

tecturally satisfying to them. They enjoy building to great heights and usually make towers. They use much symmetry and they try to decorate the building with colored objects. They don't usually name it, but even if they do, the building still does not become part of their play.

5. Buildings are named and used for dramatic play. It is at this stage, when the need arises in their play, that they begin to think of more detail in their buildings.

6. They try to reproduce buildings they actually know.

7. They work as a group to produce complicated cooperative projects, with each building serving a different purpose.

We found many individual differences in the way our children approached the blocks. Some of the children took to them enthusiastically and immediately went to the shelves, began pulling out blocks, lining them up, piling them, loading them into wagons and wheeling them about, and experimenting with them. Others watched and observed the way the blocks were being used. By the end of the first week, most of the P children had begun to use the blocks in some way.

In the heterogeneous groups, the D children were much more reticent, although they were obviously observing the use of the blocks and enjoyed putting them away. When the D children had had about two weeks of observation, the teacher would sit down on the floor with an individual child and she herself would begin building. After a while, she would ask the child to suggest where to place a block or request him to bring her one, and little by little he would become involved and also begin building. Usually other children would join the teacher on the floor and several would begin to use the blocks. The teacher rarely left at this point. She would remain to encourage, praise, suggest, and help, and, even if she left, would come back frequently to see how the child was getting on and to show her deep interest in his work. Some children would be stimulated to start using the blocks by a suggestion from the teacher that they build a "house" for the doll, the car, or the turtle. Some children needed more encouragement to begin than others; some needed a clear protected space and an initial pile of blocks provided by the teacher; others needed just an invitation to build; while some needed more time to observe and to help others build.

The teacher always took the block-building seriously and showed much interest and enthusiasm for what the children were constructing. She would discuss their buildings with them, would show them to the other children, and would make suggestions if she felt the child was ready. She spent a good deal of her time around the block-building and always tried to be aware of what the children were doing. At a later stage, the block-building became the topic for the group discussions—what the children had built, what was still needed, and their plans for the next day.

The beginning of block-building in the homogeneous D group was a much more difficult process. In spite of many attempts to spur the children to build, they did not approach it spontaneously. At first the teacher sat down on the floor with some blocks and began building by herself. The children watched passively. In the second stage she invited one child to join her on the floor. She gave the child a block and told him to place it wherever he wished. She then placed a block near his and again requested him to place one. This continued until some sort of nameless and formless building was built. Yet, in spite of these exercises in the use of blocks, there was still no building on the children's own initiative.

The teachers then decided to introduce the subject of blocks and block-building at the discussion period. Each child was given several blocks of the same type. The teacher arranged a march around the room, each carrying one block. This was followed by organized calisthenics. The blocks were arranged in a long narrow row and the children walked on them, trying to keep their balance; they placed blocks on their heads, shoulders, etc.; they jumped on them and banged them on the floor rhythmically. All of this was designed to familiarize them with the feel of the blocks. After the calisthenic period, they built a collective "building." Each child was asked to place a block wherever he wished. At first the blocks were placed in a scattered way around the room. When the first child placed his block next to another one, the teachers were enthusiastic: "It's beginning to look like a building." If a child persisted in putting a block far away from the others, the teachers called it a "fence." After much encouragement, the first collective effort produced a tower.

Other discussions dealt with the various shapes of the blocks and their names. They played a game where the teacher drew various shapes of blocks in chalk on the floor and the children had to place the appropriate block within the space. Another game was to look at the shape of a block and name an object in the room having the same shape (the window was like the unit block, the triangle in the music corner was like the triangular block, etc.). They played a kind of domino on the floor with the blocks. All of these games and collective use of the blocks helped to familiarize the children with the material. Group discussions and collective building during discussion time went on for some time until all the children began to use the blocks freely during the work period.

The initial stages of experimentation with the material lasted for several months and consisted of piling for the sake of piling, building for the sheer pleasure of using the blocks. At a later stage, the buildings began to represent something specific—a house, a car, a road. The final stage was when the children began to play in and with their buildings and to use them functionally. The teachers stimulated this by asking questions like:

"Where do you eat in this house?" "Is there a road for this car to drive on?" When the questions were premature and the children did not respond, the teachers did not press but waited for a more appropriate moment.

Another method of stimulation was by quietly bringing an accessory material to a block building: the teacher would bring a miniature table and chairs to a "house" and thus spur the activity; she would bring an auto to a long row of blocks, thereby making it into a "road"; she would bring miniature people, thus raising the question of where to put the sidewalk.

Very gradually the block-building began to take the following forms:

FEBRUARY 1968: Homogeneous D Group

Immediately after her arrival in the morning, Annette goes to the blocks and builds a closed courtyard. Rachel uses the blocks to build a building similar to Annette's. Rina does likewise. They finish their buildings and decorate them with dominos, colored cubes, small dishes and pots. They seat themselves around their buildings and play on their "flutes" (triangular blocks).

JANUARY 1968: Homogeneous D Group

Teacher approaches some boys who are building and says, "Do you want to tell me about your building?" They answer, "A bus." She asks, "Where is the bus stop?" She makes a bus stop sign on cardboard and attaches it to a pillar block that happens to be there. This spurs them to bring chairs, small fences, and a driving wheel. They begin building the bus. Other children are standing at the side, doing nothing but watching. Teacher suggests that they too ride on the bus and gives bus tickets to the driver to distribute. All ride passively. Teacher asks, "What do you see out of the window?"

Annette: Laundry.

Rachel: Lawn.

Reuben: Wind.

David: Strong wind.

They continue driving, making sounds like "trr-trr-trr."

MARCH 1968: Heterogeneous Group (from the teacher's diary)

Aron (P) built a small auto. He attached a piece of electric wire to the "pedal" (a block on the floor of the auto) and the other end to a small wheel he found in the "miscellaneous box." He attached this to the "window" of the car. When teacher asked, "What is this?" he answered, "The gears of the car."

Danny (P) and Aron (P) built a long building next to the auto. The courtyard of the building had a complete floor. Aron explained, "This is a shed for the auto." Danny said, "A garage." They bring more small automobiles and place them in the garage courtyard. Later they add airplanes.

APRIL 1968: Heterogeneous Group

Uri (P) builds a very steady building of unit blocks. There is a low seat in the front with a driving wheel. He adds four wheels and an extra one for a spare.

Teacher: Where are you going?

Uri: I want to go where you see the Mirages flying in the sky. I want to see how they fly. Afterward, I'll go to America to see my Ruthie.

NOVEMBER 1968: Heterogeneous Group

Rachel (P) and Orly (P) build a house for the new doll which Orly brought from home. There is a small room and a second floor with a balcony. They enlarge the house and add stairs. The stairs make them think of the building they are in, and they say, "We built the YMHA."

They prepare a parking space for cars. They add furniture, doll clothes, and dishes to their building and begin to play. Remarks like, "Here the children sleep," "From this door you go to the nursery school," "Mommy stays home and makes lunch," are made.

Teacher, who has heard the remark about this being the YMHA building, brings Uri (P) and asks what other buildings are near the YMHA. Uri says, "The fire station."

He builds a building with a large antenna but can't find a fire engine. Teacher makes a fire engine by drawing and cutting one out of cardboard which she tacks on to blocks. He continues building the garage for the fire engine and brings tools to "fix" the vehicles.

Sarah (D) and her cousin (who is visiting for the day) build a tall building and call it the "library." The building is decorated with pieces of cloth and mosaics, but no reference is made to its use as a library.

The three building groups decide to connect their buildings with a road, from the YMHA to the library, from the library to the fire station. Sarah adds a parking lot for the library.

Teacher suggests to Ron (P) that he build the filling station nearby. He agrees but does not build.

In the discussion time, they tell about their buildings and especially about the road connecting the buildings. The teacher leads a discussion on roads, means of transportation, walking and riding, near and far.

MARCH 1969: Heterogeneous Group

There has been a big spurt in building. For the past three days they have been building a hospital—the block-building play is combined with play in the doll corner.

The doll corner has become Hadassah Hospital, with Dorit (D), Yael (P), Orly (P), Tamar (P), Yossi (D), Naomi (D), and Aliza (P) participating. There are beds with sheets, aprons, signs, a medicine cabinet, a receiving room with telephone. Each child has a specific role.

In the block corner an ambulance is built with a driving wheel, a sign, a signal light, and a cot inside. There is a stop light on the road between the ambulance and the hospital.

Active play between the ambulance and the hospital takes place. The ambulance is bringing a wounded man to the hospital. They notify the hos-

Cooperation and consultation.

pital that they are on the way. The "receiving room attendant" gets ready, the "doctors" organize themselves, and there is active discussion on how to carry on the work.

Orly: We have to put a key near the medicine cabinet so that the doctor can take the medicine out immediately.

Yael: No. We have to leave it open.

Orly: It's impossible. Then everybody could go and take medicines.

There is also play about giving birth. Dorit lies down and feeds her doll from a bottle after she gave birth with the help of Orly.

At the same time, Nissim (D) builds a Hadassah Hospital using the small cube blocks with many accessories.

The sick people in the "houses" being built nearby are brought to Nissim's hospital by Chaim's (D) ambulance.

MAY 1969: Heterogeneous Group

Aliza (P), David (P), and Yossi (D) are building a large block of flats—a tall, long, narrow building. Lively discussion and much consultation on where to place each block follows. Dror (P) joins them.

When the building is finished, the play begins to disintegrate and they are on the verge of drifting off. (On the porch of the building they had placed miniature people.)

Teacher (approaches): What do these people do? Don't they go to work?

David moves the man from the porch directly to a car standing in front of the building.

Teacher: How did the man get from the fifth floor to the car?

David: He'll go down by elevator. (He moves the doll from the fifth floor slowly as if it were in an elevator.)

Dror: Maybe we'll make an elevator.

They take a small box, cord and a pulley and prepare an elevator. They move the doll from the top floor to the ground in the elevator.

An argument ensues when Yossi takes a car and places it in the elevator and wants to bring it to the top of the building. David doesn't allow it and after some discussion, they decide that an elevator is for people and that it's a good idea to use a derrick for the car.

The play around the elevator and the toy derrick continues for a long time.

One of the problems always facing the teachers was when to step in and when to give the children time to solve the block-building problems themselves. If a child was having difficulty in getting the principle of the bridge, or keeping a wall from falling, or solving a balance problem, or (at a later stage) making a door or window or staircase, the teacher had to decide which child was "stuck" and needed the encouragement of her help and teaching, and which child would eventually be able to solve the problem himself. It was not the same for all the children and thus there was no absolute rule for the teachers; it required utmost flexibility and sensitivity to know at what point not stepping in would produce frustration and when stepping in would stifle the child's own initiative and thinking.

Arrangement of the Block Corner

We found that by making certain arrangements and rules, we facilitated the use of the blocks, made it more tempting, satisfying and avoided frustrations.

The block corner was in a very conspicuous spot in the room with much open space around it, yet was placed in an area so that it was not necessary to cross it to get to something else. Where possible, the block corner was somewhat set apart through the use of block shelves and low fences, and this helped to give it a protected feeling. The area was expanded as the children needed more and more space for their block building.

Each type of block was kept separate, and where possible, stored on different shelves. As previously described, the blocks were arranged on long, low shelves which were designed to fit their size and number. The goal was to store the blocks in an orderly and clearly defined arrangement. Where possible, they were stored lengthwise so that the children could clearly identify their shapes. The longer and heavier blocks were kept on the bottom shelves, and we tried not to crowd the shelves too much so that the children could have easy access to the blocks.

We found that it was very helpful when the space for each type of block was marked by a drawing of the type of block belonging there. This drawing was tacked to or pasted on the appropriate spot and helped the children to keep the blocks in their proper places. We did not use all the types of blocks produced by the manufacturer; some were much too complicated and difficult to work with at this age level. At the end of this section is a list of the types and quantities of blocks we found appropriate.

On the block shelves, or near them, were a number of accessory materials—small, colored cube blocks and mosaic tiles for decoration; miniature furniture (later the children made their own furniture in carpentry); miniature people and animals (these, too, the children later made by themselves of pipe cleaners, cloth, and plasticene); small automobiles, trucks, airplanes, dishes, and pots; squares of cloth (for covering the dolls, making curtains, etc.); and samples of rugs. In addition, the teacher had ready such items as small boxes, hose pipe, rope, cord, scissors, ice cream sticks, pieces of wood, pulleys, rubber tubes, cardboard cones, medicine bottles, stones (for money), old radios, clocks, and electric switches. Plasticene was an important accessory near the blocks for making trees, dolls, and dishes.

There were some special techniques and rules that the teachers used with the block activity, which made it more pleasant and productive. These were:

1. The children tended to begin building immediately up against the block shelves, impeding other children from getting to the shelves. It was important to teach them not to do this, and a good way to remind them was by making a chalk line or pasting some adhesive a small distance away from the block shelf beyond which no block-building was allowed.

2. At the beginning, children crowded together and built too closely to each other, thus interfering with each other's work. A good way of handling this was by chalking off an area on the floor that was assigned to a particular child. Sometimes we found that by having his own area clearly marked, a child was stimulated to build. After a while,

when the children were accustomed to the organization necessary for block-building, the chalk demarcation became unnecessary.

3. The children became discouraged when there were many unused or fallen blocks scattered about on the floor, because they had difficulty in distinguishing their own building. Our answer to this problem was for the teacher herself to unobtrusively pick up the strewn blocks and put them away. We felt that if we asked the children to stop in the middle of their work period to pick up, the chances were that they would become distracted and not go back to their work. If the teacher was always alert to keep the block floor fairly clear, each individual building stood out and the child was able to view his work.

4. When a block building collapsed because of an accident, we found that the most reassuring way to keep the child from becoming discouraged was to quickly help him to reconstruct it and make no issue of it.

5. Some children tended to collect all the blocks of a particular size before they began to build. Rules had to be made to allow a reasonable amount of preparation, but no hoarding. Here, too, a certain amount of flexibility was needed because different children had different work habits which we wanted to respect. Certainly, each child was allowed a reasonable pile of blocks beside him before he began to work.

6. An effective way of stimulating dramatic play around a block-building was by making a sign for it: "Grocery Store," "Uri's Garage," etc. The children loved dictating these signs.

7. The children frequently requested permission to leave their buildings up for the next day or even for a whole week. In deciding when to allow this, the teacher had to take a number of factors into consideration: What was the block situation in the nursery; could so many blocks be spared? Was the building an integral part of a play scheme that was being added to every day, or would it become stagnant and unused? Was it very important for this child to have a feeling of achievement by seeing his own building standing as a testimony to his ability?

8. Cleanup time became a very enjoyable part of the block play when it was properly presented. It was also a good learning experience because the children learned to categorize, to sort, and to keep order; they learned responsibility and the carrying out of an assigned job, cleanup sometimes was used as a language lesson.

First of all, it was important that cleanup time be highly organized and specific. The children were warned about ten minutes before that it was soon going to be time to cleanup, and they were warned again five minutes before. Sometimes there was an organized tour around the room examining each building.

When the time for cleanup came, a bell was rung, or a piano chord struck, or a special putting-away song was sung. The children all gathered around the teacher as assignments were given and volunteered for. There were many possible variations in assignments: (a) Some children were assigned to the accessories, some to the long blocks, unit blocks, etc. (b) Blocks were arranged in wagons and driven to the block shelves; they were loaded on one long block and pushed, etc. (c) They were arranged in "delivery" packages, of three, four, and five blocks to a child. (d) Children were assigned to clean up different areas of the room. (e) An assembly line was arranged. (f) The children were asked to state in a full sentence what they wanted to put away that day. Until they formulated a whole sentence, they did not begin putting away.

When the job was done (and it was amazing how fast it was done), the children and teachers had a good sense of achievement as they looked at the neat floor and shelves.

Our Block Set

We did not order the routine set of blocks arranged by the manufacturer, but rather the sizes, shapes, and numbers we felt most appropriate to the age level we were working with.

We started with fewer blocks (because of our low equipment budget) but soon found the number to be entirely inadequate and used the bulk of our limited equipment money for the acquisition of more blocks. Both teachers and children were frequently frustrated by the insufficient number of blocks. The teachers estimated that twice the number we had would be more or less adequate. (As it was, we added cardboard and wooden boxes to the block corner to make up for the lack of blocks.)

The following is the breakdown of the types and numbers of blocks we used:

Unit blocks	100	
Double unit blocks	60	
Half units	24	
Half units	24	
Triangles	30	
Ramps	20	
Ramps	20	
Long flat boards (for floors, roofs)	20	

(twice the length of the double unit)

Flat boards (also for floors, roofs)	20	

(the length of the double unit)

Thin pillars	10

Thick pillars	10

Others	10

etc.

We made a very clear division between the use of the unit blocks indoors and the hollow blocks outdoors. There were several reasons for this:

1. The unit blocks take up less room, and thus more children can be involved in active building indoors.
2. The unit blocks are flexible and can be used more easily to express complicated ideas. They lend themselves to the addition of more details and more imaginative use of accessory materials.
3. The unit blocks impel the children to use more skill and to solve more engineering problems, to develop a sense for numbers and physical laws.
4. The most important function of the unit block is that it stimulates symbolic play and thinking (the preparation for reading which deals with abstract symbols and thinking in abstract concepts). With the hollow blocks, the child uses his whole body and real objects, whereas with the unit blocks he uses symbolic doll-size people and miniature objects.

If the young child has both materials at his disposal indoors, he would tend to use the hollow blocks because he has the immediate satisfaction of a massive, finished product which he has produced (not too much skill is required). The room then would become filled with the large hollow blocks, which are quickly used up by only a few children, and thus the process of building and adding and changing the building is usually cut short.

The hollow blocks, because of their massivity, seemed to be more appropriate for large muscle activity outdoors. Combined with large crates, long boards, ladders and wagons, the children created large imaginative buildings which they could climb over; they pulled and pushed heavy objects; they created huge houses, trucks, airplanes, etc., which they actually could get into in order to play their dramatic roles.

TRIPS

We scheduled at least one trip every week. The trips outside the nursery were as important to the curriculum as anything that happened within it. They provided the raw material, the first-hand experience upon which the rest of the program was built. Since the curriculum was the study of the children's immediate environment, the trips were their laboratory. They also served to broaden the children's horizons as they became ready for wider and wider areas of interest. (Both teachers and children enjoyed the trip as the high point of the week.)

Each nursery took different trips depending on their immediate neighborhood. The nursery near the fire station visited it frequently; the nursery near a construction site made regular visits to watch the progress of the building processes; the nursery that included a child whose mother was a radio announcer went to see the radio station. The trips always were planned as an integral part of the events and interest that arose in the nursery. They started from the simplest and "closest to home" items and, gradually, went far afield.

Each outing was carefully planned. Whenever possible, the teacher made a preparatory trip to prepare and explore the area, to investigate the conditions, the best time for the visit, the people who could be interviewed and helpful, the special items to be observed, the technical arrangements that had to be made.

Each trip was preceded by a discussion with the children in which the need for the visit was clarified. They would review the questions they wanted answered and the items that particularly interested them. After a while, some of the children themselves would suggest a trip when a question that needed clarification would arise.

During the trip, the teacher tried to encourage the children to ask questions of the workers. (The workers had often been prepared for the visit by the teacher and requested to answer questions simply.) The focus of the visit was kept clearly in mind, and, in addition, the teacher and children were alert to the various sensory details of each experience. (The teacher would suggest that they smell, feel, and listen to a specific sound.) Throughout the trip, there was much verbalization by the teacher, who also encouraged the children to express in words what they were seeing, hearing, and experiencing. The teacher tried, wherever possible, to dramatize and thus underline each part of the experience.

The excursion was followed by group and individual discussions in which the experience was recalled in all its details. Play that reflected what had been learned on the trip sometimes took days and weeks in coming and the teachers learned not to hurry it. The children sometimes dictated stories about various aspects of the trip and frequently used the experience in their painting and other art products.

Some trips had to be repeated several times until the salient items could be absorbed and understood, and the children themselves would request a repeat visit when they realized that they were still confused and unclear about necessary pieces of information.

One of the problems that frequently arose for the teachers was how to handle the children's interest in distracting sights on a trip which had a specific goal in mind. Since the trips always had a clear purpose and focus, the question before the teacher was how to react to extraneous attractions. She recognized the importance of the children's interest in other events, and yet it was necessary to remember the goal. The teacher noted and praised the child's alertness and awareness of new things, stopped to look and comment, and gently suggested that they would come back to investigate this new subject but that they now are hurrying to see _____. In her individual work with the child she again tried to show him that what he had noticed and said was important and would be taken into consideration in future planning. In recall of the trip with the children, the side issues also were recalled.

It was important that each teacher planned at least a weekly trip, usually on a specific day. Without such a rigid schedule, trips tended to be put off. Sometimes there was almost a daily "trip" when something particularly interesting was happening in the neighborhood. There were a number of trips that the teacher felt could not be well handled and absorbed by the children in a large group. On such occasions, the group was divided into two, and two tours were made. Whenever possible, several parents were invited to join and assist in the outings.

The following is a partial list of trips that were taken in our nurseries, more or less in chronological order. Of course, not every nursery made each of these trips.

"Trip" to get to know the nursery, inside and outside. We looked at everything (including the toilet, storeroom, and kitchen), named it, examined it, and, in group discussion, we talked of "where we had been this morning." This "trip" was sometimes done repeatedly in individual work with the children.

A trip outside the gate of the nursery to the opposite side of the street. The children examined the building on the opposite side, looked at the nursery from across the street, compared the two buildings and the two yards.

"Trip" to visit a sick child. This was an effective way of giving individual attention and a feeling of importance to that child. The children examined his house, his toys (if there were any), spoke to his mother. (This visit had its dangers and its difficulties in our situation where the children came from two very different social levels.)

Trip to see a baby. When the subject of babies was the central theme, there were two "trips" to a home where there was a new baby. The children watched him being fed, watched the bathing process, examined his body, looked at his clothes and diapers, watched the preparations for his bottle, and examined his crib.

Trip to see a building site nearby. When this trip was made early in the first year of work (a second story was being added to the opposite building in one nursery and a youth center was being built across the street from another nursery), the teachers found that the children were unready to absorb or understand what was happening. They were unequal to the job of seeing the separate and various operations taking place and only reacted to the noise and the confusion. It was only toward the end of the first year of the program when the children were already attempting representational building that this trip was planned again, and then it became a very meaningful experience, which was repeated many times, as the pipes were put in, as the cement was made, as the stones were placed, as the tiles were laid, etc.

Trips to the grocery store. This was a frequently repeated outing. Since the children participated in the preparation of the morning snack, small groups would go out with the teacher or the assistant to buy food.

Later, when the store project was the central interest, the trip to the store became much more focused—to see how the foods were arranged, to observe the money transactions, to watch the delivery trucks, to follow the way a telephone order was handled, to look at the pedlars' wagons (where this was in the neighborhood), to study the supermarket and how it was organized, to watch the Arab women selling vegetables that they carried on their heads.

Trip to the carpenter. The carpenter was a familiar and beloved figure. There were numerous trips to his workshop to see how he worked and to collect scraps of wood.

Trip to see the road and the sidewalk. The question of the uses of the road and the sidewalk arose during the block-building. The trip clarified what each was for and how people and vehicles use them. Another trip was taken to observe how a road was being paved.

Trip to observe road signs. This subject, too, came up during the block play. The children went out to see a "safety zone," traffic signs, a traffic policeman.

Trip to the main traffic road. The goal of this trip was to observe the various kinds of vehicles. The children differentiated between various different types of cars, buses, trucks; they identified an ambulance, a postal truck, a fire truck, a police car; they noted the speed of different cars, characteristic sounds of the motors, opposite directions of traffic.

Trip to the gas station. The children noted the gas pumps, the gas meter, the water pump, the air pump, the attendants (in one gas station there was a woman attendant), and the restaurant connected with the gas station.

Trip to the garage. Here, the children watched how the cars were raised, how the mechanics worked, how tires were fixed.

Trip to the bus stop. Children watched how people waited in line, how they climbed onto the bus, how they paid. On another trip they also rode on a bus, watching these processes. They looked at the numbers of various bus lines and went especially to see the teacher's bus stop.

Trip in the teacher's own automobile. The children were taken out in small groups to see how the teacher started her car and how she drove.

Trip to the railroad station. The children felt the steel of the train, learned the names of the cars, looked at the tracks, and examined the train signals and the engine car. They saw how the cars were attached, went to the ticket office to see how tickets were sold, and listened to the loudspeaker announcing the arrival of a train. They differentiated between freight and passenger trains. They talked to the station manager and to the track attendant. Finally, they had a short ride on the train without leaving the station.

Trip to the airport. (For details, see pages 136–39).

Trip to the health clinic. This was a trip that we repeated. The children found much satisfaction in becoming acquainted with the real aspects of a health clinic, the roles of the doctors, nurses, pharmacists. It helped them to work through some of their fears.

Nature trips. Trips into the nearby fields were taken at the changing seasons to see what was happening—to look at the trees, the leaves, the insects, and the birds. Specimens were collected, put on display, and labeled.

Trips to father's place of work. When the discussions on salaries and employment took place, the children went to see where some of their fathers were employed.

Trip to learn about electricity and water. When the children had become alerted to the details of buildings, they were interested in how the electricity and the water entered. They climbed up on the roofs of houses to see the water tanks, and they went out in the streets to see the electric lines and where they led.

Trip to see the neighborhood (Neighborhood project). The children took a short walk for the purpose of observing all the things there are in their neighborhood. They looked at the housing—apartments and small houses —and went to see some of their own homes; discussed their location in the neighborhood; examined the roads and the street names and the numbers of the buses going to this neighborhood. They noted the grocery, vegetable, butcher stores, the hairdresser, and the health clinic. Later, they added the synagogues, the schools, the nurseries, the large market with its stands, the electric and telephone lines.

During the work on the model of "the neighborhood," numerous trips were needed to enable the children to clarify where certain buildings were, what a specific building looked like, where the roads were, etc. In one nursery the problem of how to build the large synagogue occupied the children and required several trips; in another nursery, which was situated in a large community center, the building and its grounds needed much study before the children succeeded in constructing a small model.

The children became so accustomed to thinking of a trip as a way of finding out things that they began to relate differently to outings they took with their parents. Frequently they would come back the next day with a full, verbalized description of what they had seen and done, and in this way the other children heard about kibbutzim, the Old City, Haifa, the Dead Sea. We saw in this a very important achievement.

AREAS OF INTEREST

We found that a fruitful way of stimulating more interesting and varied play and of widening the children's horizons and scope of information was by choosing a topic that most of the children were interested and involved in and expanding it as a major "area of interest" for several weeks. This was also one of the most effective methods both for seeing all of the detailed aspects of familiar things and for understanding how various items and processes lead into and relate to each other—how, for instance, a car is related to a gas station, to a road, to a truck, to transportation of people and goods, to delivery to stores, to houses of people who buy in the stores. Expanding any particular subject led us to more interests and concepts. As we dealt with a particular "area of interest," it affected most of the activities of the nursery. The discussions, trips, play, games, language activities, stories, and individual work usually reflected the subject that was the major focus of interest at that time.

Nevertheless, some children continued with whatever interest happened to absorb them more, and for example, at the same time that the train was the central focus, there would be children continuing to play baby or zoo or something else. We found, however, that even the children who did not participate actively in any particular activity did get a great deal out of each topic through observing what the others were doing, listening to the stories and discussions, and participating in the trips and games. We usually found that the new information and understanding of relationships appeared later in the children's play and talk.

As we planned the development of an "area of interest," we kept several objectives in mind. It was not enough that the children have experiences, and opportunities to relive the experiences, in their play; we wanted them to learn specific aspects of the subject. We used the "area of interest" program to facilitate their thinking and reasoning abilities. Sometimes as we tried to plan a specific subject, the gap between the children's primitive concepts and knowledge and the sophisticated concepts we wished to introduce seemed enormous. Subjects like transportation, the economics of daily life (buying and selling, production and distribution), electricity, a house and how it is built, our neighborhood and all its aspects, seemed overwhelmingly complicated for our young children and yet essential to help them understand and feel at home and at ease in their world.

In the planning of each topic (which was always a topic that grew out of the children's play and interests), we tried to clarify for ourselves the basic concepts and information on the subject, and then what were the simplest, most appropriate ways to present them. The goal always was to help the children organize their isolated bits of information into clear concepts and sets of relationships. The principle was to present the material and to stimulate the children through trips, discussions, and stories (the *intake*), and then to stimulate them to work through the information and experience in play, in art expression, and in discussion (the *outgo*). In this way, information became organized into one understood whole. We were always gratified to see how many concepts the children were able to develop when the subject was presented well.

The following excerpts from teachers' diaries are some of the "areas of interest" we developed in the course of the work and which were covered in all four of our nurseries. We began with the simplest subjects, those closest to home—the child and his own body; his family. In the course of the two years we went farther and farther afield until we were able to integrate much of what had been covered in the study of "our neighborhood."

The Child and His Own Body

This was the first topic we developed in all the nurseries in order to help the children evolve a clearer self-concept and raise their self-esteem. Since this was particularly stressed in the first days, materials and methods used are covered in the section on "Who Am I and What Am I?"

Babies

Drora (P) had reacted to a new baby sister with a change in behavior at the nursery—much crying and demanding attention. We decided that the birth of a new baby was an appropriate subject to develop for three-year-olds, many of whom were going through the same experience as Drora's at home.

Our *goals* in the area of interest dealing with babies were the following: (1) to air the ambivalent feelings around the birth of a new baby in order to reduce the anxiety; (2) to help the children develop a more positive feeling about themselves, and hence greater acceptance of the new baby; (3) to sharpen observation through studying all aspects and details about babies and baby care. The concepts and information to be introduced were the following:

1. Structure of the family—mother, father, children.
2. Baby care—feeding, bathing, diapering.
3. Growth and development—size of baby and understanding the concept of growth, infant behavior, and what a baby can do as he grows.
4. Baby paraphernalia—clothes, furniture (beds with sides, play pen, doll carriage, high chair), baby toys (rattle, teething ring, bell, ball).

TRIPS

A trip to Drora's house was planned at a group discussion on her new baby. (An interesting note was that all the way to her house, Drora talked excitedly about everybody coming to see *her* bed, *her* room, *her* toys, and she seemed to deny completely the objective of the trip that had just been discussed in the group.) Drora's mother received the group (she had been prepared for the visit). At first, attention was paid (because of Drora's need) to her room and her things. After extensive examination of Drora's toys, the children went to the baby's bed to look at the baby: "She's so small, like a doll." "Just like the baby doll we have in nursery school." We examined the baby's bed, looked at her clothes, listened to the sounds she made. We sat down with Drora's mother to talk about the baby. Drora's mother answered questions about what and how the baby eats, and that she wets her diapers. The teacher and children asked if she walks, if she talks, if she laughs.

The next day we made a trip to Ronit's (D) house to see her baby sister who is ten months old. The children noticed that Ronit's baby is much bigger, that she stands and falls but doesn't yet know how to walk, that she eats crackers which she holds herself. The following week there was another visit to Drora's house to see the baby being bathed.

DISCUSSIONS

After each visit, impressions of the trip were discussed and analyzed. The children summarized what they had seen, and the teachers emphasized the new words the children were learning. They compared the two babies and discussed how babies and children grow. One discussion dealt with a lesson in how to diaper a baby, another with how to hold a baby to protect its head. Still another concerned the fact that since a baby has no teeth and cannot chew, therefore he has to drink and suck. They talked about sucking from a bottle and from mother's breast. They examined a bottle and nipple and tested to see how it works. Another discussion dealt with babies not knowing how to walk and why there was a need for a baby carriage; they noted that a baby carriage has a top to protect the baby from sun and rain. Other discussions dealt with what a baby wears and what an older child wears, what a baby eats and what an older child eats. A visit by a one-year-old baby to the nursery evoked a discussion on crawling.

Throughout the discussions (and especially at the beginning), the feeling about babies being a nuisance was raised. At first the teacher voiced this. She talked about how pesty babies are, how they cry at night and wake people up, how busy they keep mommies. She told that some children just want to get rid of their baby sisters and brothers, wish to throw them in the garbage, in the toilet bowl. She spoke very dramatically, with strong feeling, and the children burst into laughter with much relief. They, too, voiced negative feelings about their babies. One little girl said, "If my mommy loves me, why does she want another baby?"

The teacher explained that we can love our baby brothers and sisters and hate them too and that everybody has feelings like that. There seemed to be considerable relief at seeing that other children had similar feelings. Later they were able to talk about the fun of having brothers and sisters in the house as playmates.

Having had their fill in dramatic play at being babies, the children then felt freed in the discussions to talk about the fact that they were "big" and that this had many advantages.[4]

PLAY

The play dealing with babies began almost immediately. The children were more drawn to the doll corner than to other play areas and, instead of the stereotyped play of putting dishes on the table, the play became more detailed about babies and baby care, attention to the doll carriage and beds, and so forth. The addition of new materials brought both by the teacher and the children enhanced the play considerably. Baby toys, bottles, diapers, clothes, and a baby bathtub were brought. The play became more and more detailed, some of the children were drawn to the baby role, which they played with deep satisfaction, using baby talk. Other children wanted to play the parent role.

DIDACTIC GAMES

The teachers prepared posters of babies and babies with their parents. These were placed around the room. The posters were used to stimulate individual verbal expression. A "game" was played in which each

---

[4]The homogeneous D group dealt with the same material in their discussions but began at a lower level. The teacher asked each child the name of the baby in his family. Many children did not know the name and simply said "baby."

child had to say something about the picture. Sometimes the teacher had to ask leading questions like "What is the father doing?" The teacher recorded the children's statements as well as the name of the child who had made it, and this record was then pasted onto the poster and often reread to the children at their request.

Yoram (P): The father is bending down.
Eli (D): The child is laughing.
Ora (D): The baby is laughing to his mother.
Yael (D): The child is sitting on father's shoulders. The father loves him.
Malka (D): The baby is crying with his eyes.

Cutting and Pasting Magazine Pictures. The children looked for pictures of babies and of parents and children in magazines. The teachers cut them out and the children pasted them on large pieces of paper and decorated them. Some of the cut-out pictures were prepared for the flannel board, and others were used to make a "baby album." The baby album consisted of pictures of babies, baby and mother, a baby eating, a baby being bathed, mother and baby carriage, baby and big sister, and so on. (It remained a favorite "book" in the nursery.)

Flannel Board. The flannel board pictures were used as the basis for discussions. The pictures were distributed to the children and as the subject of his picture was mentioned, the child would place it on the flannel board. The pictures were kept together in an envelope and were available to be taken out and played with at the flannel board by the children whenever they wished.

GAMES

Feeling Games. A child was blindfolded and given one of the new pieces of equipment to handle; then he was asked to guess what it was—a rattle, a bottle, etc.

Something-Missing Games. The teacher put a doll and a doll bath on the table and asked the children what else was needed; gradually they answered water, soap, towel, etc. The teacher placed doll, bottle, toys, and so forth in the center of the room, covered them with a cloth, and removed one object. She removed the cloth and the children had to say what was missing.

Books and Songs. Books and songs on babies, brothers and sisters, and growing up were introduced.

SUMMARY

The children were three years old when the subject of "babies" was expanded. They were still in the process of adjustment to nursery school, and some of them were having difficulty; many of them had younger siblings.

The intense playing out and discussions on this subject helped many of the children a great deal. Drora was visibly relaxed after playing mother extensively in the doll's corner. Danny (who had begun school still wearing a diaper and nylon pants) was greatly helped when the comparison between baby and older child was made, and he saw the considerable advantages of older children. All were relieved as they realized that the other children were going through the same feelings and experiences as themselves and that there was no need for shame or guilt. The play and interest around babies remained a favorite subject and came up many times during the year.

Family

The "area of interest" dealing with family followed naturally and inevitably from the topic of babies. The *concepts* we wanted to introduce were:

1. Recognition of the roles of mother, father, brother, sister.
2. Recognition of farther-removed relatives—aunts, grandparents, cousins.

In order to introduce the topic, the children were asked the names of their mother and father. A game was played calling each child by the name of his parent. The children loved it and continued to call each other by these names for several days. This led to discussions of their families and who is in their family, and the brothers and sisters were enumerated.

TRIP

A trip was taken to see where each of the children lived, and they classified the houses into one-story, two-story, and many-storied—low houses and tall houses. The teacher pointed out that in some houses only one family lives, and in other, big houses, many families live.

DISCUSSIONS

What work does mother do? What work does father do? Children enumerated the varieties of housework done by mother. When it came to father's place of work, many children were vague, and simply said, "Father is at work." They were asked to find out where and what. The next day they reported proudly: "My father works at Hadassah, he is a doctor." "My father is a plumber," "My uncle is an electrician." "My father is a computer."

Other discussions concerned grandmother and grandfather, and the children were induced to verbalize that grandmother is mother's mother, etc. The teacher pointed out how people could be different things—"to you he is grandfather, to father he is 'father'." The children named their grandparents and began calling each other by their names. They told stories of what happened when they went to visit their grandparents. They discussed the fact that some grandparents live in the same house with their children, others live in the same town, still others live in another town, and some are dead. Other comments dealt with how grandmother helps mother and mother helps grandmother, and that grandparents often are baby-sitters. Similar discussions took place on the subject of aunts and uncles—the sister of mother, etc. Memories of visits with aunts and uncles were recalled.

At discussion time the children played the game of "family." Children volunteered for various roles—mother, father, big brother, grandmother. When the whole family was assembled, the "family" marched along together. This was repeated several times, since all the children wanted to play a role.

PLAY

The domestic play corner began to include roles like grandparents, older and younger siblings, aunts and uncles, father going to work.

DIDACTIC GAMES

In cutting and pasting games, the children chose pictures from magazines to represent all the members of their immediate and extended families. They free-associated as they held up the pictures they had chosen. Dorit (P), showing a picture of a baby with a spoon, said, "This is my baby; she is fed with a spoon," or Dalia (P), of a picture of a baby, "This is me, when I was little." Yaakov (D) chose a picture of a boy with a school bag and said, "This is my big brother." Teacher asked, "How do you know?" "My brother has a school bag and goes to school." A set of family pictures also was collected in an envelope for use at the flannel board in group names, in individual work, or by the child himself. Picture cuttings of the members of the family were assembled into a "family album" which was placed in the book corner. In addition, poems and stories appropriate to the family project were introduced.

Auto

Play with automobiles was, of course, one of the most beloved of activities. The goals of the automobile project and the concepts to be learned were:

1. to arrive at a clearer understanding of motor vehicles;
2. to consider what makes a motor go and to learn that it is not magical;
3. to understand transportation as a means of moving people and things, of getting from one place to another;
4. to see the relationship between vehicles and other aspects of modern living.

Information we felt the children should gain included:

1. Parts of an auto—steering wheel, brakes, gears, wheels, horn, signals, headlights, keys, wipers, engine, front and back seats.
2. Fuel—gasoline, oil, water. Comparison of fuel for car and fuel for people.
3. Types of vehicles—trucks, firetrucks, ambulances, postal truck, army jeeps, buses, names of cars.
4. Roads—where they lead and road signs.
5. Sidewalks—what they are for.
6. Traffic—traffic signals, traffic policemen, crosswalks.
7. Safety—care in crossing streets, care in driving.
8. Bus—bus stops and fares, change, punching of bus tickets.

After an auto was built by the children, a heated discussion took place on what makes it go. The teacher stimulated their curiosity by asking many questions. A "trip" to examine a real car was planned.

TRIPS

The group went out to examine the teacher's car. They looked at it from the outside. The headlights, wheels, and other exterior parts were named and examined. A second "trip" to see the teacher's car was made after a question regarding the use of car keys. The children went into the car and touched the steering wheel, the seats, and the keys, and looked at the speedometer and the clock. The teacher started the motor, while the children watched the process and listened to the sounds. Additional trips were taken to see traffic lanes and road signs, a gas station, and a garage.

New equipment introduced in this project and used in play included discarded automobile spare parts, discarded electric spare parts, driving wheels, suitcases, road signs, and traffic signs.

PLAY

Play around automobiles and roads became very popular and purposeful, both indoors and out. (Sometimes information that had been observed on a trip took several days to be digested before it appeared in play.) The play dealt with cars, fueling, accidents, breakdowns and repairs, and the need for traffic rules became apparent. Roads and sidewalks were built; cars delivered people to houses, ambulances went to hospitals and trucks to stores.

DIDACTIC GAMES

To enhance perception, the teacher aroused the children to utilize all their senses as they recorded memories of their "trip"—the smell of gasoline, the color of the auto inside and out, the color of the lights, the special sign on the taxi. Posters of different types of cars were hung around the room, and flannel board games were played using pictures of various types of cars and car parts and policemen and traffic signals.

The following kinds of rhythm games also were played: the children moved like slow cars, fast cars, wheels, heavily laden trucks, and empty trucks. They played at being different types of horns, at different rhythms. The children imitated the motion of vehicles, going forward and backward, and responding to traffic signals.

DISCUSSIONS

Discussions on what makes a car go were handled on a very simple level—the water, the fuel, the key. Later on, such words as clutch and brakes were introduced. All the concepts and information mentioned above were taken up at one time or another in discussions either with the whole group or with small groups, at didactic game times or in individual work. Here is an excerpt from one such discussion in the homogeneous group:

Teacher (holding a book on trucks) tells the children how the truck in the picture is delivering tar.
Teacher (asks the children): What did the truck we saw yesterday deliver?
Aliza (D) (after much thought): Bread.
Teacher: What else do trucks deliver?
Adi: (D): Eggs.

Dalit (D): Juice.

Yosef (D): Milk.

Yaakov (D): Sand.

Teacher: What other kinds of cars are there?

Uzi (D): Ambulance.

Teacher: What does an ambulance deliver?

Josef: When my mother was sick, she went in an ambulance.

Children go on to talk of jeeps, station wagons, etc.

Trains

The subject of trains came up as a natural continuation of the subject of cars and transportation. The real interest in trains followed the trip to the railroad station, although there had been sporadic train play before. We wanted the children to learn the following concepts and information:

1. Trains are one means of transportation, and are different in certain respects from other means of transportation.
2. Trains carry baggage, passengers, and freight.
3. Trains run on tracks and have cars, engine, movable steps, and whistle. The cars are attached by magnets; trains are made of steel.
4. A railroad station has a ticket office, stationmaster, porters, wagons, loudspeaker, railroad clock, and public telephone.
5. Tracks have signals, intersection barriers, track switches, and traffic barriers.
6. The special advantages of trains over buses and trucks.

TRIP

The trip followed a discussion on trains, which centered around a large picture of a train and a story by Nahum (D) of his trip on the train with his mother. Many questions were raised—where do the trains go, what makes them work? The children went by bus to the railroad station (this later led to comparisons between buses and trains). As they entered the railroad station they were first drawn to the ticket office and the line of people waiting to buy tickets. The children went out to the platform and examined the train about to leave (they heard the loudspeaker announcing this and watched a woman running to catch the train). Later they went into the stationmaster's office for a discussion with him. He took them on a guided tour to see the trains, the tracks, the signals, and, as a special treat, arranged a little ride for them on the train. On the ride they observed how the train moves from one track to another, the intersection barriers in front of a road, how a train rides backwards; they listened to the train whistle and moved from car to car. Later they examined a freight train, looked at the mail bags and the freight, observed how the cars were attached, and examined the engine car.

PLAY

The play after the trip built up slowly, at first centering around battles as to who would be the railroad engineer. A row of blocks with the addition of tracks drawn in chalk was sufficient. Little by little, more details were added, until, after two weeks, the play and building included many aspects of what had been experienced and discussed. The children requested and were helped to make signal lights and lanterns. They moved the small set of steps from the bathroom to the playroom. Railroad workers' hats and a ticket puncher were also added.

Here is a description from the teacher's diary of one day's play:

APRIL 1969: Heterogeneous Group

Ari (P) and Amos (P) built a closed train out of blocks. Moshe (D) built the track and the shed where the tracks are switched. He worked quietly, without speaking. Teacher saw that no play was developing and suggested that they carry freight on the train. They loaded the train.

Avi (P) and Chana (P) built a bus to carry people to the train. They placed dolls in the bus and when there weren't enough dolls, they prepared plasticene dolls with the additional help of Ronit (D) and Galia (D). They locomoted the dolls from the bus to the train. The play lagged occasionally and teacher's presence stimulated it further.

A passenger train was built by Galia (D) and Ronit (D). Each car was numbered. Shira (P) built a small station, and a small doll sitting on a block was used as the ticket agent. Yosef (P) meanwhile announced he will be the locomotive driver of Galia's train. Ron (P) became enthusiastic and played the conductor, inspecting tickets. Teacher became a passenger with five children and they went to "Haifa." Shira (P) joined them and little by little the others all came along.

At some point in the play, the passengers went by bus No. 13 to the train, the bus stopped for a railroad barrier, some of the passengers visited the "aunt in Haifa" (in the doll corner), and some children stopped at Yael's (D) stand to buy ice cream.

DISCUSSIONS

Discussions dealt with the children's impressions of their trip—the types of workers at the railroad; train transportation; the motor and its fuel (diesel and coal, electric trains); what the tracks look like; differences between trains and other means of transportation; the feeling of riding on a train and the frightening feeling when you move from car to car and feel the wind; the differing speeds and varying destinations of the trains.

Nahum (D) told of how it feels to be in a tunnel. The teacher used pictures of trains and railroad stations to stimulate the discussions.

Stores

The goals of the interest project on stores were for the children to learn:

1. to differentiate between different types of stores;
2. to understand the concept of buying and selling;
3. to understand the concept that stores have to be supplied and that deliveries are made by trucks;
4. to classify items.

We wanted the children to learn that there are a variety of kinds of stores—grocery, supermarket, vegetable store, butcher shop, shoe shops, clothing shops—and to begin to identify the details of the stores—shelves, cabinets, counters, storeroom, refrigerator, shopping wagon, shopping basket, scales, cash box, cashier, money and change, opening and closing time of shops, show windows.

Trips

The purpose of the first trip was to see shops in general, so the class went to the shopping center to look at display windows. Subsequent trips were to particular shops to buy specific things according to a list the teacher and children had prepared (previously they had examined the kitchen to see what was needed). They noted that some things are packaged and others have to be weighed; that in a supermarket there is no salesman, only a cashier. They noticed that there were different types of scales; that cans have pictures on the outside showing you what is inside. The children chose, bought, and paid for their purchases.

Play

Although there had been some store play before, it was interesting to note that after the trip to the grocery store, the play at first dealt with the storeroom and the trucks delivering goods. The children used all the collections of cartons and boxes that had been saved for pasting and classified them for delivery to the store. In the store they built shelves and arranged the goods. (The group discussion period concentrated on reviewing the trip as well as on how to build steady shelves and arrange the goods. The teacher felt that the problem of how to make a shelf steady

required specific consideration.) After this, the children began collecting
and bringing to the nursery heaps of empty cans and boxes of foods and
cigarettes. The following excerpt from the teacher's diary describes the
play several days after the trip to the grocery.

OCTOBER 1968: Heterogeneous Group

Jonah needed some help in building shelves for his store and Chaim helped
him very skillfully. Danny was the driver of the milk truck and delivered milk
to the store.

Chaim went to collect supplies for the grocery, and pulled everything out
of the odds and ends box. Jonah and Chaim quickly arranged the supplies
according to the types of products. Each shelf contained a different type
of food, and the children even remembered that they needed a refrigerator
for the milk and various types of cheeses.

Most of the children became interested and enthusiastic. More boys came
to work in the grocery shop, and the girls all came rushing to buy. Jonah
decided to "close the store" until it was all organized.

It was suggested to some of the girls that they build houses to which
they could bring the food, and they did this impatiently. Then each took a
shopping bag and "money" to the store. Two "grocers" had been chosen—
Jonah and Chaim. Reuben declared himself the cashier (this was a familiar
role since he had been the ticket-seller on the bus).

It was interesting that the children accepted the presence of the cashier
even though they knew that in the neighborhood store mother pays the
grocer directly. They paid *both* the grocer and the cashier. The cashier also
took on the job of guard and watched that nobody left the shop without
paying. The girls bought wildly and filled their shopping bags with all sorts
of products.

We insisted that the buyer must state clearly what he wanted. He must
not point and say, "I want this," but rather, "I want soap."

The store play became more complicated as it continued for several
weeks. At one point many children were involved in making "cakes and
lollipops" out of plasticene, and "candies" wrapped in colored paper. They
dictated signs which read "Open for business," "Closed for holiday." They
used the scales and commented that some things are weighed and other
things come prepared in packages. They noted that sometimes you order
"give me a pound of . . ." and sometimes "give me a dollar's worth of . . .".

After the initial enthusiasm, the grocery store became part of a wider
play scheme: the "drivers" *always* stopped off to buy cigarettes, and the
"nurse" in the "Baby Health Station" came to buy lollipops for the crying babies. Later a shoe store was added to the play scheme, and there
was much measuring of shoes as well as classifying according to size, color,
and type (rainboots, sandals). (Later the children's experience in setting up
shops and buying and selling was the basis for the "market" they arranged
at Purim time.)

The didactic games played included a grocery store puzzle, a vegetable store puzzle, and games that taught use of scales and measuring equipment.

Airplanes

The stimulus for the interest unit on airplanes occurred in the heterogeneous group in 1969.

A plane flew by one day, and Amnon (P) immediately started to build an airplane in the yard using a crate and long boards. Several children joined him. David's (P) father had just gone abroad, and David had accompanied him to the airport, coming back full of talk and impressions of airplanes. There were several days of sporadic play and building of airplanes, but the group discussion and play indicated large gaps in information and much interest in knowing more about the subject. We decided to concentrate on and expand the subject. A trip to the nearest airport was arranged.

The goals for the airplane project were:

1. to deepen understanding of intercontinental travel;
2. to help the children understand the concept of speed;
3. to explain the purposes of airplanes—transport of people and freight, and as a war machine.

We introduced concepts and words dealing with aviation—airplanes, pilot, flight, airfield, takeoff, landing, distances, and speed of travel—and encouraged the children to notice specific details—wings, tail, propeller, wheels, headlights, windows, landing-stairs, runway, observation tower, waiting room, radio communication, steward, stewardess, navigator, maps, safety belts, windsock, meteorologist, fuel.

TRIP

The trip to the airport was timed so that we were there during a takeoff. (The airport was a small one, used only a few times a day for passenger and occasional military planes.) The first stop was the waiting room where the ticket office, restaurant, benches, and porters and their wagons, were observed in detail. Through the windows of the waiting room, the runway was carefully scrutinized. The movable landing-stairs, the plane door opening, the passengers climbing into the plane, and the stewardess collecting tickets at the entrance to the plane were noted. The children observed how the baggage came to the plane in separate wagons and was deposited in the plane through a back opening. When the plane took off, the children were excited by the noise, and we watched long enough to note that the wheels were retracted when the plane was in the air. We also watched a military plane land and noted the differences in the color, size, and noise between passenger and military planes. The children commented that there were no passengers.

(The airfield was too far from the nursery to make frequent visits, although we felt that there were so many impressions that several trips were really needed in order to absorb them. It was necessary to make do with much recall and discussion, as well as the use of pictures and books.)

In group discussions, things that were seen on the trip were talked about, explained, and discussed in detail. If they were not understood in a first discussion, they later were clarified, and thus the level of the discussions was raised very slowly in easy stages.

NEW EQUIPMENT AND MATERIALS

After the trip, we introduced new pieces of equipment to facilitate and stimulate the play in order to incorporate the new information and concepts that had been acquired. In the doll corner, we added small suitcases, and miniature toy airplanes were added to the small table blocks. During the course of the project, ladders for the landing stairs; pilots' caps, goggles, and earphones; long boards for wings; insignia for the planes; lanterns and signal flags for the landing strip; and a cloth bag on a pole for a windsock were introduced in the block corner. A telephone receiver was used as the radio transmitter. Maps were brought both for the pilots and the passengers, as well as newspapers and magazines for the passengers. Tickets and signs were made. (Many of these accessories were added at the request of the children or were brought by them on their own initiative.) In addition, for use with the clay, ice cream sticks (for wings), small flags, and buttons to be used as headlights were made available as the need arose.

Cuttings from newspapers and magazines were arranged on large posters which were hung on the walls, and an airplane album was made, which included pictures of various types of planes; of pilots, stewardesses, and airfields; of the interior of a plane and its seats; of the pilot's cabin with its radio and other equipment.

DIDACTIC GAMES AND PLAY

We introduced the subject of airplanes in the group games and in didactic materials in order to teach the new words dealing with aviation in a structured way. An airplane jigsaw puzzle and an airplane lotto were made out of magazine and travel folder pictures. Pictures related to airplanes were cut out of magazines and folders and prepared for use with the flannel board. They were distributed to the children, and the teacher began an improvised story. When the subject of his picture appeared in the story, each child placed his picture on the flannel board. For example.

> *Teacher:* "Yoran went with his parents to a far-away land. (Amnon (P) adds: "to the United States.") He went there in a big airplane. Does anybody have a picture of an airplane?" (Ronit (D) places her airplane on the board.) "They took many suitcases with them. The porters took the suitcases and put them on the wagon." (The child who had a picture of a suitcase and the child who had a picture of the wagon placed their pictures on the board.)

We also played a flannel board game in which each child was given a picture of an airplane accessory. The teacher would ask, "Who has the picture of the instrument through which the pilot talks to the observation tower? Can you remember what we call it? After the child names it, he is asked to place it on the flannel board. The game continues using various accessories.

The "What's missing?" game also was played in this project, the teacher drawing with chalk a picture of a plane or a part of a plane and asking, "What's missing?" and the children naming the missing part.

Rhythms and games in which the children assumed various roles also were used. For instance, in one, the children are planes—they fly; take off from the floor and spread their "wings"; take off from the airport and return to it; land and rest on the ground. While flying, the "plane" changes course, speed, and height. In the middle of the flight one plane needs fuel and receives it from another plane in the air. In another game, the children are pilots—they get up in the morning, wash, shower, dress, and eat; go off to the airport; climb into their planes and start the motors; talk through radio communication and look at maps. Finally, the children are passengers—they arrive with both heavy and light suitcases; porters take their bags; they buy tickets, and climb onto the plane on imaginary ladders, sit, fasten their seat belts, and look through the windows; the stewardess delivers food on a tray.

Appropriate songs, records, stories, and word puzzles dealing with airplanes were presented. In carpentry, each child made a plane which he took home, and in art work, an airplane mobile, paper airplanes, and paintings were made.

The following is an example of how one day's play incorporated many of the concepts and information that had been studied.

> Amnon (P) built a plane for the third day running and requested some help in adding two red headlights. This interested several children and by the end of the morning every child in the group was involved in airplane play. Yosef (D) also built a plane—smaller than Amnon's and also added red

headlights. Tally (P) joined Amnon's plane carrying a suitcase. Several other children joined, also carrying suitcases.

Amnon built an observation tower with the brick blocks in the form of a square. Udi (P) built another observation tower, but accepted the suggestion that he join his building to Amnon's and he moved his whole building over.

Danny (P) built a weather vane out of several blocks. He took long, flat boards and placed them one on the other in the form of a flower. He explained that with the aid of this insrument which turns around, he will know which way the wind is blowing and then he will announce when to land.

Danny (P), Ilan (P), and Drora (P) were stewards and gave the passengers tickets. Amnon's plane landed in India (this was Udi's suggestion). Yosef's plane flew to America. When the passengers were seated, the stewardesses distributed food.

Meanwhile Udi had become the flight controller in the observation tower. Both he and the pilot had telephones and communicated with each other frequently to discuss when to take off and land. The observation tower was also in touch with Danny and his weather vane to get information on the winds and this was reported to the pilots.

"Our Neighborhood"

Toward the end of the second year of work, we planned a final project that we called "Our Neighborhood." We believed that it would, in effect, be a review of the two-year curriculum that had concentrated on the children's daily lives and environment. Such a project would serve to recall the various bits of information the children had gathered and also would help them to summarize and integrate the knowledge they had acquired. The neighborhood project lasted about two months.

Our *goals* in the neighborhood project were:

1. to examine the buildings in the neighborhood and think about their purposes;
2. to understand why buildings are where they are and how they meet the needs of the people in the area;
3. to understand the concept of "neighborhood" as a unit made up of homes, and services for the people living in the homes;
4. to learn what goes on in a neighborhood and how it is all related.

We wanted the children (1) to learn words that describe items and relationship of items in the neighborhood—near, far, small, large, high, low, wide, narrow, crowded, in front of, behind; (2) to understand the interrelations of people, businesses, and services in the neighborhood, to realize that there are many houses and only a few stores to serve many people; and (3) to discover what elements make up a neighborhood—the children's houses, the stores, market area, baby health station, nursery school, schools, youth center, synagogues, roads, buses, police, hairdresser, carpenter, workshops.

The teacher introduced the subject by pointing out to the children how well they had been building houses, cars, stores, bus stops, and roads, in the nursery school. She then asked, "What do we call a place where there are many houses together?" "What kind of buildings are there in your neighborhood?" "Why did the city build roads?" The purpose of the questions was not to obtain an immediate and complete answer, but to stimulate the children to examine the neighborhood and its various buildings. The children, of course, were unable to answer all the questions, but they expressed the wish to go out and look at what is in the neighborhood and to learn the names of things.

TRIP

The class went to see where some of the children live, and they noticed that houses have numbers and streets have names. They learned the word "neighborhood" and began to understand what it comprised. They then went to the shopping center where they noted the various types of shops and the fact that they were concentrated in one area, and they again discussed the purpose of the shops. In group discussions following the neighborhood trip, the children talked about the trip and listed what they had seen. This discussion led to a decision to build a "neighborhood" in their block play.

PLAY

The next morning, the teacher delayed the "planning period" until most of the children had arrived and then they were reminded of yesterday's trip. It was decided that each child who wanted to would build his own house, and the others would build other buildings in the neighborhood. In trying to remember what was in the neighborhood, the children listed houses, roads, and the nursery. As the teacher pressed their thinking further, some children volunteered to build cars, a grocery, a garage, a hairdressing shop. The children were ready to rush off and begin building, but the teacher stopped them and said, "But in a neighborhood, houses are not just built anywhere. There's a plan." Out of this came chalk markings of streets and a plan for where each building should be, also marked in chalk.

The children then rushed off to work and very soon the shortage of blocks became apparent. They began to add large boxes, pieces of wood, cardboard boxes, and anything available in the nursery. After some period of building, the teacher again stopped the children for a short intermission to see what was being built and to decide whether buildings were interfering with each other. Each group told what it had built. The building phase of the project lasted about two weeks and entailed numerous trips to examine specific buildings and their special features, in order to be able to reproduce them more accurately.

Group discussions at this phase dealt with the building and the play and, in effect, were reviews of what had been discussed at various times during the two years.

> *Teacher (turns to Dafna, who has been building a house):* Tell us about your building.
> *Dafna:* We built a house. I'm the mother and Aliza is the baby.
> *Teacher:* Have you arranged to furnish your house yet?
> *Dafna:* Yes, we have a bed, a table, chairs, and curtains.
> *Teacher:* What are you doing now?
> *Dafna:* I want to feed the baby cereal.
> *Teacher:* Where will you get the cereal?
> *Dafna and others:* The grocery. (Dafna takes a basket and goes to the grocery.)

> *Teacher (to Naomi):* What did you build?
> *Naomi:* I built a hairdressing shop.
> *Teacher:* What do you do there?
> *Naomi:* I cut hair.
> *Teacher:* How do you know what kind of haircut to give?
> *Naomi:* I ask how they want it.
> *Teacher:* Children, be careful; remember to tell Naomi how to cut your hair or she might cut it too short if you want it long. (In this way, the children were being encouraged to talk, and often they themselves took over the teacher's role in making conversation.)

The play included imaginary trips on the bus to the health clinic, visits to the grocery and the hairdresser, and an elaborate nursery school with miniature equipment including pictures on the wall, tiny bits of plasticene on the table, a place to hang clothes, a toilet, kitchen, and outdoor equipment. Later, the neighborhood expanded to include a supermarket, various food shops, and a very active restaurant where actual cooking took place. Signs with the family name appeared on houses and shops. A rule was made regarding a ride on the bus—"You can't ride on the bus unless you pay," but some children stole onto the back of the bus.

Discussions and play again went into the details of buying and selling, how you earn money and who spends it—problems that had arisen in the play. The question of supplies for the shops was dealt with. The next phase dealt with geographical orientation—the exact position of

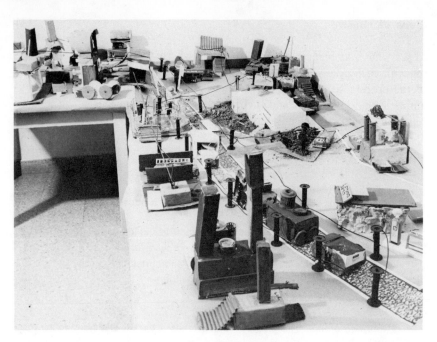

"The Neighborhood" models, as developed in each of the four nurseries.

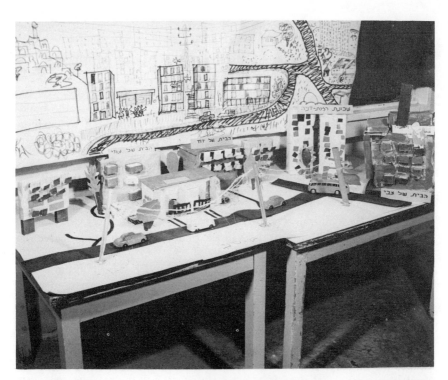

roads in the neighborhood and which buildings belong on which streets. This, too, entailed several additional trips.

After the general orientation was clear, the children delved into greater details of the neighborhood, such as the water tanks on the buildings and the electric lines and poles. The children went out to examine how the electric wires ran into the houses. They translated this detail in miniature to their block buildings.

THE MODEL NEIGHBORHOOD

While the children were deeply involved in the subject, the teacher suggested that in addition to their block building, they also could build a miniature model of "our neighborhood."

A large sand table was set up for the model. The buildings were made of cardboard, cigarette boxes, match boxes, plasticene, and small interlocking plastic blocks. The first building to be made was the nursery, which was placed in the center of the box. Small groups then went out to examine the details of the buildings near the nursery—the synagogue, the youth center, etc. They studied their geographical positions in relation to the nursery, and this necessitated arranging on the table (using wet sand) the contours of the neighborhood with its hills and roads. The children then approximated the relative positions of the miniature buildings they had made—close to, far from, behind, higher, and lower than the nursery. The houses were built with much attention to detail, including miniature "people" on the balconies. Little by little, the shops, the health clinic, the fire station, the bus line, the electric wires, and other details were added. (In the heterogeneous group, the P children added automobiles in front of their houses, and the D children, not to be outdone, added their "uncle's" truck or the bus used by the teacher.)

The "model" neighborhood was in a central part of the room and many discussions took place around it. The children began to play with the model itself; they added people made of plasticene, wood and pipe cleaners, small automobiles, street signs, trees. The teacher introduced a rule that if you play with the model you must *say* what you are doing:

> Danny, holding a doll in his hand says, "I am leaving the house. I am passing the store. Now I am going near the fence of the park. The road is going uphill."
>
> *Teacher:* How do you feel, going uphill?
>
> *Danny:* Hot, my legs hurt.
>
> *Teacher:* Yes, going uphill makes a person feel hotter and sometimes our legs hurt if we are going fast. What else is happening on your walk?
>
> *Danny:* Here is the synagogue. Now I am going into the gate of the nursery.
>
> Yaakov takes a police car from the police station and announces that he

is "driving around the neighborhood, now I am on the main road and going to Hadassah Hospital."

The children enacted fires and fire engines, accidents and ambulances, and visits to each other's houses on the model table. The need to keep the "neighborhood" neat and clean also was brought up in the course of the play. In their paintings and collages, some children also used the theme of the neighborhood.

The end of the year found us at the height of interest in the project, which had opened wide areas of questioning and thinking. The children had had to express in words what they thought, what they were doing, and what they intended to do. Even the most passive children had become involved in the fascinating topic, and they all had had a positive experience in cooperation and in maintaining protracted interest in a defined subject. They learned that each building has a purpose, and they realized that it pays to ask questions and find things out. They began to understand that they are a part of everything that happens and that everything affects them.

One of the teachers said, "I finished the year feeling that the questions are still wide open and that the children are ready to find out more and more."

OUTDOOR PLAY

"Might this be a waste of time?" was a question frequently raised by our teachers when evaluating some activity. We were so aware of how much we wanted to accomplish in the short space of two years that we felt we could not afford to waste a moment. Therefore, we worked to make the outdoor play period an integral part of our intensive program, as important as the indoor one. It was not used just as a recess and relaxation period, even though the outdoors lent itself to "letting go" more freely—to running, shouting, climbing, falling, and rolling around. The purpose of the outdoor equipment was to encourage active movement, a sense of release, and the free use of space to develop strong bodies and physical skills.[5]

At the same time, the outdoor equipment also was designed to stimulate imagination and creative use of materials. The materials lent themselves to be made into whatever the children wanted—boards, sawhorses, crates and large hollow blocks became houses, space ships, and fire engines. Lengths of cloth and canvas would close off a crate for absolute

[5]For a detailed description of the equipment, see pages 85–86.

privacy, would become a tent, or would be hung up to make a shady spot. The sandbox and the waterbox with all their accessory equipment were always attractive corners. In addition, large paintbrushes and cans of water were used for "painting with water"; there were pulleys for hauling blocks; tires and inner tubes for rolling and swinging; tree stumps and large rocks arranged in stepping-stone fashion for balancing and climbing; wagons and wheelbarrows for pulling sand, blocks, and children; and ladders of different lengths which could be attached to the crates and trees for climbing. At first the large boards and sawhorses were arranged by the teachers in ever-different combinations of inclines and horizontal positions as a spur to courageous balancing, sliding, and climbing activities. Later the children themselves arranged them in the combinations they wished.

In good weather the children were encouraged to take off their shoes and wallow in sand, water, and mud. Afterward they would wash their feet and all the equipment with the hose. They learned how to take off their shoes and socks and line them up neatly. When the paints, clay, and carpentry were moved outside, the outdoor period became an extension of the indoor play.[6]

Outdoors, the children engaged largely in dramatic play. The outdoors play followed the same slow development that it did indoors. At first, the children spent their time just moving blocks from place to place, using wagons and wheelbarrows and occasionally shouting out, "For sale, for sale," as if they were peddlers. Later, the play often reflected the "area of interest" that was preoccupying the children at the time. Accessory materials in the form of dolls, dishes, cartons, wheels, and headlights were always available, and the teachers played the same interested and stimulating role outdoors as in the dramatic play indoors. The outdoor play often would be planned in advance by the children and occasionally also would be discussed afterward in the final group meeting before going home.

Here are some excerpts from the teachers' diaries and the observer's notes in the first year of the program:

OCTOBER 1967: Homogeneous D Group

Today, for the first time, the children began to use the hollow blocks outdoors for building. With the teacher's encouragement they built a long wall of two-block height. The boards and sawhorses were also used more purposefully and they loved climbing on the long ladder. [At the same time, the P group was beginning to use the hollow blocks.]

[6]Much of the yard equipment (which had to be locked up during the night) was piled onto a large moving "storehouse" which was wheeled out daily, and this arrangement made the teacher's job easier.

Using blocks, crates, and boards in outdoor play.

OCTOBER 1967: Heterogeneous Group

The P children are building a car out of hollow blocks. They sit in it and drive to the "university." At the "university" they jump off, run to the pool, and dive in. They also "swim" and "fish" in the pool.

NOVEMBER 1967: Homogeneous D Group

The blocks have again been placed attractively by the teachers but no one touches them. Finally Ofer begins to build with the hollow blocks and says, "Kids, kids, bring me more blocks." Yaakov delivers blocks, carrying them on his back like a laborer. Yossi asks, "Me, too?" Ofer says, "Come on!" Gabi joins and drags the waterbox. After they have finished collecting all the blocks, they leave the play. However, when Hanna and Simcha go over to play with the blocks, Ofer calls out from far away, "No, it's mine." Teacher intervenes and convinces him to let the girls play.

MAY 1968: Homogeneous D Group

There are two groups playing side by side in adjoining crates. Gila and Aliza call their crate an auto, and later change it to a kitchen.

In the second crate, Ruth and Dalia bring chairs and announce, "It is Independence Park." (This was a few days after the Independence Park celebration for Independence Day.) Ruth goes around the yard collecting children to come to Independence Park. When the children are seated, Dalia and Ruth dance and sing for them. Jonah takes a rubber tube and makes announcements to the group as if he were using a microphone.

Ruth requests the children to sit down on the lawn. Teacher gives them green burlap and they arrange it on the ground as a lawn. The children sit and sing "Flags All Over," Jonah announces over the microphone "Israel." Gabriel carries a long stick and says, "It's a flag."

JUNE 1968: Heterogeneous Group

Ehud (P) and Shlomo (P) build a car of hollow blocks. The front end is long and low, the rear end high. Children come and go and sit in the car making car noises. Shlomo and Ehud add colored cones to the car as decoration.

Next to them Danny (P) builds an "airplane" which really resembles one. He sits in it and announces, "I'm flying to the sky." To teacher's questions he is able to define that "in an airplane you go to faraway places, in a bus you go to near places. I'm going further than a bus could go."

In another corner Amir (P) and Uzi (P) build a helicopter which is difficult to distinguish because of its square shape.

LANGUAGE TEACHING—UNSTRUCTURED

Teacher and Child Relationship As It Affects Language Development

An understanding smile, a comforting pat, a hug, a sympathetic look, the drying of a tear, and laughing together were some of the teacher's first steps in stimulating the children's language development. In the language area, just as in all others, we felt that the teacher-child relationship was an important factor. If the teacher succeeds in demonstrating to the child that communication between them is pleasant and rewarding, then he will be more eager to use language as a tool for establishing contact.

Naturally, we created an atmosphere in which the child was exposed to a great deal of talk, but we felt it was equally important to remember that he needed the experience and encouragement of being listened to by somebody interested in what he had to say. Sometimes the listening process was very difficult for the teachers; it required patience, real interest, and readiness to try to understand because often the children spoke unclearly, pronounced poorly, and expressed jumbled ideas. With children who were silent, it required infinite persistence on the part of the teacher to maintain some means of contact, both nonverbal and verbal.

Each child was reached individually every day and talked to for at least a few minutes. His clothes, his appearance, his work, his home experiences were subjects used by the teacher to try to evoke a response. Even if she received no response, she continued the "conversation," sometimes with the comment, "You'll tell me another time."

NOVEMBER 1967: Homogeneous D Group

Nissim is the most retarded of all the children in speech, in activity level, and in making contact with people. His home is one of utter neglect both physically and emotionally. The teacher spent a good part of this morning with him, giving him food and trying to induce him to enter a conversation.

The teacher and children are spreading chocolate on bread. Nissim sits opposite the teacher.

Teacher: Do you want to eat, Nissim?

Nissim: (No answer).

Shmuel: I want to eat.

Teacher: (To Shmuel) Take a piece of bread, Shmuel. Now I'm talking to Nissim. (Turns to Nissim) What do you want to eat, Nissim? Do you want bread?

Nissim: (No answer).

Teacher: (Points to the bread) What is this?

Nissim: (Moves his lips).

Teacher: Br . . .

Nissim: (Whispers) . . .ead.

Teacher: You want to eat bread?

Nissim: (Nods his head).

Teacher: Here's a piece of bread with chocolate. Did you know that this is chocolate?

Teacher: Is it good?

Nissim: (Nods and takes the piece of bread).

Nissim: (Nods and holds on to the bread which he hasn't yet tasted).

Teacher: Shall I cut your bread for you?

Nissim: (Nods).

(Teacher cuts the bread in half and Nissim begins to eat.)

The teacher goes on to talk to the children about the brown color of the chocolate, about what happens when you cut the bread in half, about eating breakfast. Nissim listens interestedly.

After this interlude he stays close to the teacher for the rest of the morning. By the end of the morning, after persistent, protracted efforts are made to talk to him and activate him, he is able to arrange a vase of flowers and even to say the words "flowers" and "yellow."

DECEMBER 1967: Homogeneous D Group

Teacher (as she greets Yoav on a rainy morning): When I came to school, my face got wet in the rain. Is your face wet too?

Yoav: (Doesn't answer, but smiles).

Teacher: May I feel your face and see how wet it is?

(Both of them feel his face and wonder at its wetness. Teacher wipes him with a towel.)

Though the teachers realized how important good language development was for the ability to communicate, to think, and to understand concepts, they realized at the same time that by demanding verbalization prematurely from the children, they might cause greater withdrawal or rebellion. The teachers needed great sensitivity in order to know when to show the child that she accepted him without his speaking and when he could bear pressure to participate more actively.

The teacher used simple, clear, short sentences, believing that the child learns primarily by hearing. When the children listened to good, simple language, they were stimulated to imitate it.

Yair (as he touches his cup): Hot.

Teacher: Yes, the tea is hot.

He is delighted that the teacher understands and responds. Later he ventures to say, "Tea is hot."

The P children had always been exposed to a great deal of talk at home, and in the nursery we tried to give the D children a similar experience.

The teachers always tried to remember to state what they were doing and to translate the children's gestures into words:

"We're making sandwiches. We're spreading the margarine on the bread." All join the teacher in chanting, "Smush, smush, smush. Smooth, smooth, smooth."

A child pointed to beads. Teacher asked, "Do you want to string the beads?"

The teachers were careful to use correct grammar and to introduce new words appropriately: "The dog *barks*," "Let's see how the pussy *laps* his milk." They did not hurry the children to use correct grammar and pronunciation, realizing that this would come at a later stage, but believed that the important thing was to get them to attempt to express themselves.

We found several techniques that were helpful in getting the silent child to begin verbalizing. Group singing and finger games, which the teacher introduced very frequently at the beginning of the nursery program, often swept the silent child along, and he was participating before he knew what he was doing. This was equally true of poems and chants which were recited by the group as a whole. Rhythmic motions, too, were often accompanied by some appropriate rhythmic words by the teacher, and the children were often charmed into joining in.

> The children were rolling plasticene and banging at it with their fists. Teacher chanted to a familiar tune:
>> Rolling, rolling
>> Rolling today,
> and to a vigorous, rhythmic tune she made up at the moment:
>> Banging, banging, banging, banging
>> Harder, harder, harder, harder.

Sometimes instead of talking, teachers and children would express themselves in operatic language. The children were quick to follow the teacher's lead in this and enjoyed it very much.

At all times, the teachers were aware of their role as the stimulus to the children's use of language. They tried not to miss any opportunity to express in words or to evoke in words whatever the children were experiencing. Even the routine toileting and washing of hands were accompanied by much talk or rhythmic chanting.

The snack time, especially, was put to use for language development. The children were divided so that there was a teacher at each table, and the teacher used this opportunity to encourage discussion, humor, and imagination, and to play language games with them. Just as with adults, eating together produces conviviality, and talking together is a natural outcome. This was exploited in the interests of developing the children's readiness to talk.

NOVEMBER 1967: Homogeneous D Group

Teacher: I see a red tomato on Eli's sandwich. I see a red tomato on Orit's sandwich (and so on around the table). (The children are delighted as their names are called and also by this rhythm of the teacher's chanting.) What do you see, Eli?

Eli: (with some prompting from teacher) I see some cheese on Orit's sandwich, I see some cheese on Haim's sandwich, (and so on around the table).

or
Teacher: I'm so hungry I want to eat all the sandwiches. I'm so hungry I want to eat a whole horse.

Yoram: I want to eat a whole house (children laugh).

Teacher: I want to eat a whole elephant (children laugh).

Menashe: I want to eat a whole watermelon (everyone is interested and beginning to babble).

or
The children are eating green pepper. The teacher talks about the color and asks all the children to look for green things in the room. Some children don't know the color. The teacher hangs up a picture of a green pepper and the children play the game at subsequent snack times and go on to other colors.

The teacher literally taught that words could serve many purposes. Frequently she gave instructions in words only, with no accompanying gestures, repeating and sometimes asking the children to repeat the instructions.

The teacher also tried to introduce the concept that words could be used in settling arguments. When two children were fighting, she would demand that they explain in words what had happened. Sometimes the combatants were too overwrought, but some other child or children would explain. The motto "Say it in words not in blows" became the motto for every argument, and, of course, the teacher tried when possible to be there before the blows began in order to help them to "say it in words."

After the children began to talk more easily with each other, with the teacher, and in group discussions and at play, the teacher began to concentrate on correct grammar and pronunciation. She would demand whole sentences and correct pronunciation and would request the right word.

MARCH 1969: Homogeneous D Group (from the teacher's diary)

At clean-up time we gathered all the children together and asked them to state what they were going to clean up. Oded said "the blocks."

Teacher: Which ones?

Oded: The long ones.

Teacher: Now say exactly what you are going to do.

Oded: I'm going to put away all the long blocks.

And so on through the whole group. The children loved it and, after a few days, this statement in whole sentences became the regular procedure at clean-up time.

OCTOBER 1968: Heterogeneous Group (from the teacher's diary)

In making the plans for the morning, Daniel (D) said, "I will be an auto."

Teacher: You will be an auto? Where are your wheels? Where are your headlights? What did you want to say?

David (smiling): I will *build* an auto.

JANUARY 1969: Homogeneous Group (from the teacher's diary)

Hannah, who for a full year had not uttered a sound except to scream, has still never addressed one word to the teachers. Her progress nevertheless has been remarkable. She is talking to the children freely and is actually the leader in most of the play in which she is involved. She is interested and alert to everything going on.

I decided to take drastic measures to break the last barrier—the talking to adults.

Hannah had organized store play and had assigned roles to the children. She turned to me and wordlessly, requested toy money. I said I don't understand—will she please say it in words. Hannah looked surprised, turned around and found something else to do.

Each time she turned to me, I shrugged my shoulders and said I didn't understand. I had much doubt and misgiving at what I was doing (so much so that I didn't confide this to anyone on the staff). Hannah seemed very insulted, for a while stopped playing and went about with her thumb in her mouth. For two weeks it looked as if she were going to revert to her original behavior. I was about to give up.

After two weeks she arrived one morning and motioned for me to pin on her name tag. I again shrugged my shoulders that I didn't understand. "Would Hannah please say it in words?" Hannah muttered, "Put it on for me." I said "What?" Hannah repeated it in a louder voice. I embraced her, told her how happy I was, that I knew all the time that she knew how to speak and how happy I am that now I will be able to understand her and do what she requests of me.

I announced to the class at discussion time that Hannah had spoken to me. When the attendance was called Hannah answered in a strong voice (for the first time!). From then on, she addressed me whenever she needed me and later on was able to converse with me just casually.

MAY 1969

Hannah remained with very limited language facility—about two-and-a-half year-old level—she used no sentences. Whenever she spoke, I saw to it that she received instant satisfaction and attention to all requests.

Her face changed, she looked much happier, with joy in her eyes, whenever she spoke. She became even more active in play and was one of the most effective leaders.

Experience—The Base for Language Enrichment

In line with our belief in "learning by doing," we expected that much of the learning of language would take place in a natural, spontaneous way in connection with real experiences and events. We thought it was far more preferable to talk first about the cat and dog with which the children were familiar rather than the cow which was for them an abstract concept.

Introducing new words alone was not enough, since words are only a symbol for real things and for our young children too many words still had to be experienced before they could be truly understood. In line with this, much of the program was designed to develop the child's ability to perceive his surroundings, to make him familiar with a variety of experiences and materials and with the words that go with them. We felt that a direct, vivid experience, even if it was nonverbal, would serve as the base for the development of clear and intelligent use of words and concepts.

The experiences and trips were accompanied by and necessitated a great deal of verbalization. There was much talk in preparations for a trip; there was the discussion about the experience afterward and then playing it out in free spontaneous play. Getting the children to tell about their experience or trip, to put it into words, was not easy, and expression of ideas was a slow process. Our young underprivileged children and even the privileged ones had to be helped to verbalize ideas and experiences even though they were able to use words readily in their social relations.

The teachers were aware that some young children still enjoy talking just for the sheer pleasure of it. Others are motivated by their immature need to relate everything to personal experiences, whether it seems relevant to the discussion or not. The teachers did not consider this talk out of order but understood that the child's experience is much more meaningful to him if he can relate it to something from his own life.

MAY 1968: Homogeneous D Group

The group is talking about their trip to the main road and the kinds of cars and traffic they saw.

Chaim: My uncle has a car and he took me for a ride.

Teacher: It must have been fun riding in your uncle's car. Was there a car like that on the road today?

And she leads the group back to the discussion. (She did not ignore him, nor did she tell him that what he said was irrelevant. Instead, by answering him in the way she did, she was really telling him that she values him as a person, that his experiences are important, and that she is glad that he is participating in the discussion.)

The major bulk of the language learning took place around the children's free play and regular activities where they could acquire and use words in a spontaneous and meaningful way. We also used some formal teaching of language and concepts, often on an individual basis, but this was largely for the purpose of emphasizing and exercising the concepts with which the children already had some familiarity. The structured aspect will be discussed later.

It was easy for the children to experience and learn conceptual words in their play, as they built with blocks and made *tall* and *low* buildings, put furniture *into* the house, made gardens *outside* the house, and used *short* and *long* blocks. The teacher used these opportunities for emphasizing words after the children had had the opportunity of actually sensing them in their own bodies and muscles. When the children were excited by a new measuring scale, for instance, how natural it was to learn the words and concepts *heavy* and *light, many* and *few*. They also learned words that express likenesses and differences.

NOVEMBER 1968: Homogeneous D Group

A rake is being used in the yard and the children are raking.

Teacher: What does that rake remind you of?

Ophir: A fork.

Teacher: Yes, and yet they are different. What is different?

(No answer.)

Teacher: Do we eat with a rake?

(Children laugh.)

Eli: No, you rake with a rake; you eat with a fork.

They examine a fork and a rake, compare the prongs and the handle, talk of large and small.

APRIL 1968: Heterogeneous Group

The children are making a cake. All the ingredients are laid out on the table. As the children are beating the whites of the egg, they say it is white like milk. They compare the beaten egg whites and the milk in its container. Uri (P) says, "And the yolk is yellow, like lemon."

When they talk about the color of the cocoa, David says, "The brown is stronger than the white because when you put the brown in the white, it turns brown—it swallows it."

In addition to the planned experiences, the teacher used random, unplanned events to further the children's observation, language, and thinking. The teachers knew that focusing the children's attention, observing and commenting on things together would help them to discriminate about and differentiate what they were seeing and would give them many more things to talk and think about.

NOVEMBER 1967: Heterogeneous Group

A stray kitten comes wandering into the playground. The children begin shouting, chasing it and trying to catch it by its tail. The teacher takes the kitten, puts it on her lap, and a few children gather round her. She pats and calms the kitten and then allows the children who wish to pat the kitten. She keeps using the word "gently, gently."

Teacher comments on how soft and warm the kitten is. Each child has a turn to feel it. They examine her fur, face, and tail. They talk about her color. Teacher suggests they examine her feet.

One of the children is sent out to get a dish of milk for the kitten. The children watch her drink, and teacher points out how the cat's tongue goes in and out of the milk. Teacher asks the children if this is how they eat.

They laugh and show how they eat. They listen to and feel how the kitten purrs. Later they wrote a story of the kitten:

A kitten came to our school.
She is grey and soft.
She has a little nose.
She has little feet.
She has a little tail.
She eats with her tongue,
Out and in, out and in.
You pat her gently.

The teacher makes a poster for the room with a picture of a kitten and the children's story underneath it. She reads the story when the children ask for it. The children later played kitten in their free play. Afterward, this chance experience was expanded in group discussions, and the kitten was compared to the children. A poem about a kitten washing herself was introduced.

Play as a Means of Language Development

Free, spontaneous play was one of the most provocative tools conducive to the development of the children's language. Play, by its very nature, stimulated conversation among the children, brought on the flow of words in an easy, natural, and spontaneous manner. The play forced the children to talk to each other and to clarify their thinking. Sometimes a teacher listening to children playing intensely is astounded at the extent of thinking they display and at their rich use of language.

The children learned many words and concepts as an outcome of their many vivid experiences in the nursery. Through their first-hand experiences, words became an integral part of their lives. They had begun to grasp the use of word symbols rather than purely physical behavior. The phase of first-hand experience and expression in play and words was an indispensable step (time-consuming though it might have seemed) in achieving real learning and thinking.

LANGUAGE TEACHING—STRUCTURED

The previous section explained our basic method in the encouragement and development of language usage as *doing, experiencing,* and then *verbalizing.* In addition to the natural teaching and learning that took place in the actual day-to-day living in the nursery, we used many techniques to stimulate richer language and greater discrimination, imagination, and thinking to help the children reach higher levels of thought and expression.

1. Sharpening Perception

We played many games designed to help the children to develop all their senses, to be able to perceive the details of what they sensed, and to verbalize what they experienced. The ability to perceive accurately and to recognize differences was basic to richer language and ability to form concepts.

VISUAL

One Thing Missing. This time-honored game is a favorite and is helpful in the focusing of attention and concentration. The teacher places several objects on the floor and names them, and the children repeat the names after her. One child goes out of the room, the teacher removes one object, and when the child returns, he is asked to remember what is missing.

Describing a Child. One child stands in the middle of the circle of children and each child says something to describe him: "He has black hair," "red shoes," etc. The child also is encouraged to say things about himself.

Policeman Game. The policeman game helps to sharpen observation and stimulate descriptive language. In it, the teacher goes to the "policeman" and describes her "missing child" (she describes one of the children without looking directly at him). The "policeman" must find him from among the children according to the description. Later the children themselves can play the "mother" and do the describing.

Looking Out The Window. This game sharpens observation and stimulates imagination and originality in language expression. The children gather at the window and state what they see. The teacher encourages imaginative statements like, "the leaves are dancing to the music of the wind," or rhythmic statements like,

The streets are wet,
The cars are wet,
The trees are wet,
The coats are wet.

Change the Picture. The teacher draws a shape, such as a rectangle. While the children close their eyes, the teacher makes some change in the shape; such as adding a line along the side of the rectangle. The children open their eyes and say what she has done; this game helps sharpen the child's visual perception.

Color Discrimination. The teacher puts four different colored circles on the flannel board. She then either removes or adds one, and asks the children to say what color has been removed or added.

Human Expression. This game helps to make the children sensitive in perceiving human expression. The teacher names an expression—an angry face, a smiling face, a crying face, a sad face, a disappointed face, and asks the children to make the face and describe it—mouth down, teeth bared, etc.

AUDITORY

The following games help develop discrimination and awareness of gross and subtle sound differences.

Voice Sounds. One child puts his head in the teacher's lap. Another child tries to disguise his voice and says, "Tick, tick, who am I and what's my name?" The first child must try to recognize his voice.

Animal Sounds. One child imitates the sound of an animal—barking, meowing, braying, buzzing, crowing, chirping, cockadoodling. The children identify the animal. (Sometimes the teacher has to suggest what animal the child should imitate.)

Human Sounds. One child makes a human sound—singing, humming, laughing, crying, whispering, shouting, walking, coughing, sneezing—and the other children identify the sound.

City Sounds. The children close their eyes. They tell what city noises they hear—automobiles, trucks, car horns, the kerosene wagon bell ringing, feet walking on pavement, construction sounds.

Listening to Silence. The children are very quiet with their eyes closed, and are asked to tell what they hear—trickle of water from a faucet, fly buzzing, distant automobile, birds chirping.

Sounds of Weather. The children listen to the wind, the rain, the thunder, and describe it. The teacher encourages imaginative, picturesque language.

Musical Instruments. The children close their eyes, and the teacher plays a musical instrument. The children state which one.

Kinds of Sounds. This game consists of the classification and description of different sounds:

High—"Squeaky door," "scream," "chalk scratching."
Low—"Thunder," "drum."
Soft—"A whisper," "walking on tiptoe," "a kitten purring."
Loud—"A shout," "an explosion," "all the blocks falling."

The teacher asks such questions as, What is a scratching sound, a buzzing sound, a crashing sound? What is the difference between talking and shouting? What is noise?

Subtle Sounds. The teacher presents various objects—a large stone, a button, something metal, something plastic, sand, gravel—which she places one at a time in a box and shakes. With their eyes closed, the children guess what the object is.

FEELING

A box with various objects is prepared by the teacher. A child closes his eyes and is given an object to feel, identify, and describe—cold, hot, wet, hard, rough, smooth, round, sticky. All the children feel the object and describe it in words.

SMELLING

The teacher prepares jars containing various objects with distinctive smells and the children close their eyes, smell, and identify what is in the jar—a flower, a lemon, coffee, cinnamon, onion, cocoa.

TASTING

The teacher prepares distinctively tasting things—salty, sweet, sour, sharp, oily—the children taste the items, state what each is, and try to describe the sensation it produces.

2. Classification and Differentiation

We played games that helped the children to classify and differentiate the familiar things about them. They identified and listed things in the room by category: hard, soft, metal, round, furniture, wheeled, people (teacher, boys, girls), transparent, opaque, green, red, liquid, etc. The children were asked to name the "largest" thing they could think of, the "smallest," etc. "What is fuzzy, rough, sharp, flat?" etc. We also played a game of opposites: cold-hot, near-far, dark-light, fat-skinny, long-short.

The children's answers were vivid and imaginative; when asked to enumerate hot things, for example, they listed in quick succession: warm bread from the oven; sun; the iron; hamsin (hot desert wind); fire; flame; campfire; melted chocolate; hot tea; lit cigarette; lit match; gas fire; stove.

3. Language for Pleasure

At odd moments, in group discussion, and during the "quiet time," with individual children, we used other structured ways of stimulating the use of language for pleasure, for expression of imaginative and original thinking, for humor.

Rhyming Game. The children loved making rhymes using their names: "Ruthy toothy," "Udi foody," "smelly Eli." There was much laughter as they played this game excitedly.

Alliteration. Rachel once said "big black ball," and the teacher repeated it, asking if anyone else could say something like that. Soon came "dolly's dry diapers." The teacher encouraged them to look for words beginning with specific sounds.

HUMOR—THE RIDICULOUS GAME

Teacher: Did you ever see a dog with glasses? The children immediately catch on: Did you ever see a horse that flies? Did you ever see a monkey with a coat?
Teacher: Did you ever see a cat give birth to puppies?
Children (immediately): Did you ever see a fish that gives birth to birds? Did you ever see an elephant as little as a kitten?
Teacher: Did you ever see a blue tomato?
Children: Did you ever see a red lemon, etc.

THE SIMILE GAME.[6]

This game was a great favorite of teachers and children. Children not yet bound by the stereotyped expressions that adults use ("red as a

---

[6]Claudia Lewis, *Deep as a Giant—An Experiment in Children's Language* (New York: Bank Street Publications, [n. d.]).

beet," "fast as lightning," etc.), are delightfully able to think freshly, spontaneously, and originally. The teacher said, "Uri said, 'It was loud as when you hit a drum.' What is the loudest thing *you* can think of? Loud as _____?" The answers came:

> Loud as an airplane flying low; a lion roaring; a whistle; when you scream; when we break down all the block buildings at the same time.
>
> Hard as the tiles on the floor; the wall; the pillars on the building. And then, hard as a bone (pointing to his arm).
>
> Soft as dough; sponge; plasticene; butter; glue; cheese; spinach; cotton; a flower.
>
> Round as an orange; my head; candy.
>
> Red as a tomato; red paint; mommy's lips.
>
> Quiet as a clock; when you close your eyes; when you wake up in the night; when the sun shines.
>
> Low as earth; sand; a flower.
>
> Frightened like a baby is frightened of a cat; a dog; an elephant; a giant; a tiger; a snake; a lion.

The children loved this game and came back to it often, almost never repeating themselves.

4. Creativity

All of the program was designed to encourage the children's original and creative thinking. The "What Can You Do With" Game is a structured game designed to develop flexibility in thinking, which is one ingredient of creativity. The teacher took an item and asked the children, "What can you do with it?"

> What can you do with a block? Build with it, kick it; hit somebody with it; put things on it; wet it; throw it; slide on it like a skate; make a shelf; pretend it's a gun; use it as a hammer; beat it like a drum.
>
> What can you do with this paper napkin? Make a blanket for the doll; make a hat; tear it; crumble it; wipe your mouth and your hands; clean your shoes; blow your nose; throw it in the toilet or the wastepaper basket; cut it; fold it; throw it into the wind and watch it blow away.

5. Games to Stimulate Verbalization and Understanding of Words

Sometimes through games we stimulated the children to use words more fluently. Such games included:

Television Game. One child is the television actor. Another is the announcer. The actor performs—eating, playing ball, crying, going to sleep, etc., and the announcer describes to the "audience" what the actor is doing.

Giving Instructions Game.*   In order to overcome the children's tendency to respond to words automatically, this game was designed to help the child think about the meaning of words. The teacher gives a child a command, but he must not carry it out until he repeats the words. He then obeys the command which he has verbalized.

> *Teacher:* Take the yellow crayon.
> *Child:* Take the yellow crayon. (He then takes the crayon.)

Silent Verbalization Game.*   This game was meant to help train the children to think in words rather than just to respond to concrete things. The teacher would hold up a picture of an object. The children would look at it and would voicelessly say the word to themselves. The teacher then would put away the picture and ask a child to say what the picture had been.

6. Creative Writing

Writing down what the children said always spurred their verbal expression and their richer use of language, imagination, and originality. Their "stories" were then read back to them or displayed on the wall with an appropriate picture or an illustration made by the children themselves.

The Dictating Game.   It helped the children to organize their experiences and impressions if the teacher asked leading questions. She would help them recall an experience by asking how did it feel, smell, sound. Knowing that children sense an experience most vividly through their muscles, she would try to get them to recall their muscular sensations. She would use this technique after a trip or some memorable experience, when she would ask the group to dictate a "story" about the experience. Sometimes she would initiate a topic: "Yesterday was Hamsin (hot desert wind). "How does the sun feel on a Hamsin day?"; or "How did you feel when you put your hands in the clay?"; or "How did you feel when you walked into a puddle?" Limiting the topic to something very specific helped the children focus their feelings, and the exercise was more successful than when trying to report a lengthy experience.

---

*The games marked by an asterisk in this chapter were designed by us after reading the ideas expressed by Marion Blank in her article, "A Tutorial Language Program to Develop Abstract Thinking in Socially Disadvantaged Pre-School Children," *Child Development*, 1968.

The following is a dictation from the homogeneous D group at the beginning of the program in November 1967:

> Because it is a windy day, the children have to go inside. Teacher seats everyone and they talk of why they had to go in. She suggests they tell about the wind. Each child contributes a sentence while the teacher records and later reads back to them:
>> What a strong wind!
>> The wind blew me into the sand.
>> I fell down because of the wind.
>> How the sand came into my eyes!
>> How the papers flew!
>> Whoof, whoof, whoof (imitating wind sound).
>> It made me sneeze.

Here is a dictation entitled "The Field Fire," dictated in the second year of the program:

> *Oded (P):* We went to see the field after the fire.
> *Ruth (D):* We saw a black field.
> *Zvi (P):* We saw black soot.
> *Chaim (D):* We saw a black tire.
> *Gabriel (P)* We saw many, many black shoes in the field.
> *Uri (P):* The shoes were burnt.
> *Teacher:* Black as _____?
> *Ruth (D):* Black as the strap of your watch.
> *Dafna (P):* Black as our guinea pigs.
> *Ron (P):* Black as an automobile tire.
> *Uri (P):* Black as tar.
> *Teacher:* How did it smell?
> *Edna (D):* It smelled like cheese.
> *Chaim (D):* The smell of the guinea pigs.
> *Gabriel (P):* The smell of smoke.
> *Dafna (P):* The smell of burning hair.
> *Oded (P):* The smell of burnt thistles.
> *Gabriel (P):* It was a big fire!
> *Ruth (D):* The fire was red.
> *Uri (P):* The fire truck came.
> *Edna (D):* The fire truck was also red.
> *Gabriel (P):* They attached a long, black hose.
> *Chaim (D):* White water came out.
> *Uri (P):* They sprayed "fountains" of water.
> *Teacher:* And the fire was extinguished.

Describing a Picture. The teacher would make a poster using an evocative picture—a mother and child, a family playing, two children fighting, an angry face, delicious-looking food. At a group meeting, she then would ask each child to say something about his associations with the picture, and she would record the child's statement with his name. The children's dictation would be pasted underneath the picture on the poster, and the children frequently asked for it to be read back to them. Sometimes a picture would be examined, discussed, described fully, and then removed. Afterward, the children would be asked to describe the picture from memory.

Stories Stimulated by the Children's Drawings or Pictures. The teacher distributed to each of the children some picture cut-outs (pictures of children, animals, airplanes, automobiles), and a large quantity of colored paper to cut and paste. Each child used the cut-out pictures he was given as a stimulus to create a scene by adding colored papers which he cut to the appropriate shapes. The children made houses, lawns, flowers, trees, airplanes, airfields, antennas, etc. When the cutting and pasting were finished, all the children looked at each picture in turn, and the one who made the picture (or sometimes another child) told a "story" about it.

MARCH 1968: Heterogeneous Group

Chaim (D) uses a picture of a cat and a bar of chocolate to start his picture. He constructs a house around the pictures and adds an airplane flying above.

Yossi (D) tells the story about Chaim's picture: "The airplane is flying to the airfield. The cat is in its house. The food is for the cat. He wants to eat the chocolate."

Chaim corrects him. "The chocolate is not for the cat. When the man, 'the pilot,' goes down, 'lands,' he will eat the chocolate."

Eli (D) (who had taken a long time to begin verbalizing) used pictures of a bunny using a telephone, a baby, an airplane, and a boy lying down, around which he added a house, flowers, a girl, sky, and earth. Here is his story:

"Here on the bottom is earth. Here is a bunny telephoning in the house. Here is an airplane flying to the airfield, and here is a little girl going into the house to eat. Here is the blue sky and the red poppies. Here the boy played a lot of football and wanted to rest, so he lay down. The baby is in the house and the big boy is outside playing football."

Reactions to Music. Sometimes beautiful, imaginative language was stimulated by music. The children would lie on mats listening to the phonograph. The teacher would tiptoe over to a child, sit near him, and write down what he told her about the music: "I am dreaming about floating in the sky," "I am dreaming about the sea and swimming," "I am bicycling in the air."

Children's Own Books. Each child had a book about himself, decorated by him, with his photograph and his name on the front cover. Inside were stories written by the teacher about what he had done, photographs of him in various activities, pictures drawn by him, and stories which he had dictated. The children loved sitting down with the teacher to dictate their "story." Sometimes the story was read to the others.

STORIES AND BOOKS

"A story a day" was a principle in the nursery. Talking about, telling and reading stories was a fundamental element in our *daily* program. We considered it an essential tool for developing the children's vocabulary and their ability to concentrate, for stimulating them to think and to express themselves verbally. From the first day, the book corner was set up as an attractive and important part of the room. At the beginning, the books were largely picture books and attracted the children to handle them and turn the pages.

Since some of the D children had never before had contact with a children's book and had never listened to a story, it was necessary to introduce them to stories and books in slow stages. They had to be taught to respect books, how to handle and look at them, and even how to turn pages. From the beginning, the children were attracted by the books and would pick them up, idly turn pages (though barely looking at the pictures), carry them about and then drop them, apparently unaware that they were doing so. (At the beginning, some of the children used the holding of books in the library corner as an escape from the activity in the nursery.)

It was clear, after several attempts, that most of the D children were unready to have a story read to them even when it was one based on their own familiar experiences. They loved the preparations for story-reading and the intimacy of the group, but they lost interest very quickly when they were unable to follow what was happening. In that case, the teacher then used the book not so much as something to read from but as a starting point for group and individual discussion about the pictures and the children's associations aroused by the pictures. Little by little the D children learned to pay attention to more and more details in the illustrations. In the mixed groups, the comments of the P children who would name things and make remarks about the pictures would arouse the D children to examine the pictures with sudden interest.

The teachers used the children's facial and verbal reactions to the stories and illustrations to gauge what they had understood and where additional explanation was necessary; each child's comment and reaction was treated as very important and interesting. Some children, though, were not yet ready even for this beginning story period, and no child was ever forced to remain in a story-telling group. We found that interest in stories and books grew when the story group was smaller and when there was more opportunity to note each individual child's reaction. Very often, a story was "read" to a child in an individual session as a means of arousing his interest and ability to concentrate.

At first, the picture books that were presented dealt with pictures of children engaged in various activities, families and babies, toys, cars, and animals. Many of the picture books were compiled by the teachers themselves from magazine pictures, and, at a later stage, they were compiled by the children.

When the D children had learned "how to look" at a picture, the teacher began introducing a story. At first she told the story in her own words and only gradually moved over to reading from the text with the aid of the pictures that were held up before the children. Even then, the "reading" of stories was not yet an exclusively verbal experience; the teacher had the children accompany the story with appropriate gestures, sounds, and songs—moving their feet when the story told about walking, knocking on the door when there was knocking, imitating the sound of a dog barking, etc. The stories had to be presented most dramatically, with much repetition.

The first stories dealt with the familiar and immediate life of the child, the "here and now,"[7] and only later did the stories lead the child out to a wider and less familiar world. Our assumption was that a young child views the familiar as fascinating, and since for him his everyday life is full of adventure, he seems to have little need for the more remote fantasies created by adult writers.

Even though the information and vocabulary acquired through reading are good in themselves, we wanted primarily to present books as highly enjoyable, as an art form, as literature and not as text books or encyclopedias. The elements of adventure, drama, suspense, pleasing sound, and repetition of pattern were important ingredients in the literature that we sought. The *suspense*, of course, could deal with the exciting question of whether the cat found a home or whether the girl made a friend, but the suspense was there. The *adventure* could deal with a balloon as it escapes into the sky, with the sad experiences of a broken automobile, with a steam shovel's life and ways, but there was always the drama of a "hero" and his struggles with the world.

Though the books and stories served also to enrich the vocabulary

[7]For a full and illuminating discussion on the essential elements which contribute to good children's literature, see the introduction in Lucy Sprague Mitchell, *Here and Now Story Book* (New York; E. P. Dutton & Co., Inc., 1921).

and add information, the books were chosen primarily on the basis of whether they would provide the children with an enjoyable literary experience. The element of *pattern* and of *rhythmic repetition* added greatly to the art form of the story and to the children's delight. A story that had a repetitive motif or a refrain, that used alliteration and a clear pattern, was a story that had a literary appeal to our young children. (The story of The Three Bears, for instance, is a classic because of its beautiful and satisfying form.) Another component particularly appealing to the children was the element of *enumeration* when it was placed in an attractive pattern—even enumerating what they ate for breakfast or what clothes they were wearing, if accompanied by a unifying refrain, which the children could recite with the teacher, was most exciting and interesting. We also tried to find stories with a very clear story line, made up of very simple units that placed together made the story, since the children were not yet ready to follow a long and involved plot.

Humor in the stories, of course, was greatly appreciated. Gross exaggeration, palpable incongruities, and pleasant repetitive nonsense words were all elements of the humor that appealed to our young children.

The *content* that was most satisfying dealt with the elements of the children's daily experiences placed in a form that both responded to their own questions, interests, and wish to understand and at the same time raised further questions. Successfully interesting context was more than just the imparting of information; our teachers found that some of the most successful stories were those that they themselves composed from the daily experiences of the children.

We arranged a regular story-telling time at the end of the day, as the children rested on straw mats before going home. Whenever possible, we tried at this time to divide the group in half with each of the teachers reading or telling a story to part of the group. In addition, as has been described previously, stories were read to small groups and to individual children at available opportunities—sometimes in the middle of the morning work program; frequently, outdoors; sometimes in "quiet time"; or during the individual work period.

Aside from the enjoyment of books as literature and as pleasure, books also were introduced and utilized as a source of information. Books, catalogues, and pictures were consulted when needed in connection with trips, special topics, and problems that came up in play or blockbuilding.

QUIET TIME—STRUCTURED LEARNING EXPERIENCES

It is long-established practice that nursery schools provide many types of games, puzzles, lottos, geometric shapes, and other didactic materials for the children. With recently augmented interest and awareness of the need to develop specific skills in perception and concept formation, these activities have taken on added importance in a nursery program. In a structured way, the children can be stimulated to learn, measure, match, classify, group, sort, arrange sequences, and identity items. Such structured drill is important to underline and firmly establish the skills that the children are naturally acquiring in their day-to-day use of materials.

We felt it necessary to supervise closely the use of the structured materials. By arranging a "quiet time" during which such materials were offered, we were able to observe their use carefully and also to stimulate more children to use them. We had several goals in our quiet time. One of the most important of them was to stimulate the child to *concentrate* on a specific assignment and *finish* a job. He was made to sense clearly the adult approval of *persistence*, and his own *feeling of accomplishment* on finishing a task was encouraged and reenforced. In addition, the quiet time was used to help the children *learn skills*, to *think in terms of processes* and *sequences*, to *acquire information* (names of colors, numbers, shapes, etc.), to *sharpen perception*, and to *work in an organized fashion*.

In order to accomplish these goals, the teachers needed to plan out the quiet time carefully to determine what equipment or task should be given to each child according to his own level of achievement. Too often, if use of the didactic materials is haphazard, children play with the same material repeatedly, gaining nothing new from the experience or, even worse, they use it incorrectly with no one there to notice the errors.

We offered picture puzzles; picture sequences; color boxes (various fabrics and objects of the same color); "feely" boxes (objects of various textures); number games, dominoes, and other matching games; table blocks and construction toys; various types of form bingos and lottos; and flannel board games of shapes and colors. The teachers sometimes prepared their own games, puzzles, and exercises. They cut out and mounted pictures from magazines and old books for picture sequence stories; they prepared ingenious matching games of shapes and objects; they used large pieces of cardboard to make huge domino games that could be played on the floor.

During the quiet time, the children were divided at tables, and the teachers moved from table to table or sat at one table leading a lotto or domino game until the children learned to conduct the game by themselves. Sometimes the teachers would sit with a child or group of children until they understood the principle of a certain game or puzzle.

The quiet time also was used for other quiet activities. The teacher would present some art or craft material at one table, and the children took turns using the material. Sometimes a science experience was introduced in the science corner. At other times, a small group gathered around one of the teachers for language games or for dictating or reading stories. In any case, quiet time always was a relaxed period of the morning, welcome after the active outdoor play.

INDIVIDUAL WORK

Short structured sessions with individual children were maintained on a regular basis whenever possible. The goal of these sessions was to develop the child's ability to think. We saw in this individual contact between teacher and child an opportunity to establish a more intimate and warm relationship. Through the individual and focused attention "just to him," the child felt important and satisfied at the total attention *he* was receiving.

At the same time, the teacher was in a position to assess the child's level of understanding and thinking and his language development and skills, and to keep a close watch on his progress. This enabled her to plan what was needed to improve his particular intellectual development. This was an opportunity for the child, too, to sense and recognize his own achievements and progress. The teacher's method was to underline the child's successes and build up his confidence in his ability to achieve. In this way, the individual sessions served as a corrective emotional experience as well as a corrective cognitive experience. The child had the opportunity to think and to use his capacities without the pressure of competition, a factor that was important to some children, especially those in the heterogeneous groups.

The individual sessions were used to develop interest and skill in structured drills and games and to clarify concepts and information that were being touched on in the nursery program. Sometimes the child used the time to review and repeat something he had been doing in the nursery in order to further enhance his grasp of it. The table games, table blocks, pictures, drawing materials, and dolls were all used as a means to develop the children's cognitive capacities as well as their use of language.

Sometimes the teacher prepared materials on the table before she began the session but at other times she would request the child to fetch specific objects in order to train him to be able to follow more and more complicated instructions; at times the teacher would plan the content of the sessions, at other times she would take a cue from the child at the moment of the session.

DECEMBER 1967: Homogeneous D Group
Teacher sits with Ron and tries to find out what he remembers of what he had just been doing in the outdoor period.

Teacher: What did you build in the store room?

Ron: Succa

Teacher: How did you build it?

No answer. She asks further questions but gets no answer.

She requests him to bring the small table blocks. He brings the box and, at the teacher's suggestion, removes several blocks and scatters them on the table. Teacher instructs, "Take a big block, the biggest one."

He does this, stands it up and teacher adds another block to his "building" and little by little, together they reproduce the "succa" he had made. The teacher accompanies all their actions with words. When they have finished, Ron "decorates" the succa with colored blocks.

Teacher then says, "Take the smallest block," and they continue in this vein with teacher heaping compliments as he carries out the instructions. (Perhaps Ron has still not learned to tell the story of his building, but has made a step in this direction.)

DECEMBER 1967: Homogeneous D Group

Teacher tries to involve Yossi in the topic that the group had just talked about in the discussion period (she had noticed that he was restless and had not participated.)

She takes out a picture album on "The Child and His Body" and asks him to tell her about the picture of a child.

Teacher: What do you see?

Yossi: Eyes.

She asks further questions and finally leads him to say the word "child".

Teacher: I wonder why the child keeps his hand in his mouth?

No answer. After several more such questions teacher realizes that her questions are premature. She goes on to ask about the names of the various parts of the body. He answers correctly but is unable to answer when she asks, "What do you do with your eyes?" or "What do you do with your legs?", etc.

She notes that he was restless and that her approach was wrong. She decides that next time she will use a doll or something more concrete and that she will teach him to use the words "to see," "to walk," as he observes how his own organs function.

SEPTEMBER 1968: Heterogeneous Group

Yoav (D) is very shy and constricted when in the group. When alone with the teacher (this is a new teacher for him in the second year of the program), he speaks in a very low voice and his language is sparse and restricted, but he manages to express himself.

At his request, they play picture domino (in the group he does not dare join the domino game and generally tends to play with equipment after the children leave it). With difficulty, he is able to verbalize, "This is a house next to a house, a flower next to a flower."

DECEMBER 1968

Yoav chooses to look at the book on automobiles. He knows the names of all the types of vehicles and says what each one's function is—"This is a truck carrying tar to make a road," "This is a steam shovel to make the road smooth." He demonstrates with his hands how the wheels turn. Teacher requests him to draw a circle, and he takes paper and crayons and draws a small circle and comments "like the wheel." He draws a large wheel and then other wheels. At teacher's request, he points out the biggest wheel without any difficulty. He then draws a square "like the body of a car in the picture" and announces "this is not a triangle."

The conversation continues on the subject of automobiles and then goes on to trucks. At the end of the session, he takes a truck with him to go out and play.

JANUARY 1969: Heterogeneous Group

On the table are colored mosaic stones.

Teacher (to Judy, D): Give me a large red stone. Judy carries out the instruction.

Teacher: Now give me all the large red stones. Judy does so.

Teacher then requests all the small yellow stones. Judy carefully leaves all small blue and red stones and picks only the small yellow ones.

Teacher fingers the medium-sized stones and says, "This is not big and it is not small. It is medium-sized." She has Judy repeat the word "medium" and then requests her to collect all the medium ones no matter what color. Judy does this and together they build a large building of the large stones, a tower of the little ones and a fence around their buildings with the medium stones. While building they repeatedly use the words large, medium, small.

The individual work sessions were used also for structured language teaching of words such as below, behind, etc., and specific concepts such as colors, numbers, etc.

Aside from the drill in categorization, comparisons, and understanding of sequences that was provided by the didactic materials and the selected drills from the work sheets, we tried to provide some additional exercises designed to develop abstract thinking, logical thinking, and thinking in terms of cause and effect. Games of *categorization* included *categorizing* food, clothing, transportation, jobs. Later we moved on to using *exclusion*—what is *not* a vegetable, *not* furniture, *not* round, *not* made of glass.

Selection Among Alternatives.[8] The ability to *select* is an important element in thinking. We drilled in selecting specific objects with specific characteristics. The teacher would place three pictures of balls, three pictures of cups, two pictures of balloons, and two pictures of flowers on the table. She would say, "Give me two cups and a ball," and then, "Give me two balls and two red flowers." Later the instructions were more complicated, making choices from more alternatives: "Give me a chair and two

---

[8]Some of the following drills were devised according to principles presented by Blank and Solomon, 1968, and by Bereiter and Englemann, 1966.

automobiles." "Give me something made of glass and something that moves," etc.

Forms and Colors. An envelope with several colored circles, squares, and triangles was presented to a child. He removed the cardboard pieces and placed them on the table, and then the teacher asked, "Give me a circle." "Give me two squares." "Give me a green square and a red circle." She presented questions regarding discrimination of form color in increasing complexity and stopped where the child failed.

Relative Word Concepts. Individual work was carried on to see whether the children had truly understood relative concepts. The teacher built a tower of three blocks and said, "Give me the *highest* block." "Which is the *highest*, which is the *lowest*, which is the *middle* one?" The teacher worked with the child until the concepts were clear. Similar work was done with words like *under* and *over, next to, in front of,* and *behind.*

Making Comparisons. The teacher presented a long ribbon and a short ribbon and asked the child to state which ribbon is *longer*, which is *not longer*, which is *shorter*, which is *not shorter*. Both teacher and child then looked around the room for lengths to compare—longer board, shorter board, longer dress, shorter dress. Another exercise was for the teacher to present two paper bags, one filled with cotton, one with sand. The child held each in his hands and was asked to state which is *heavier*, which is *not heavier*. The same was done with blocks and other items.

Cause and Effect. We looked for exercises with which to drill the children in thinking in terms of cause and effect and collected simple action pictures that implied sequential action, something that had happened before and something that would happen next.

For example, we used a picture showing a kitchen with a cat climbing onto a cupboard. In the kitchen are some cups that have been displaced by the cat; two have already fallen and broken on the floor and several are in the process of falling. In the doorway is a child looking upset at this. The teacher asked several questions: "What does the boy see in the kitchen?" "What is the cat doing?" "Where were the cups before?" "What will happen to these cups (she points to the cups in the process of falling)?"

The child's answers at first ranged from "There is a cat in the cupboard and he takes a cup and it breaks and another cup and another cup and another cup," and "The child sees a cat, a chair, and that thing for garbage," to "The cat threw the cups down and this one broke a little piece and another one was broken into many pieces on the floor." There was much work to be done in helping the children to see sequence in events and to recognize causes and effects.

"How do you Know" Game. "How do you know that the clock is working?—"Because it is ticking."

"How do you know that there is a bus outside?"—"Because I hear the tu-tu-tu."

"How do you know that there is wind today?"—"Because I see the trees moving; because it is cold."

"What Would Happen If" Game. "What would happen if you hit this clay cup you just made?" "It would go smash shumush."

"What would happen if you went out without a hat in the rain?" "The water would come on my hair, in my face, in my eyes."

"What would happen if you put another block on top?" "It would all fall down."

"What would happen if we heat the water on the fire?" "What would happen if we didn't light the stove today? Why?" "Why do we wear sweaters in the winter?" "What will happen if we use the paint brush without wiping it?"

Such games and questions were designed to develop logic in thinking through compelling the children to organize their observations and understand their significance.

SCIENCE

In every contact with his physical environment, the child has an opportunity to acquire scientific knowledge. We saw it as the teacher's job to make the children aware of and to underline these casual everyday encounters with the facts and laws of nature and science. The teachers tried, first of all, to heighten their own knowledge of and interest in these phenomena. They were then more readily able to respond to and arouse the children's curiosity, questions, and investigations.

The goal of the "science teaching" in the nursery was not so much the dissemination of information and facts as it was the establishment of the "scientific method" as a way of viewing and trying to understand phenomena. The very nature of the nursery program and setup created the background for the "scientific method." The teacher's frequent naming of things by their *exact names* and her encouragement to *observe* things were already a step in *defining* and *classifying* phenomena.

The organization of the equipment in the nursery; the *classification* of similar things into groups according to their use, shape, and color; and the routine of putting things back into their definite places were the foundation for *order in thinking*. Similarly, the division of time into a regular schedule were the basis of learning that first things come first, that one thing follows another, and that there is *relationship between events*.

Of course, it was impossible to relate to every passing event and phenomenon, but we tried as much as possible, not to let things go by unnoticed. Rather we would stop, notice, ask questions, and examine. When we felt that the children had learned some of the "scientific approach," we added a "science corner" with specific and structured equipment such as magnets and magnifying glass so that the children could experiment in order to widen their information and horizons.

Life in the nursery presented opportunities to touch on all the scientific areas that are later covered in the schools. Of course, scientific questions had to be presented in a manner suitable to the capabilities, interests, and understanding of a nursery-age child. The level of our "science teaching" was largely in the area of observation, description, and classification, and only in some cases was it followed by analysis, measurement, and examination of causes and effects. Since areas of scientific knowledge overlap in everyday life, we did not confine ourselves to any one science or organized curriculum. Yet in reviewing some of the subjects touched upon, we can divide our "studies" according to various sciences.

In learning about his body, its various parts, and their functions, we can say that the young child was learning the foundations of *anatomy*. In this area, we did the following:

1. Purposeful observation of one child by another and verbalization of what was observed—one head, two eyes, two ears, etc.
2. The child's examination of himself in a mirror, touching and moving parts of his body, and again verbalizing what he was doing—I am smelling with my nose, I am walking, jumping, and running with my feet, etc.
3. Listening through a stethoscope.
4. Measuring temperature on a thermometer.

All these and other activities helped the child to become more aware of the parts of his body.

Zoology was studied as we tended the animals in the nursery. There was much interest in any animals that came our way: a stray cat, a pet dog, a porcupine, an insect found under a stone. In addition, there was a permanent animal corner where "our" animals were housed. There, the children learned how to feed and care for animals, and they observed each animal's special needs and way of life. Guinea pigs, white mice, fish, turtles, insects, chicks, and birds, all added to the children's knowledge and experience. (Of course, not all the animals were in the nursery at the same time.) With the stimulation of the teacher, the children were guided to make detailed comparisons, ask questions, and look for answers by themselves.

Questions of birth and death came up naturally as these events occurred. The children asked questions and expressed feelings and ideas. Even though we may not always have succeeded in answering all their questions, we felt that the opportunity to discuss these matters openly and matter-of-factly was to the good.

Botany was investigated as we collected flowers, leaves, and thorns. We observed plant growth in the garden and in our house plants, and we went out to observe the nearby fields during the different seasons. The foods we ate also were examined closely. Games were played such as: "I have something red and round and smooth and you can eat it"—a tomato; "I have something long and yellow and white inside"—a banana; "I have something long and green and white inside"—a cucumber. The major interest in botany centered around the familiar foods the children enjoyed eating. They learned to distinguish between a root (radishes) and a leaf (lettuce). They learned to classify fruits and vegetables, and they peeled fruits and vegetables and compared the seeds.

Collections of stones; examination of building materials, earth, and sand; and the addition of water to all of these were our studies in *geology*. As the children sieved the sand, added water, climbed on rocks, and banged rocks together to make different sounds, they developed deeper interest in these elements and were aroused to question and to experiment.

> The children sat in the sand corner and dug a deep hole. Aaron said, "It is a tunnel." Ron, "No it's a deep hole." They continued digging and reached earth. Aaron, "Under the sand is black earth."

In many aspects of the children's activity they were exposed to the laws of *physics*. They were fascinated by the wheel—the steering wheel, the wheels in their bicycles and wagons, the automobile wheel, the pulley wheel in the derrick.

They loved seeing the insides of an automobile, of their moving toys, of clocks, of locks and keys; they used pulleys and pumps and thus were learning some elements of *mechanics*.

Aside from the enjoyment inherent in water play, the children also were made aware of the properties and changes in *water*. They observed and experimented with how some things float in water and how other things sink when they are heavy. They studied *states of water* as they boiled water; watched it steam and observed it condense; examined ice and watched it melt. They observed evaporation as they watched wet

Children discover the laws of physics.

things dry in the sun. The children pumped water through hand pumps, moved it from place to place through pipes at various heights, and drank through straws. They watched water react with soaps, and they experimented with various liquid and powdered soaps. They made large bubbles and small bubbles and watched how they burst. All of these experiences were observed and discussed.

Heterogeneous Group

Teacher: What are the things we can tell about water?

Jonathan (D): It is transparent.

Edna (P): It is like glass.

Yehuda (P): It is like a bottle.

Uri (P): It is like transparent, thin material.

Ruth (P): It flows.

Dorit (P): Stones sink in water.

Eli (P): Soap floats on water.

Jonathan (D): It makes bubbles.

Heterogeneous Group

Teacher: Does water always flow?

Benny (P): It flows from a bottle.

Nili (P): From a pitcher.

Danny (P): From the faucet.

Ilan (P): In the freezer it is ice.

Teacher: Does the ice flow?

Benny (P): The ice is hard and cold.

Teacher: How does the ice become water?

Danny (P): Let's put the ice in a warm place.

Naomi: (P): Maybe on the stove.

The *weather* was a daily subject of discussion as the children arrived in the morning. Frequently the teacher asked how the weather made them feel—do you feel hot, cold, wet, sweaty? The teacher discussed with the children what clothes keep the wetness out and what clothes get wet. There was a large thermometer in the nursery which they sometimes looked at. They discussed the radio weather forecasts and imitated them.

> Ari announced in the voice of a radio announcer: "It is seven o'clock, here is the news! Tomorrow it will be below zero!"

The snow, of course, aroused much excitement. The children collected packs of snow and brought it into the room to examine it. They went out to see how the snow was disappearing: "The water is going into the earth." "The rain devoured the snow." They described the snow: "It is white like sugar." "Like salt." "Like an undershirt." Teacher: "What will happen if we heat it?" "It will melt itself." "It will be like ice cream."

Interest in *electricity* began with a broken flashlight. In another nursery it began when the record player did not work and they discovered there was an elecricity failure in the nursery. The children were interested in learning about the electric outlets and the wires that led to the record player, to the electric stove, to the bell; about the electric wires in the walls that led from the electric lines in the street and about batteries. In some of the nurseries, they learned how to make an electric connection with a battery and a bulb and later they wired a bell.

Transformation of matter was observed when the children mixed paint powder with water, prepared paste and clay, cooked puddings, made food spreads of cheese and vegetables, made dough and baked it. They observed that by mixing materials you could create something new. Reviews of what they had done, how they did it, and what the results were helped them to understand cause and effect. They observed that they could repeat the same process and get the same results and that they could change some of the ingredients or quantities and get different results—for example, if they added more water to the clay, the clay was softer. The cooking process produced many effects—the egg becomes hard; the potato becomes soft; the egg white which is soft can be beaten to be stiff; the cocoa makes the cake brown; the dough is soft before baking, rises, and becomes stiff after baking. A chance incident was exploited when possible.

A plastic bag accidentally was left on the stove. The smell brought a few children to the kitchen. They and the teacher discussed what had happened. Zvi (D) said, "Once a candle fell in the fire in my house and became pudding.

The discussion led them to decide to try various materials on the fire to see what would happen. They placed pieces of plastic from a food container, cord, nails, pieces of candle, matches, into a tin can and put it on the fire.

Zvi (P): It's like a pudding.

Romi (P): It's puree.

Zvi discovered that not everything melted—the nail remained whole and so did the match and the cord!

The plastic melted and took on the color of the blue candle melting near it. The teacher helped them to mix the brew with a long stick. They removed the tin can from the stove. Danny pulled the stick out of the brew and a long plastic string was formed which he pulled as far as the next room, to the children's incredulous amusement. They left the stuff to cool and kept coming back to observe it. At first they commented that it is soft and then Romi came running in to announce, "It is frozen."

Naomi (P): It is cold.

Danny (P): You can't mix it any more.

Teacher suggested that they try to take it out of the tin can.

Danny: It is a stone.

Naomi: It is plastic, it's hard.

They managed to remove it from the can and commented that it had taken on the form of the can. They lifted it and examined it. "It is transparent in some places." "It is green." "It is blue."

Children enjoy cooking and discovering laws of chemistry.

Teacher agreed that all these descriptions were true. "There is a nail." "It is nice, let's make more."

They continued for several days with various experiments of this nature.

Mathematical concepts which are absorbed without the child being aware of it were brought to the children's attention in the nurseries. *Numbers* and *amounts* were used daily:

Give me one bead.

Let's put two beads in each cup.

Each child puts away one block. Later you can take one block in each hand.

When we set the table, each child has one chair, one plate, one cup. On each side of the table are two plates, two cups, etc. In each plate the server puts three olives, one piece of bread, one-half of a tomato.

Fluids are measured out from a large pitcher to a small pitcher, from a small pitcher to a cup. "Fill the cup half-way, if we fill it full it may spill."

Distance was measured by *many* steps, by *few* steps; later by *long* steps and by *short* steps. Heavy and light blocks and weight differences in different objects and materials were an introduction to concepts of *weight*. *Geometric forms*—squares, triangles, and rectangles—were named and used in games and puzzles. At each child's individual drawer, we placed a symbol instead of the child's picture—

and he learned to recognize his own symbol. Apples divided into halves or quarters, oranges divided into many segments gave some idea of *fractions*.

In addition to the daily incidental experiences that the teachers underlined to develop conceptual scientific awareness, there was a science corner where several planned materials were concentrated. There were magnets of various shapes; interlocking wheels; pulleys; colored cellophane transparencies; batteries; candles; a scale; and a large magnifying glass. The magnifying glass was used to examine sand, stones, hands, bugs, leaves, etc.

From the Teacher's Diary:

We used the cellophane transparencies to look at the sun, the sky, the clouds, at each other. Each color was named, colors were combined, and the children saw how the combination of blue and yellow made things look green, etc.

NOVEMBER 1968: Homogeneous Group

The nails fell from the carpentry table. Teacher suggested the children use a magnet to help pick them up. The magnet was tried with other materials and the children discovered that the magnet does not pull everything, only iron. They looked about the room for things made of iron to see if the magnet could pull it.

The use of these special materials enriched the children's knowledge and stimulated them to experimentation and awareness of phenomena.

RHYTHMS AND MUSIC

The music sessions were a favorite part of our program. They engendered spontaneity and freedom and induced a *joie de vivre* that was sensed and savored by all.

Although the music teacher conducted demonstration lessons with the children, her chief function was to train the teachers to conduct their own music program. Thus, they were able to introduce a music session at any moment of the day they found appropriate. At first, the teachers were doubtful of their ability to do this, but the training sessions and sample lessons with the music teacher bolstered their confidence and they found the frequent use of music a valuable asset. The enthusiastic response of the children to the music experience also enhanced the teachers' self-confidence.

In the following section Leah Helner, the music teacher, describes elements of her approach and some of her sessions with the children as recorded by the teachers.

Every educator brings to the children her own special personality and her own special gift for educating. This gift can be useful only if she creates an atmosphere of security and warmth. By lavish praise and overt affection on the part of the teacher, by her active participation with the children (whether this means rolling on the floor, singing the same game song thirty times, or "becoming" a balloon), a joyous atmosphere will be created. Any restraint or reservation by the teacher will be reflected by withdrawal and lack of enthusiasm in the children.

Following are some of the techniques I used during the year. They are typical of many others and it is hoped that the examples themselves will suggest the hundreds of possible variations.

The Warm-up

The session usually begins with simple rhythmic movements and gradually the children are led up to an "ecstasy of movement" involving the whole body. After such a warm-up a child seems to be happily receptive to further activities.

DECEMBER 1967: Heterogeneous Group

. . . Leah came at 9:30. She began by putting a Paso Dobles record on the phonograph. Each child in turn made any movements he liked with his arms and legs; the other children were invited to imitate him. Then Leah invited each child in turn and danced with him. The children were delighted and laughed out loud. . . .

DECEMBER 1967: Heterogeneous Group

Leah put a Pasa Dobles record on the phonograph and asked the children to walk around the room, keeping time with the music. They came back to the centre of the circle, bent down, clapped their hands on the floor, still keeping time, then walked around "stretching high" and "bending low" alternately. When the music stopped the children sat down and Leah put on another record. The children touched various parts of the body, again keeping time. At the end Leah said, "Now we are nice and warm." The children were happy and laughing. . . .

In the warm-up, recorded music is used, thus freeing the teacher to participate fully in the activities. The children's attention is drawn to the music. The strong rhythmic pulse of a Paso Dobles suggests strong stamping, pushing, pulling, clapping movements that the leader initiates. Here is a wonderful opportunity to act out aggression and anger both verbally and physically without feelings of guilt and shame. If the leader wishes to vary the warm-up, other music with different rhythmic impulses serves basically the same purpose: the waltz suggests soft, slow, rounded, peaceful movements; oriental music undulates; and the polka with its impetus to hops, leaps, and skips, invariably creates a mood of hilarity. The child is encouraged to initiate his own movements, which are highly praised by the teacher and imitated by the group. (In the course of time, the children learned to use the phonograph by themselves. One of the most satisfactory outcomes of the music program was the spontaneous way the children would put a record on the phonograph and dance freely when the spirit moved them.)

The warm-up creates a good atmosphere and also increases the children's awareness of their own bodies. It teaches them to differentiate and name the various parts of the body and helps to build vocabulary by verbalizing their actions (e.g., the child hears the words "push," "pull," and associates the word with the action). The child's ego is strengthened by his ability to participate and contribute and by the lavish praise he receives from the educator.

Singing Games and Songs

Games seem to present a special challenge to children and with careful structuring, they can be an effective tool for educating. In a game, a child is able to repeat seemingly without end and without becoming bored. He is able to sit patiently and await his turn, since he actually is participating in a passive way by watching and learning from the other children.

APRIL 1968: Heterogeneous Group
. . . Leah took out the guitar. The children were happy and alert. She sang, "Good morning, stretch your arms, play, play, play on the chairs." Everybody beat on the chairs. Leah then played the guitar and sang the following song (part of a game that required that the child rise, walk across to the leader, and strum on the guitar while being sung about):

> Here comes Ruthie, beautiful, beautiful Ruthie;
> she wears a pink blouse.
> Here comes Vered, the biggest of the big;
> she wears checked jeans.

Edna didn't want to come when her name was called, but she laughed out loud and was wild with joy.

> Here comes Yossef; he plays very nicely.
> Here comes Uri—he is so big. (Uri told Leah that his mother had bought him new shoes.) He wears black shoes.
> Here comes Etti, all in red; she is wearing a red blouse.

In this singing game, the child is made aware of his name and himself; he fulfills the challenge to walk across the room and strum the guitar; and he identifies his clothes and their colors. He is aware of himself both as one of the GROUP and as ONE in the group. His sense of identity is strengthened as he is singled out in song and as he performs the actions required of him.

Repetition and Improvisation

As the games become familiar, it is possible for the children to accept innovations and to enjoy both the familiarity and the variation. A familiar game can be very useful as well as instructive, at the right moment.

NOVEMBER 1967: Heterogeneous Group
The children walked around the room in time to a marching song and then began to run. Haviv started running wild, fell down, and hurt himself. Leah played "I ran, I ran, and I fell down," and the children danced freely.

Here a potentially unhappy situation was diverted with the familiar song, and since the game finishes with the "mother" kissing the child who has hurt himself, it also provided an open opportunity for an affectionate gesture.

FEBRUARY 1968: Heterogeneous Group

Leah brings her guitar. The children say the word "guitar." She takes off the special rainproof cover. The cover underneath is laced. Leah asks, "What is it?" "A string?" Yosi (P) says, "This is like a shoe lace." We looked for children who have laces in their shoes. Leah improvised a song about colors of laces and colors of shoes.

For repetition to be effective, the teacher must be able to see the potentials in a child's question instantly, and create a new learning situation by improvising. She can use a familiar song with the new content.

Accompaniments for Games

1. PERCUSSION INSTRUMENTS: BELLS, TRIANGLES, XYLOPHONES, DRUMS, BLOCKS

The children made their own drums using very large paint cans, heavy rubber from old tires, rope, and sticks. After they were put together, the children painted the drums attractively.

. . . Leah comes and sits down with the xylophone near Ronit and David. At the first sound, all the children begin to draw nearer to Leah who said, "I will ask you questions in song, and you will answer."

The idea of the game is for the teacher to strike the different metal lengths in any series she chooses in small sentence rhythms. When she has finished, she hands the mallet or small wooden hammer to the child to respond in any way he chooses. This exchange of question and answer can be accompanied by words. The child's ability to grasp this pre-verbal response can serve as an important step in conditioning him for communication with others.

Leah explains that the xylophone is made of metal sheets. "What objects in the room are made of metal?" Gad points to the legs of the chair. Anat runs and brings a triangle. Leah tries to "strike" the various metals" in front of her. The stove is made of metal. Most children are interested . . . Shalom tries delicately, almost fearfully, to strike the xylophone, but he understood the point of the question and answer game. Ronit surprises us by her grasp of the game and creates a wonderful relationship with Leah while playing. Eli, a shy and retiring boy, takes courage and answers forcefully and intelligently, like the bright child he is. Danny refuses to participate and shrugs his shoulders. Ofra agrees to play and participates alertly. . . .

2. OBJECTS: TOYS, PICTURES, BALLS, BALLOONS, HOOPS
 SCARVES

These materials are used mainly to stimulate the children to improvise body movements and to participate in rhythmic role-playing.

JANUARY 1968: Homogeneous D Group

. . . Leah took out a little toy donkey from her pocket. Before taking it out, she asked the children to feel it through her pocket, and to guess what it was. The answers were: "seeds," "balloons," "key." She took out the donkey, but the children were unable to name it. They guessed: "dog," "horse," "cat." In the course of the game it was suggested that the children wave a scarf and ride on a block, which represented the donkey. Eli took the scarf, and instead of waving it, spread it on the block and sat down (it had become a saddle).

Anything from a stone to a toy can be used as a stimulus. It is up to the teacher to be constantly alert and to realize that a musical motif, rhyme, or story can be built on anything.

NOVEMBER 1967: Heterogeneous Group

. . . Leah asked for the key to the piano. She sang, "Where is the key?" "Here is the key, here it is." Leah continued singing and looked for the key on the piano. When she found it she sang, "Here is the key, here it is." She concealed the key in one child's hand and looked for it while singing the song. . . .

Goodbye

The end of the lesson can be a most important part of the session. It presents an opportunity to the teacher to single out and reach each child. This physical contact between teacher and child can be extremely significant in the development of the child's relation to the world around him. At the end of the session, while singing, the children can be encouraged to say their farewells and goodbyes in good spirits.

NOVEMBER 1967: Heterogenous Group

Leah said goodbye to the children inside the building and went out. The children went out after her into the yard. She said "Shalom" to them through the fence "with the fingers and with the hands."

As the year progressed all the children showed increased ability to concentrate on more complicated games.

Wherever possible, we went outdoors and we observed the world around us in rhymes and song. The children learned to observe closely what they saw and later to imitate, by "becoming," cars, planes, trucks, donkeys, goats, birds, trees, wind, rain.

We found that much depended on the teacher of the group. If she felt restrained, disapproving, or embarrassed, it was much more difficult to communicate with the children, since the children felt their lack of involvement and were themselves more withdrawn.

Not all of the children will be willing to participate in all the activities. The reaction of the teacher to the child will depend on the situation and the manner in which the child rejects the activity. She should joyously welcome the child to the group wherever possible; let him play alone, if that seems called for; or attract him to the group by singing welcoming songs with the other children. Becoming angry or upset does not make the child more willing to participate.

Without emotional well-being, it seems that intellectual growth will either be retarded or stunted. All children, be they deprived or privileged, will learn more effectively where learning is a pleasurable experience and where the knowledge they are absorbing is also knowledge that attracts and excites them. This excitement can be generated in an atmosphere devoid of fear, where the child feels himself surrounded by affection and approval and is able to take part in hilarious, joyful activities. The work of the teacher is to create and structure such an atmosphere—she must create daily a situation where the child cannot help but learn.

Perhaps the special playful and joyful approach to music which Leah Helner so creatively injected in her lessons both with the children and with the teachers is best exemplified in her following fanciful description of sample lessons:

Whenever

    I

am with a group of

            CHILDREN

I want our

       experience

together

            to be

               J O Y O U S

      Who am I?

                 I am Leah

      Who are you?

We are the children
I am the child
We are the children

We clap clap clap our hands
clap our hands together

We touch,
touch,
touch our knees
touch our knees together

We touch our heads with both hands,
round like a ball
like an apple, like an orange
like a cookie—like a   kiss
we touch our knees,
play them like a drum
tap
tap
tap
like a drum

We bang the floor
with our hands
with our feet
rum   ta   ram   tam   tam

we   jump   H I G H
in the sky,

REACH
for the clouds
bring a star down
bring it to your heart
let it go again
let's catch another
Let's   REACH   for the
sun on a winter day
bring it down to
warm ourselves
and let it go away

together we'll walk
      straight and tall
big steps, giant
            elephant
     lion
     steps
and STAMP hard
with A L L O U R M I G H T
                like a bear.

now

let's go galloping
       g a ll o p i ng   gall o pi n g   gall o p i n g
   like a horse
a brown horse, a white horse
    a red horse, a blue horse
fasterfasterfaster
         STOP
and   h o l d   the horse, h o l d him
  like a picture   like a statue

and now
       gallop
          again
             again
               again
and
      stop!!!!!
and
    f a l l together
and
    f a l l
      on the floor

    and r o l l   together

like a b a l l   together

curl up like a ball

        curl up like a k i t t e n

Now

     ^m e l _t

like an icecream in the sun

       like   c   s
                  a   h
                  n   a
                  d   b
                  l   a
                  e   t
                  s   t
                    on erev

like ice cubes in a glass of

                       water

    melting,

       melting

          melting   until it is

    Q U I E T

        QUIET

            q u i e t

               quiet

     sssssshhhhh

        ^sh_hh_hs h h h_{e e e} e

we've galloped

       and skipped

             and S T A M P E D

we've banged

      and j ^u ^m p e d

             and sung

and now

       ^shhhhhhhhe

      what do we hear????????????

      ? ? ? ?

   ? ? ?

     ?

    ?

I hear you breathing

       in

    and

       out

  in

    and

out   and
          in
                    out
we hear the birds
              busy with their bird things
     singing their bird songs
we hear the W I N D   BLOWING through the trees
someone is hammering
                         building a house
          someone is
walking, w a l k i n g   aw a y

the wheels of a car
               t u r n i n g a
               d n u o r

a big bus stopping

                                        and starting again

     an   a
            e
             r o   flying
          n e
        p l a
                    in the sky
                    like a   b i r d
let's ss tt rr ee tt cc hh
                         our arms and be the plane
        let's
            fly
          away   like the bird
        let's be the bus   that   STOPS
                              and starts
let's be the man that
                    w a l k s   aw a y

let's t u r n t u r n l i k e t h e w h e e l s o f t h e c a r

let's   blow about like the   W I N D

              AND
              roll
                  roll
              roll

           and blow
like leaves
               and stretch on the ground
                    and grow   l o n g
         on the ground
let's lie
   let's be
                                        still
                         still
put your legs to sleep
                                  quiet
put your arms to sleep
                                  quiet
put your back to sleep
                                  quiet
put your toes to sleep
                                  quiet
and your head
               to sleep
                    quiet
                         quiet
close your
         eyes
and dream
      dream
                  d r e a m

d r e a m
   of the oc

                    OCEAN

dream of the sky

dream of your   bed
         dream of the night
                    dream of the day
A N D . . . .
            s l o w l y
                  wake   UP!!!!!!!!
wake your legs UP
               wake your arms UP
                         wake your toes UP
                                   wake your eyes UP

W
 H
  E
   R
    E   ARE   W
                  E
                   ? ? ? ? ?

        on the
                ground
and from the ground

w e s l o w l y   r i s e   w e s l o w l y   r i s e

        first our a r m s

          then our c h e s t s

            and now on our f e e t

and UP
      on our t o e s

and we are BIG
            and Big   and B I G
    and   g h   h i
    we'll   walk walk walk h i   g
            and   h
we'll
    wave our arms
            and say

                              G O O D B Y E !

CREATIVE ART WORK

The deep satisfaction and inner joy, the sense of pride and accomplishment that each of us derives as we produce anything, however small and
commonplace, but uniquely our own, is one of the priceless pleasures con-

tributing to our sense of well-being. It was this pleasure that we wanted our children to experience and to seek later on.

The art media were a good vehicle for achieving this experience and also for strengthening the child's sense of his own individuality and capability. The important value that we wished to instill in the children at all times and especially in creative work was that each individual sees and does things in his own way and that each way is valued because it is his own expression. This meant that we did not compare work of various children but rather examined and appreciated *each* child's work and encouraged original ways of expression and effort.

The children loved the feel of and the activity associated with the creative art materials (some had to be helped to overcome their fears of the messiness). They experimented with and explored the possible uses of the materials, but at the same time acquired skill and learned good work habits. We were particularly interested in helping the child to produce something of his own because we knew it would give him a feeling of competence. This competence in handling the materials would in itself then serve to motivate him to even greater readiness to work and even greater confidence and achievement.

The art materials were introduced one at a time, and very gradually, so that the children had plenty of time to become acquainted with each material. Each was offered to small groups at a time, while the other children were busy with other activities. The teacher tried to remain close by in order to help the children become familiar with the possibilities and the limitations of each art medium.

The teacher did not see her teaching role as that of giving exact instructions and teaching how to paint or make something. Rather, she sometimes helped by making the child aware of more details, by helping him to observe or to perceive in a more differentiated way. She tried to arouse his awareness of color, design, and mood by commenting on these aspects of his work as well as by examining adult work together. She made it a rule never to ask "What is it?" but rather "Do you want to tell me about it?" in order to remove the pressure on the child to do representational work when he preferred some other mode of expression.

Painting

Painting with paper and brushes was offered at the easels or on the floor. For group mural painting, long pieces of paper were spread out on the floor for several children to work at together in their assigned sections.

In addition to paints, the children were given empty cups so that they were able to mix their own colors if they wished. The materials were arranged so that a minimum of technical supervisory help was needed. In addition, there were finger paints, and the children enjoyed experimentally painting with pieces of cotton, sponges, strings, nails, matches. Sometimes the paper was painted with colored paste on which the children would strew sand, sawdust, pebbles, or pieces of fabric.

Clay and Papier-mâché

Clay was introduced after the children were familiar with plasticene and dough. At the beginning they were involved with the possibilities of the material and spent much time rolling, banging, smoothing, and squeezing before they arrived at representational work. We tried to present the clay and plasticene as a material to be worked with in bulk and not to be rolled into thin lines and used as in drawing and outlining.

Papier-mâché work was very satisfying because of its cozy, messy feel, and the children made fruits and vegetables for their store play, plates and cups, and driving wheels.

Cutting and Pasting

Cutting and pasting was a favorite activity. Before the children acquired skill in the use of scissors, they would tear out the picture or the shape of their choice and then with deep satisfaction would apply themselves to the attractive, sticky paste. After they had their fill of this process and the accidental arrangement of pasting the picture wherever it happened to go, they moved on to planning the arrangement of the page either for decorative or content purposes. Another satisfying activity was pasting empty cigarette boxes, toothpaste tubes, bottle tops, string, small objects and fabrics in three dimensional architectural arrangements. The children loved this new form of building and would frequently paint their finished product. An additional form of pasting activity was the arranging and pasting of various fabrics to form a design.

Other Materials

Mobiles were made using pipe cleaners, colored electric wires, and paper. Pipe cleaners and plasticene were used for making small figures of people and animals for use in the block play. Chalk was another medium for art expression and was used on the floor, blackboards, and paper.

A pleasant activity which the children enjoyed and which produced attractive gifts for the parents was modelling in melted plastic. Transparent plastic cups were melted in a double boiler with some color added. When the plastic cooled the children took small lumps and molded them into pins (a safety pin was molded in). They also molded them into beads and buttons using a nail to make the holes.

There were numerous additional art experiences, some accidental and some planned. The pleasure in the work was always stressed and an attempt was made to develop in the children a sense of aesthetics.

HOLIDAYS AND CEREMONIES

The celebration of holidays in our program involved much soul-searching, thought, discussion, and experimentation. On the one hand, we all knew the importance and joy of developing and establishing traditions in our emerging nation and were aware that our celebrations and holidays are an important means of creating a unified culture. We knew the crucial role of the schools and the influence of the educational institutions in integrating the various cultural traditions and in the slow creation of a unified national identity and mode of celebration and holiday.

On the other hand, we knew our three- and four-year-olds. We knew what interested and absorbed them and what they were capable of understanding and thinking about. We knew that we wanted our curriculum to be geared to their interests and their capabilities. We did not wish to confuse them or to impose a program that, though based on a well-intentional desire to transmit our heritage, might prove too complicated for children of this age. The question was how to reconcile these two needs, how to introduce the spirit of the holidays and yet remain on the level of our three- and four-year-olds' capacity for understanding and participation.

One thing became clear: we did not think it would be fair to the children to cut down on the rich experiences they were having during the nursery day. If we gave to each holiday a week or two of preparation and digression from their usual program, there would be insufficient time left for the program which had been carefully designed to meet the children's emotional, intellectual, and social needs.

Yet it was important for the children to know that there was a holiday, to recognize some of the symbols, to know some of the words, to sing some of the songs. We carefully sifted the traditions of each holiday in order to choose what would be meaningful and comprehensible. The historical background of the holiday was usually too far removed and too abstract for these young children. From our experience, we knew that all the stories of the holidays become jumbled together and confused. We decided that what would impress the children and be remembered by them would be the special foods, the distinctive symbols, and some of the songs and atmosphere.

Where possible we used the holiday symbols as a learning experience—the candles for Chanukah led to discussions on light and how it can be produced; the costumes for Purim led to games of changing one's appearance, changing one's facial expressions, and learning how you look different and yet are the same; Shavuot and Tu B'Shvat were an opportunity for drill in classification and differentiation through examination of trees and fruits and their differences.

There were certain entrenched traditions in Israeli nursery school teaching of holidays that we felt needed reexamination. One was the amount of time and active preparation given to each holiday. A second was the practice of having carefully prepared celebrations and performances for the parents, and another was the matter of elaborate gifts for parents ostensibly prepared by the children but in effect planned, designed, and largely executed by the teachers. Because our energies were primarily directed to the day-to-day work of relating to each child, trying to understand him, and planning appropriate activities which would facilitate his understanding of his everyday world, we asked ourselves whether diverting these energies to intense activity in preparation for each holiday would be justified.

We came to the conclusion that two or three days before a holiday was sufficient time in which to introduce the atmosphere, the symbols, and a few appropriate songs of the holiday. Usually the children themselves would indicate when to introduce the subject by beginning to talk about what they had observed in the streets and in their homes. Work in the nursery went on as usual and the subject of the holiday was introduced during the discussion time and in the rhythms and songs period. We often found that the experiences of the holiday came out more in play and talk after the holiday, when the children would report their experiences and often play them out.

We knew that the parents had been accustomed to expect an elaborate celebration and enjoyed seeing their children perform. But we also knew how upsetting it was to many children (who still fear even one or two strangers) when their nursery fills up with a noisy crowd, and when they must make a public appearance and are unready for it. It also seemed wasteful of the teacher's and children's energies to have them rehearse a prepared role that in no way is expressive of themselves and their own originality. In addition, we considered the parent's own anxieties in concern for how their children would "perform." We decided that the celebrations, either with or without the parents, could and should be spontaneous, simple, fun, and, above all, on the children's level.

Although we knew that the parents were accustomed to expect the children to come home from the nursery with appropriate gifts for the holidays, we did not want to sacrifice the children's spontaneity and originality in order to produce a finished product that would meet the parent's adult standards. There were times when our teachers felt the children were entirely unready to produce a gift, and at such times in order to avoid disappointment for the parents, we ourselves prepared a gift that the children delivered in the teacher's name. For the first Rosh Hashana, for example, the teachers prepared greeting cards for the parents and the children took them home. On other holidays, the teachers tried to arrange gifts that were products of the children's ongoing work.

It was clear that in order to make such basic changes from standard nursery school procedure, we would have to obtain the understanding and cooperation of the parents. Before many of the holidays a parent's meeting was called in which we would discuss what the children could understand of the holiday and what was too difficult; what activities they were capable of and what they were unable to do. We found that these meetings were a wonderful forum for sharing with the parents some of our thinking about children. We talked about how some children still fear strangers and crowds; how some have not yet developed enough belief in themselves to perform publicly; how we would like to avoid the parent's own anxieties about their children's performances; and how a finished product in the form of a gift would only be a reflection of the teacher's skill and not really something of the child's own original expression. It gave us an opportunity to show the parents how much we valued their children's spontaneous and original creations. We discussed with them how important it is to the child to see that his products are valued in the home—what he feels when something he has made is thrown out, made fun of, hidden, or destroyed, and how he feels when it is made a fuss of and displayed proudly.

We planned the holiday celebrations with the parents and found that they were ready to play a very active role in performing for the children, playing games with them, cooking with them, and preparing decorations. The parents responded so well to these discussions that they were ready to forego the "performance," but came to be active participants themselves instead. They even agreed not to come to the first celebrations in order to avoid too much excitement while the children were still involved in adjusting to the nursery. We found that we were able to discuss with them that it would be preferable to leave younger sisters and brothers at home so that the nursery child could be the important focus when the parents did come to visit him. We planned that when the children would be seated, they would be in a circle of children facing children, with the parents sitting in a wider circle each behind his own child.

All of this evolved out of much discussion and basic agreement among the teachers, but nevertheless, when it came to actual practice, some of the teachers found it very difficult to flaunt the conventions and deviate from the parent's expectations. They were constantly examining their consciences as to whether they had failed as teachers if they did not meet the expected standards. Once, after a Shavuoth holiday when the teachers had decided that bringing the children to the municipality party for all the children of Jerusalem would be too hot, crowded, and confusing, they were very disturbed at what they had done when they met together the following week. The other children in town had all been dressed up in white shirts with wreaths on their heads, and our children had been denied that experience.

Since the teachers were particularly sensitive to changes in the mode of celebration of the holidays, we found that if each one was free to make changes to the extent to which she felt ready, she was able to implement her program with conviction and carry the parents along with her. The teachers all moved along at different rates, depending on their own personalities. They learned by their experiences, and they watched the children and their reactions, and, as a result, made gradual changes. In mutual discussion at the weekly meetings, they influenced and reinforced each other and developed more awareness of the children and their needs.

Rosh Hashana and Yom Kippur

Rosh Hashana (New Year) comes right in the midst of the difficult period at the very beginning of the school year when the child is going through the throes of separation from mother and home and trying to adjust to the new conditions of attending nursery school. He has not yet made this adjustment and it seemed very inappropriate at this point to introduce the concept of a holiday to three-year-olds.

Rosh Hashana was mentioned about two days before the holiday, when the symbols of honey and greeting cards were introduced and the song which all of them were hearing in the street ("Shana Tova Umetuka" —"A Good and Sweet Year") was sung. We chose these symbols as a bridge with the home, since we knew that there would be honey on the table at home at this season and that greeting cards could serve to relate home and nursery and bring them closer together in the child's mind. The teachers prepared cards and on the eve of the holiday gave one to each child for his family. There was a short ceremony of eating honey and singing Shana Tova (Happy New Year). The focus of the discussion was that "tomorrow is Rosh Hashana and we don't come to school."

In the second year, when the children were four years old, we again made no elaborate references to the holiday. We felt that the children were too young to develop the post office subject (this was the greeting card season), and that the flavor of the holiday would be discussed better after the children had experienced it. The teacher brought a poster of a child mailing a letter. An address and a stamp were clearly marked on the envelope. There was a short discussion on the picture and on the purpose of the stamp. The teacher brought stamps, and each child placed one on the envelope of his card as the teacher wrote his address (not all children knew their addresses). The whole group went to the corner mail box to post their cards. The children all reported when the cards had arrived at home.

After the holiday, we were pleased to see that the children were beginning to become aware of more details.

> *Yossi (D):* I went to synagogue.
> *Teacher:* What did they do there?
> *Yossi:* Pray.
> *Teacher:* How?
> *Yossi:* With a book and a skull cap.
> *Teacher:* What else do they do?
> *Yossi:* They pray and they sing. Also with a shofar (ram's horn). (He made a fist, held it to his mouth and imitated the sounds of a shofar.)

Several of the children then began to imitate the shofar and, later, the swaying of the prayers.

Succot

The symbols of the holiday were the succa, the decorations, the fruits. In the first year, the subject of Succot was not taken up in all the nurseries before the holiday. The homogeneous group still was not at a stage of much awareness of what was happening around them nor were they ready for discussions. They were still very involved in adjusting to the new surroundings in the nursery. In the nurseries where more readiness was shown, the awareness of the holiday developed as some children came with the news that they were building a succa at home. The teacher questioned, "Who has seen a succa? What is it made of?" In order to answer some of the questions, they went out the same morning to examine a succa nearby. This trip was repeated—the first time they watched it being built, the second time they saw it finished and decorated They were invited to sit down and refreshments were served in the succa. Play on the subject of Succot began after the holiday. The children built succot outdoors out of crates decorated by colored blocks; they collected branches and made the roof of the succa; they wanted to "eat" in their succa.

In the second year, before the holiday they actually built and decorated a real succa in some of the nurseries. Again, after the holiday there was discussion of their succa experiences during the holiday. Play around the building of succot appeared in all the nurseries. They also used art and scrap materials to make miniature succot out of plasticene and match boxes.

Chanuka

In one of the nurseries, the subject of the holiday began in the group discussion when two children brought candles one morning.

The teacher shows the candle.
Aron (P): It's almost Chanuka. Mommy bought candles.
Teacher: When do you light candles?
Yossi (D): On Sabbath you light candles.
Teacher: Good, Yossi. When else do we light candles, many candles?
Galit (P): We have a Chanuka menora (the Chanuka candelabrum).
Teacher: Yes, we light candles in the menora on Chanuka.

The children were asked to bring Chanuka menoras to the nursery and they were put on display. The children examined them thoroughly, and the different ways a Chanuka menora could be made was pointed out.

The subject of light and dark came up. The teacher darkened the room and lit a candle; one of the children said, "It's like electricity." The children watched the candle get smaller as it burned and the nursery become dark when the candle burned out. They experimented to see which burns longer—a match or a candle. They also saw how one candle could be lit from another. One of the children said, "He gave him light." (Each object and activity was carefully named and verbalized.)

The next day the teacher brought a large spinning top (another Chanuka symbol) and added it to the display of candelabra. They tried it out and had difficulty making it work; they talked about how the top turns around. In rhythms, they practiced turning around and each tried turning another child around like a top.

One of the mothers was invited to the nursery to make pancakes (another traditional Chanuka symbol). The children watched fascinated as each step in the process was explained. They distinguished between sweet pancakes and salty pancakes.

In the first year, the parents were not invited to the Chanuka party, because it was felt that the children would be disturbed by such an exciting experience so early in their school adjustment. There was a small celebration where they darkened the room, lit the Chanuka menorot, sang Chanuka songs, played with tops, and ate pancakes.

The second year the symbols again were introduced, but this time the children went much deeper into the subject of light. They talked of electricity, candles, sunlight, fire. They experimented to see what catches fire and what does not—rocks, cloth, water, matches, metal, and so forth. When they watched the candle burn down, one of the children, looking at the dripping wax, said, "Look at the water." This brought on the question of what the candle is made of. The children took tightly rolled pieces of cotton and dipped one in water and one in oil to see whether they both would light.

In talking of the symbol of the top, the children moved on to talk of what else turns around; they mentioned wheels, a carousel, buttons, marbles, hoops, balls. In rhythms, they made motions of turning—one leg, one arm, two legs, two arms, whole body turning.

The children went out into the fields to gather material to make menorot. They gathered branches, large stones, pebbles, and acorns, and each child combined his own choice of materials to make his menora.

In the second year, we wanted the Chanuka celebration to be very warm and family-like. We arranged small groups of children and parents around tables set up with the makings of pancakes and a small kerosene stove on which to fry them. Each group worked on their own pancakes. (Some of the teachers felt this was too difficult to implement; others did it successfully.)

The rest of the celebration consisted of an impressive ceremony around lighting the candles, followed by amusing games played by both the parents and the children. They played games such as trying to eat a candy hanging from a string; two parents feeding jam to each other blindfolded; and pancake-eating competitions. The children loved seeing the parents "perform."

In one of the nurseries, the ceremony ended with the distribution of gifts in an amusing way. A huge top filled with favors for the children was arranged on a pulley. As each child in turn reached to get his gift, the top would be yanked up to the ceiling to the great delight of the children. In another nursery, the teacher neatly combined dance, learning colors, and the symbol of the holiday by using a large hoop hanging from the ceiling with many colored ribbons hanging from it. The children all remembered their own colored ribbon and danced a dance holding on to the ribbons, thus turning the hoop around.

Purim

Purim was the most difficult holiday to plan and to change. The traditions for celebrating Purim in nursery schools are so well-known and entrenched that any change seemed to be unthinkable. The highly-organized party, the performance, and elaborate costumes have been considered by Israeli teachers and parents as essential ingredients of the Purim celebration.

Yet our previous experience with young children had taught us that many of the children could not possibly understand many of the costumes which they and their friends wore—a pirate, a Dutchman dressed in national garb, etc. We found that they were frequently very frightened at the masks, were puzzled and fearful of their friends dressed unrecognizably, and were subdued by the big crowds of parents and relatives in the nursery.

We decided to try a new approach to the holiday, one that would be more appropriate for three- and four-year-olds. This time the children would be the ones to decide spontaneously how they would "dress up." We planned that we would ask the parents to help us in gathering together all sorts of old clothes and odds and ends and that at the Purim celebration itself we would put these things on display and let the children choose and dress themselves up to their heart's content. In essence, that was all that the Purim celebration would consist of.

PARENTS' MEETING

It was with trepidation that we approached the parents' meeting. Would they accept this new plan? Would they cooperate or would they object that they enjoyed preparing the children's costumes and that they did not want their children to miss out on the fun the other children in the neighborhood were having?

Since some of the teachers were themselves torn as to whether this was a good, workable idea or not, the parents responded in exact ratio to the teacher's own enthusiasm. Where the teachers were themselves very convinced of their proposed plan, they succeeded in arousing much enthusiasm and participation among the parents and much interest in making it work. The parents were delighted that they were relieved of the burden of scrounging around and preparing a costume and also of the heavy expenses involved in making it. Many of them were pleased at the idea of letting the child dress up as he wanted. Some of the parents liked the idea but were concerned about "what the neighbors would say." Nevertheless, they went along with the rest. The parents were asked to send clothes, hats, jewelry, feathers, cowboy belts, funny objects, lipsticks, toy guns. (Some bundles arrived the very next morning after the parents' meeting and were already an indication of the parents' enthusiasm and interest in the project.)

The teachers who were themselves unsure about leaving old traditions (and at the staff meeting had used the argument that parents would not want to relinquish the pleasure of dressing up their children) had greater difficulty in arousing the parents' enthusiasm. One of these teachers introduced the subject to the parents by saying, "Don't be upset, but we have a new suggestion for Purim." In that group, naturally, many parents objected to the plan on the grounds that they had already prepared costumes for the children.

The character of the Purim party was therefore different in each group. Some nurseries gave themselves over completely to the new idea; others had some of the children come already costumed, but, wherever possible, there was an attempt to influence the parents to dress the children in something they could understand and enjoy.

PURIM ACTIVITIES IN THE NURSERY

After the bundles of clothing and costume materials began to arrive, the teacher prepared large boxes to hold them, and the children and teachers examined the things and arranged them in various categories. The children spontaneously began playing at buying and selling clothes, using toy money and dressing up. They examined themselves in the mirror and then later changed to something else, usually announcing who they were.

The group discussions preceding the holiday dealt with the many ways people appear—different clothes which change people's appearances, different emotions which change their faces. The children practiced making angry faces, sad faces, smiling faces, pouting faces. They looked at many pictures of people with varying moods expressed in their faces and discussed what their faces seemed to convey, and the children tried to imagine why they were feeling the way they were.

As an additional holiday activity in each of the nurseries, one of the mothers came and prepared traditional Purim cakes with the children. The children helped prepare decorations for the nursery, blowing up balloons, making noisemakers and masks.

THE PURIM PARTY

The nursery was arranged as a giant market place. There were booths with decorative displays of clothes and jewelry. Colorful skirts were hung on lines about the room adding to the gay atmosphere.

The children arrived uncostumed, with the parents, in the afternoon. Buying and selling began immediately, with some of the parents assigned as salespeople. The children made choices and shouted, "I want the red hat," "I want the black shirt," etc. After the "buying," the children and parents went off to the "dressing room" corner, and parents helped their children to dress, tied sashes, painted moustaches when the children requested, and so forth. This was done in a relaxed manner with much fun and laughter. Some of the parents, too, put on costumes; others dressed up only in funny hats.

The party was not highly planned but had a very spontaneous atmosphere. After everyone was seated, the teacher led a group discussion with the children on the preparations for the holiday. The children then paraded in their costumes. After that, musical instruments were distributed, and the parents and children in turn played the instruments and sang. The teacher told the story of "Caps for Sale" and the parents acted it out to the great amusement of the children. Records were put on, and the children and parents all joined in the dancing, some parents with their children, some parents together, some children together. Then, refreshments were served. Afterward, instead of going home in the costumes they had created (as we had expected they would), the children spontaneously took off the costumes, arranged them in large boxes, and asked, "Will we dress up again tomorrow?"

The children had been natural and relaxed. The parents had enjoyed themselves tremendously and one of the P fathers wrote a letter to the teacher saying:

> I feel I must write to you about how impressed I was by the very special character and quality of the Purim party at the nursery today.
>
> I was particularly struck by the spirit of spontaneity and improvisation, especially the costumes created by the children and the wonderful spontaneous dancing. It is unnecessary to add that spontaneity and creativity are precisely the qualities which are so important in a system of education which aims to develop a child's full personality.

The teachers who had carried through this celebration were so delighted that they succeeded in exciting the other teachers, and the next year all the groups celebrated Purim very successfully in similar fashion.

Passover

Since the Passover school vacation begins so long before the holiday itself, it seemed premature to discuss it much so far in advance.

The theme we introduced was the family nature of the holiday, the Seder (ceremonial meal), and the cleaning fervor around Passover. We taught "the four questions" (a short section of the ceremonial reading traditionally chanted by the youngest child at the Passover Seder table) and we cleaned the nursery very thoroughly. The children loved the responsibility and the activity of using buckets of water. On the last day before the vacation, the children were served matzot and grape juice for the final snack, and these were talked of as special foods of the holiday.

Independence Day

The Independence Day holiday was presented as something happy and proud without going into any complicated explanations of statehood, independence, and birthday of the state, since the children were entirely too young to understand such concepts. Where such a discussion was attempted (among highly developed P children), the following excerpts will illustrate the confusion:

Teacher: What is a state (Medina)?
Dany (P): Like a "mangina" (a melody).
Ishai (P): Like independence.
Anat (P): It's a state and independence.
Teacher: The state is my house and your houses, Jerusalem, Haifa, Eilat, the fields, the trees.
Eli (D): And Tel Aviv.

Because of the insistence of the mothers in the homogeneous group, in the second year this group went to Independence Park to join all the other kindergartens in Jerusalem for a public celebration. From the teacher's report, we gather that the buses were very overcrowded, and the children were confused and subdued though they did not cry. They were not able to respond to the instructions given over the loudspeakers and generally were relieved to go home. When asked to recall later what had happened, the impression was that of many, many children and airplanes. The other groups celebrated the holiday by marching around the room and the block carrying flags.

Welcoming In the Sabbath

We celebrated the Sabbath Welcome with a very short ceremony. Friday was cooking and baking day, and sometimes the children made a cake for the Sabbath Welcome. The ceremony itself consisted of lighting candles and singing a song. Usually the discussion that followed dealt with the rest day that was to come, what plans the family had, and what they had done on previous Sabbaths.

Birthdays

The number of birthdays in the nursery is equal to the number of children, of course, and that means a lot of birthdays! We debated whether to combine several birthdays into one big celebration (and thus not disturb the normal routine), but decided that the whole point of the birthday celebration, which was to give to the individual child a feeling of importance, would be lost. We decided, instead, to concentrate the individual birthday celebrations into a short span of time around the ten o'clock snack. In this way the celebrations did not disturb or radically change the daily routine.

Most of the children had some idea of the concept of "birthday party" before they even attended the nursery. Some of the first dramatic play in the nursery (which even preceded the first actual birthday party) was a reflection of the children's concept of this important event which they seem to have known about from their older brothers and sisters. They would organize a "party," imaginary sweets would be distributed, usually there would be singing and dancing, but there was seldom a "birthday child."

The goal of the birthday celebration was to make the individual child the center of interest. On the day of the birthday, the children all fussed around him, noticed his fancy clothes, and wanted to sit near him even though normally he may not have been popular. It was interesting that some children grasped this opportunity of power and began giving orders, whereas others became particularly shy on this day.

The birthday party had several ingredients:

1. For each child's birthday, a poster was made with home snapshots of him at various stages of his development, in addition to pictures of him in the nursery.

2. A little time before the "party," most of the children would participate in preparing an album of their own drawings to present to the birthday child. The teacher would then sit with the children as she collated the album, and they would talk about the birthday child, examine the drawings each child had prepared and plan how to decorate the tables and the special chair of the birthday child. They loved the special chair and one of the children said "like a king."

3. At the same time the teacher would prepare a wreath of flowers for the child's head, and the children would carefully measure the wreath to fit his individual head size. The children seemed to enjoy such preparations for the party more than the celebration itself.

4. The ceremony was kept very simple. It consisted of eating the birthday cake, singing and dancing, some games, and a talk with the mother of the child. The mother would tell stories (which the teacher had helped her to prepare) of special events that had occurred in the birthday child's life, and of how he had grown. Sometimes the child himself would talk about himself, "I used to crawl and now I walk," etc.

A gift from the nursery—usually a book, or crayons and paper—was hidden, and the child had to find it by responding to calls of hot and cold, as he approached the hidden gift. When it was found, the children played a game of guessing what it was by its shape, feel, and sound. We also played an imaginary gift game in which each child would act out an imaginary gift and the other children would have to guess what it was— a ball which they "bounced," an auto that moved, a jump rope, a doll they held in their arms, beads they strung.

5

Parents

WORK WITH PARENTS WITHIN THE SCHOOL SETTING

Most educators would agree that in order to improve the level of the culturally deprived child, it is almost as important to work with the parents as to work directly with the child. In recent years, educators, psychologists, sociologists, and social workers have expended much thought and energy seeking effective methods for direct and intensive work with parents. Many interesting and helpful experimental projects have been proposed and put into practice. This work has covered a wide range of activities which include:

1. Parents' cooperatives where the parents play an active role in the teaching and the day-to-day activities of the nursery.
2. Seminars and workshops with parents where problems of child-rearing are discussed,
3. Direct work with children at home by professionals, while parents are present to observe the methods,
4. Teaching culturally deprived parents how to intellectually stimulate their children at home,
5. Direct supportive and advisory assistance to individual parents,
6. Arrangements for play groups run by mothers, sometimes with professional guidance.
7. Activation of parents to attend, observe, and assist in the nursery activities,
8. Setting up of parents' rooms in nurseries. (An integral part of the Head-Start nursery program is the parents' room in the nursery. Mothers can bring along their younger children and spend the morning in the parents' room in an atmosphere of warmth and acceptance, drinking coffee, exchanging recipes, and teaching one another other skills such as sew-

ing, knitting, and hairdressing. At the same time, a professional worker is present, and the mothers are stimulated to think about their important role as mothers. In a casual way, the physical, emotional, and intellectual aspects of child care come up for discussion. Most important of all, the mothers enjoy and benefit from being related to as important people in their own right.)

Clearly, work with parents is essential for an effective program to alleviate cultural deprivation. It seemed to us that the disadvantaged parents, too, required an opportunity for a corrective experience in establishing gratifying relationships with people. They, as well, needed opportunities to build their own self-esteem and sense of dignity; it was essential for them to be respected, listened to, empathized with, and encouraged to make and implement plans for themselves. We believed that through such a personal experience, they would be more equipped and ready to relate to their children in similar ways. At the same time, it seemed to us that the disadvantaged parents needed to be exposed to and motivated toward a new view of the role of parent—a view that would include awareness of a child's needs for emotional security and intellectual stimulation as well as for recognition of his individual personality, unique traits, and needs.

To our deep regret, the structure of our research project prevented us from applying this approach intensively and from utilizing some of the aforementioned intriguing and probably effective procedures. Since we already had many variables in our research plan—the heterogeneous groups, the compensatory curriculum, two teachers in a group—we were unable to introduce the parents into the curriculum because we felt it would then be impossible to determine the specific effect of the various other factors. We had to content ourselves to remain within the normal procedures of parent work in Israeli nurseries.

Within this framework, however, we were very aware of the importance of contact and work with parents. We tried to bring them closer to the nursery school and to the teachers and to share with them our observations about their child, in order to assist them to understand and help him. In addition, *we needed the parents* in order to help us know each individual child and his needs as well as to become acquainted with each family and its specific ethnic and cultural values.

We found that within the structure of our nurseries, the best means of approaching our parents was through the personal contacts of home visits and informal chats as well an occasional, more formal appointment at the nursery. In addition, there were parent meetings which dealt with the ongoing work at the nursery and touched on the principles of our educational philosophy.

We approached the parents with the basic assumption that all parents are vitally interested in the development of their children and in helping them to progress. We realized that if we were to be effective, it would have to be on the basis of honest, mutual respect for each other. This meant never talking down to parents or giving them orders, but being careful to speak to them in such a way that they would understand us and our objectives. We constantly tried to communicate our belief in the parent's important role in their children's development. In our contacts with the parents, we tried to help them to understand what is normal behavior for children of this age and what are children's physical, emotional, and cultural needs. We felt that many of our parents needed a warm and supporting relationship with the teachers, and, of course, all the parents were accepted with the utmost respect and consideration essential for their (and our) self-esteem.

At first, some of the D parents were suspicious of the teachers as authority figures (some of them had themselves been school dropouts and feared teachers and schools), but as the contacts proved to be friendly, helpful, and accepting, the parents began to appreciate and enjoy talking to the teachers about their children and later about themselves—or sometimes vice versa. We felt we had achieved something when some of the parents came to talk to the teachers about their personal problems.

The contacts began before the opening of the nursery, with the first home visit of the teacher which was designed primarily for teacher and child to become acquainted. The next contact was the child's visit to the school (before the opening of the nursery) and the initial parents' meeting to discuss the problems of adjustment to nursery school and to the first days at school (see pages 28–29.) We tried, wherever possible, to keep administrative work at a minimum (at least when the children were present) and to keep the teacher-parent contacts on a friendly, informal basis. Parents were urged to come to the nursery to observe or to help whenever they could manage the time. They were always welcomed and usually were served coffee.

The teacher tried to make at least one additional home visit during the year. She also tried to visit the home if a child or mother was ill for an extended period, or when she felt that she needed additional insight into what was happening at home in order to understand the child better. Information was exchanged, problems of the child were broached, and solutions were sought. During these encounters, the teacher usually learned a great deal about the family and the child. Here are excerpts from a teacher's notes on one such home visit:

FEBRUARY 1968

I informed Naomi's mother that I would be visiting after school this morning. (We had decided to make this visit in order to get more information because of Naomi's very slow progress in the nursery.)

Naomi is a thin child with large eyes; she plays either with Uri (her neighbor) or alone. She spends most of the time wandering alone in the nursery, sometimes singing or talking unclearly to herself. Uri is very attached to her and when he sits down, he always saves a place for her near him. She is less attached to him. When he is at the nursery, she plays a bit with him (in the doll corner); when she is alone, she usually plays in a stereotyped way with puzzles and table games. Naomi has wet her pants several times at the nursery, and we have begun to remind her to use the bathroom and to accompany her there. In a conversation with her older brother, he revealed that mother burns the soles of Naomi's feet with matches when she wets. We saw some scars on her feet but it wasn't clear whether these were from burns or not.

I accompanied Naomi home after school. The house was orderly and adequately furnished. The heating stove was burning and there was food cooking on it. Mother wasn't home but was at the neighbor's where, it seems, she spends a great deal of time.

Mother invited me into the living room and spent much time between the kitchen and the living room bringing refreshments. She almost never sat down, and when she did, it was very difficult to engage her in conversation. It wasn't clear whether this was because she is not accustomed to make much conversation or whether she didn't choose to.

The children range from ages nine, eight, and four-and-a-half, to Naomi (three-and-a-half). They helped themselves to the refreshments as they wished with no objections from their mother.

In the sporadic conversation that did take place, mother told that father does not have steady work, that she had worked as a domestic but has stopped because of a bladder infection. Her husband buys the food for the family; she hardly goes out, and she complained that her whole family lives far away in Galilee and it is difficult for her alone.

I encouraged her to talk about her feelings of being alone and later I broached the subject of Naomi's wetting. Mother acknowledged that the problem has lessened considerably recently but Naomi still occasionally wets at night. I talked of how encouraging it is that the symptom is appearing less often and how, with patience, it will pass. When parents become angry at this symptom it usually makes it worse. Naomi's mother nodded but did not seem to accept this statement fully.

I left in a friendly atmosphere but felt that mother was relieved that the visit was over. (The contacts continued as Naomi's mother began to trust and confide in the teacher more and more and felt that she at last had somebody to whom she could pour out her troubles.)

We had several parents' meetings during the year. Attendance was usually very high (especially in the homogeneous group), and included many fathers. Refreshments were always served. At the meetings various aspects of the program were discussed. When a particular "area of interest" was being developed in the nursery, the parents often were informed of it. There was usually a parents' meeting before a holiday to plan with them how the holiday would be celebrated in the nursery.

One very successful meeting, which was held in each of the nurseries, was one in which the parents themselves used the materials in the nursery—the clay, paints, blocks, doll corner, books. They learned how to prepare finger paints, play-dough, and clay. It was amazing how much both the D and P parents enjoyed playing with the blocks and in the domestic corner and how they took on dramatic play roles with enthusiasm. They left their paintings, clay work, and block buildings for the children to see the next morning. This experience, of course, aroused the parents' interest and understanding of the children's play.

Usually, after a parents' meeting there would be much greater interest on the part of the parents to pay individual visits to the nursery. Many of them especially eager to watch the music and rhythms periods of which they had heard so much from the teachers and the children.

In several of the nurseries a much-appreciated gathering was a picnic for all the families of the nursery. Fathers, mothers, and siblings came carrying picnic baskets. There was a gay atmosphere with much food, humor, games, and music, and the parents were delighted and asked for more such events.

In each nursery there was a parents' bulletin board with announcements of meetings; photographs of the children in action at the nursery; material on the "area of interest" occupying the children at the time; lists of recommended books; requests for parents to contribute things like old pots, plumbing pipes, blankets, sheets, empty cigarette boxes. In addition, most of the financial transactions with the parents (bills and receipts) were handled through the bulletin board.

Little by little, many of the parents drew closer to the nursery and participated more actively in its program. Mothers came to help bake the cake with the children on Friday and several came to make Chanuka pancakes with the children; on the day that the children made chips for their "restaurant" a mother was invited to come and help. Fathers with special skills were asked to help and to teach. One father came to teach about electricity and helped the children set up a chain of lights for their buildings; another invited the children to the garage where he worked and then came to visit the nursery, bringing discarded automobile spare parts; still another father took the children on a ride in his bus. A mother invited the children to the broadcasting station where she worked. Parents performed for the children on holidays, took animals home to care for them during school vacations, and helped out on trips. Mothers helped sew and iron curtains and aprons for the nursery. Some came to help when a teacher was ill (in some cases they were paid for this). Other parents helped by allowing the children, as a group, to visit in their homes to see new babies, to see how a house is constructed, and to look at special things in the yard.

A difficult time with the parents arose when we decided to switch teachers for the second year of our program. (This had been decided in order to offset the effects on the research results of each set of teachers working in a different style, and also because we thought it would be beneficial for the children to be exposed to a new set of teaching adults and thus widen their experience in developing relationships.) The parents had become very attached and loyal to their first set of teachers and invariably found the second set to be inferior. We held parents' meetings to explain the reasons for the switch and what the benefits to the children would be. We also arranged for home visits, with the previous teachers coming to introduce the new teachers. In spite of these preparations, the new teachers had to work very hard to overcome the initial opposition of the parents.

The most emotional and dramatic event in the two years of the research program was the final parents' meeting. The parents of all four nurseries had never met together before, but we decided to have one climactic event to mark the end of the program. We had been concerned as we planned the evening over how the D parents would feel as they mixed with the better-dressed and more articulate P parents (although they had been meeting together in their individual nurseries), and we even debated seriously as to whether we should plan such a meeting. However, we decided that the binding, common interest in their children would overcome any awkwardness.

We used the large auditorium of the YMHA (where one of the nurseries had been located). An attractive exhibition of the children's work was arranged, including the four large table models of "Our Neighborhood." Also on display were a large block scheme which had been built by some of the children; paintings; collages; woodwork; clay work; the children's individual books; photographs of the children at work; and posters of poems dictated by the children. The parents were overwhelmed when they saw the extent of the children's skills.

The program was good-humored and varied. There was a talk on what the children had "learned" in their two years at the "university nursery," including the use of words like physics, mathematics, geography, etc. One of the teachers read from some of the children's dictations and quoted some of their original and creative uses of language. Excerpts from some of the delightful moments of play which had been recorded in the observations were read. A hilarious aspect of the evening was when one of the teachers asked for volunteers among the parents to be "pupils" and "parents" for a demonstration of how parents should teach their children. The parents were dressed for their roles, and the teacher guided the "mothers" in teaching their uncomprehending "children" how to examine the number of legs there are on a table and how to construct a block building with a window.

At one point in the evening several of the P parents spoke very movingly of their appreciation of the program and of what it had done for their children. But the high and emotional point of the evening was the finale led by the music teacher. She began by giving a demonstration lesson and succeeded in getting all the parents literally to dance while seated in their seats. She spoke of how much she had enjoyed working with each of their children and that each one had revealed his own special personality. Then she announced that she had composed a song especially for the evening and wanted everybody to participate in singing it. To a very catchy tune she sang:

> We are all in Israel, Israel, Israel,
> I come from . . . (and pointed to a father who said: "I come from Poland")

The teacher enthusiastically said, "From Poland" and had all the parents join in singing "I come from Poland." She went on to the next parent and the next and the next and as each country was mentioned there was applause, and the audience sang out louder and louder and prouder. "I come from Kurdistan; I come from America; I come from Afghanistan; I come from Morocco; Chile; Israel; Yemen." Altogether some thirty countries were named.

As the singing went on, some of us in the staff had tears in our eyes as we realized that perhaps through our work we had contributed to giving a feeling of dignity and self-esteem to our children and their parents.

Epilogue

What happened? Did the D children change their attitudes to themselves, to adults, to other children? Did their self-esteem improve? Were they motivated to move from passivity and aimlessness to more interested, active, and exploratory behavior? Did they modify their thinking from magical acceptance to a more scientific, logical approach to facts? Did they acquire a tendency to examine reality and observe details of events and processes? What developments took place in the areas of concentration span, development of initiative, leadership, creativity? Was there more use of language as a means of communication? These and many other questions no doubt arose in the reader's mind as the problems of the D children were described and as the method of work with them was outlined.

In trying to evaluate how effective the procedures described in the book were in eliminating the deficits, many problems arise. It is more difficult to assess the impact on the children when, in addition to cognitive gains, one considers it equally important to consider such complex questions as establishment of self-concept, ego strengths, initiative, creativity, and ability to relate to others. How much is measurable quantitatively and translatable into hard data? Can the wide and generalized effects of this experience be measured by how a child performs some specific tasks, and if so, what should these specific tasks be? Is it not possible that, in some areas, descriptive observations may reveal more of how the whole child functions than specific tests? In the literature of educational research these broad questions arise repeatedly and have as yet found no definitive answer, although many alternative methods to quantitative analysis have been suggested as means of evaluation.[1]

---

[1]See the following: Herbert Zimiles, "An Analysis of Current Issues in the Evaluation of Educational Problems," in *Disadvantaged Child*, vol. II, ed.

Although it can be expected that the final report of the research project will present quantitative measurements of the children's development wherever possible, many of the questions raised above will perhaps be answered best by descriptive and qualitative evaluations based on extensive observational material.

At this stage in the unfinished preparation of the research findings of the study, this epilogue will confine itself to review, in general terms, the qualitative impressions of the changes in the D children as revealed in actual personal observations and contacts, as well as in the hundreds of written daily observations by trained observers. These preliminary findings and perceptions are a combination of the author's observations and those of the teachers and the research team. They are descriptive in nature and are not a substitute for hard data and quantitative research results. Those will be published as soon as they are fully compiled and evaluated.

The maturation factor (the children were two years older) must be constantly borne in mind as the changes in the children's behavior are enumerated. In the final report and evaluation of the research results, this factor will be taken into account as the children are matched with their peers who were not exposed to the same research setting. Nevertheless, the strong impression we received was that many significant changes could not be attributed to maturation alone.

We will look at the same areas of behavior that were described in Chapter 1 (pages 7–13) where the differences between the D and P children at the beginning were outlined and will describe the D children at the end of the two-year program. Of course, as in the earlier section, we are describing general trends and characteristic behavior in the group as a whole, and it must be stressed that these ranged in quantity and quality within the wide gamut of individual variations that is to be found within a group of forty-eight children.

PHYSICAL APPEARANCE

There was a subtle but very striking change in the outward appearance of the D children. At the beginning, close observation had revealed that there

Jerome Hellmuth (New York: Brunner/Mazel, Inc., 1968); E. B. Omwake, "Head Start—Measurable and Immeasurable," in *Disadvantaged Child*, vol. II; Miriam L. Goldberg, "Problems in the Evaluation of Compensatory Programs for the Educationally Disadvantaged," in *Education of the Disadvantaged*, ed. A. Harry Passow (New York: Teachers College Press, Columbia University, 1968); Edward L. McDill, *Strategies for Success in Compensatory Education* (Baltimore, Md.: Johns Hopkins Press, 1969).

was frequently a tight, defensive quality in their movements and posture; eyes and facial expressions were often troubled, suspicious, and sometimes angry; they rarely smiled or laughed and, too frequently, seemed to be depressed. Though they were in constant motion and therefore gave a superficial impression of animation, their activity was largely undirected and haphazard (except for a need to touch everything in sight) and seemed to lack interest and enthusiasm. Often their health needs were neglected and some of them were untended and filthy. In contrast, two years later, there was a marked change. Their eyes were alive and alert; they smiled frequently and cried passionately. Often their posture had changed; they held their heads up and no longer averted their eyes; they used their bodies with more ease and abandon; even their voices had become louder and more assertive.

Surprisingly, the care at home for their health and physical appearance had improved. Somehow the teachers seemed to have succeeded in conveying to the parents the importance of their child, and perhaps this idea was what created a change in the parents' attitude to the children's well-being. Perhaps, too, the example of the teacher's own concern for the children's illnesses and lack of cleanliness had contributed, but the results were unmistakable. There were no longer cases of neglected sores and lice, and there were no flies clustered around the children. The children had learned to wipe their noses and to carry a handkerchief or ask for tissues so the inevitable, universal running nose no longer appeared. The children had even become finicky about using napkins whenever they ate. (All this progress, of course, had come as the result of slow painstaking effort.) At the end of the program, one could say that in outward appearance, most of the D and P children had become almost indistinguishable.

ACTIVITY—PASSIVITY

When the D children first came to the nursery we described them as passive, uninterested in most things in their surroundings, and unable to play; they carried toys about disinterestedly and wandered aimlessly, and their haphazard activity was essentially nonpurposeful. The P children, on the other hand, were "lively and plunged enthusiastically into the materials and activities of the program. . . . They were purposeful, interested, and ready to try new experiences."

After two years in the program, these very words could be used to describe most of the D children, with the addition of a number of other characteristic behavior patterns: they exhibited much initiative; they could carry through a long-term goal; they were frequently inquisitive and asked questions; many were even exploratory in their examination of things that interested them. The sharp contrast between their active and positive behavior and their previous aimlessness and passivity was perhaps the most exciting single phenomenon manifested and a striking witness to the profound •hange that had taken place in the children. They had become active, awake, and more purposeful. They had moved the long distance from listlessly holding a car in their hands until it dropped, to building roads and housing schemes, remembering to move cars and buses along the "roads," as well as to provide a garage, a gas station, a bus stop, and a tow car.

The children who, at the beginning, had sat unobtrusively at tables stringing beads and doing puzzles in a stereotyped, trial-and-error fashion were later interested in making expansive and detailed buildings as well as in using paints and art materials freely and creatively. The fact that they had been able to produce miniature representations of their nursery, their own houses, and familiar landmarks in their neighborhood was proof that they had developed extensive and concentrated ability to observe as well as to request and use materials in very ingenious ways. For the most part, their play was as vital, exciting, and lively as that of the P children, even though the subjects that interested each of the groups were frequently very different. Many of them had become accustomed to ask questions, to turn to the adults for information, and sometimes when something was unclear, they requested trips to observe specific details. As new equipment and materials, such as the scale, the magnets, and the magnifying glass, were introduced into the nursery, most of the children did not hesitate to try them out, study them, and experiment with them.

RELATIONS TO PEOPLE

The suspiciousness and defensiveness that so markedly characterized the D children at the beginning of the program seemed in almost all cases to have dissolved. In its place there was frequently affection and much trust in the teachers and other adults who came to the nursery. Many would, with simple naturalness, address visitors, ask their names and why they had come, and with the same ease, when asked, would explain what they themselves were doing.

The change was very pronounced and palpable especially in their attitude to the teacher. From fear of addressing her, unreadiness to respond to any reaching out by the teacher, and shrinking away when the teacher approached, most of the children had moved to a responsive awareness of her presence, a deep trust in, and freedom with her. They used this freedom to express their attachment to her as well as to ask often for help; they sometimes were demanding and showed that they wanted "spoiling"; in most cases they seemed to expect the teacher to accept them as they were, and they allowed themselves more leeway in expressing their feelings. It was no longer possible to describe them as withdrawn and suspicious, but rather there was often an openness about them that was very appealing. Nevertheless a few children remained inordinately shy.

In their relations with each other there was also marked change. Although some of the children had played together in small groups from the very beginning, many had been unready for play with each other. Toward the end of the program, it was characteristic that the children needed each other for play and no longer gave the impression of being "loners" in the nursery. However, quite a few children began their social relations by interacting with only two or three others and continued to do so to the end. It sometimes was surprising to see how kind and helpful they were with each other, giving advice and help freely, sharing equipment, and working on joint projects. There seems to have been a true identification with the teacher and her attitudes in this area. Along the same lines, one was generally struck by the children's readiness to accept others as they were and by a real expectancy that they would be accepted by others.

There were, of course, notable exceptions. There were several cases of extreme pathology at home. In consequence, there were a few children whose disturbed behavior persisted, and who remained aggressive, silent, or disoriented.

SELF-CONCEPTS

The children seemed to have become more sensitive and aware of themselves and of other people and their individual characteristics. They began to demand their rights and to respect the rights of others. They were more conscious of their bodies and their physical capabilities and enjoyed developing their physical skills; they seemed to care more about their appearance. With their increased consciousness of their bodies, they became more careful and tried to avoid hurting themselves; when they did get hurt, they cried and demanded attention. In the area of self-esteem there was a distinct difference in development between the D children in the homogeneous group and the D children in the heterogeneous group, and each group will be described separately.

In their improved attitude toward themselves, the children in the homogeneous group seemed to have made their most deep-seated gains.

Many of them exuded an aura of self-confidence, assurance, and purpose-fulness and went about their business in a clear, definite manner and a kind of assertiveness in their decisions. Their style of play was usually positive and goal-directed; they participated with confidence in group dis-cussions, and most were ready to perform in front of others with no diffi-culties. In their everyday work at the nursery, the children had proved tó themselves and had been encouraged to believe that they were capable of doing, of achieving, of making decisions, and of sticking to goals, and this confidence had contributed enormously to their feeling of self-worth and sense of mastery.

The feeling of being meaningfully accepted and valued seemed to have become deeply incorporated into the personality of many of the chil-dren. At times, there appeared such a profound personality change that it even aroused the impression and the hope among the observers that the child's belief in himself and consequent self-assurance was now so well-rooted that only enormous adversity would succeed in quashing it. No longer was one struck by a sad quality, by a feeling that the children would prefer to "disappear into the walls." Instead we were impressed by their enthusiasm, by their apparent fearlessness in tackling new tasks, and by their pride in their work. Several of the D children in the homogeneous group developed positive leadership traits which they used in very con-structive ways, stimulating and incorporating others into their projects.

The D children in the heterogeneous group were much more diffi-cult to assess. Though they too gave the impression of having made strik-ing gains in confidence, self-assurance, and sense of mastery, capability, and achievement, something in their feeling of self-worth still seemed to need strengthening. All too often, they lacked some of the assertiveness and the sense of pleasure that seemed so characteristic of the D's in the homogeneous group. They sometimes seemed to be more ill at ease and diffident, and somewhat less sure of themselves (in spite of much teacher encouragement). There was something deferential in their behavior in re-lation to the P children; they seemed to be wary and secretly conscious of them; watchful of what they were doing; puzzled and troubled fre-quently by not understanding what they were playing or talking about. (The D's were quick to imitate what the P children were doing, often with-out understanding. For example, they went through the motions of using the toy telephone "to place a grocery order" without grasping the meaning of placing a grocery order by telephone, or they played "going fishing" without understanding the concept at all.)

There seemed to be a feeling of inferiority in regard to the P children that was all-pervasive and ever-present, even when completely unjustified. Perhaps the incident that most deeply etched itself in the writer's memory was when Pinchas, the brightest of our D children, built a very complicated airplane, replete with many complicated details and along came Ephraim, a P child, who said, "O.K., I'll be the pilot and you be the steward," and Pinchas meekly acquiesced.

None of the D children in any of the heterogeneous groups reached any leadership positions, even though some of them were very bright and positive, with definite leadership qualities. There were several children who attempted leadership but were frustrated by lack of success. Instead, there was a slightly sad and shadowy quality about their presence in the group. Most of the time they played the role of followers and seemed to be groping with a nagging sense of inadequacy.

In spite of this, the warm and encouraging relationship with the teachers, the nurturing of the children's individuality, the numerous opportunities for discovery and accomplishment through their own efforts, and the considerable accretions to their store of information and skills contributed to a marked improvement in their self-confidence, initiative, and sense of purpose.

LANGUAGE

Using words had become a natural and spontaneous means of communication for all but one of the D children by the end of the two-year experience in the nursery, and yet most of the children still showed difficulty in expressing themselves easily. Despite their much richer vocabulary, they lacked an easy flow of words; they built sentences, but their grammar remained poor and incorrect.

Nevertheless, a distinct change had taken place in their ability and desire to communicate verbally. They had moved from shrugging their shoulders as a characteristic means of expression to enthusiastic outpourings and attempts to tell about subjects that excited them. Many kept up a constant babble, talking to each other and to the teachers; and many were able to tell stories, albeit often disjointedly, to make rhymes and play with words, to express imaginative and creative similes, and even to use language for purposes of humor.

On the whole, the children's pronunciation was clearer, and they no longer "swallowed" syllables and words. Some of them spoke in sentences, although others still only spoke in full sentences when the teacher requested it. They had learned the importance of words and (without the teacher's prompting) would often ask what something was called before they would request it. Connective and relative words had become an integral part of their vocabulary and were used freely. Much more impressive than the improvement in the children's speech habits was their ability to listen and concentrate. Most could absorb and understand long stories (which they were often able to dramatize), and they could participate in an intensive group discussion for as long as half an hour.

In contrast to the P children, however, their vocabulary and the scope of their information was markedly more limited. Their store of words and knowledge seemed to be richer in areas that had been touched on in the nursery—topics which had been discussed, examined, and explained—but in most other subjects they seemed to be woefully behind the P children who received constant stimulation at home.

In other words, though their vocabulary and store of information had become much richer, it was still inadequate for their age level. It seems that the gap between the two groups in the area of information and language had even widened during the two years.

MODE OF THINKING

The fog that had seemed to envelop the D children at the beginning of the work had dissipated. They had begun to perceive themselves as distinct entities, and they were much more aware of other people and the things and events that surrounded them. It was more than mere awareness—they *cared*, and were interested in and curious about their immediate environment. They gave the impression of being much more oriented in their world and more secure in themselves. The children had learned to observe clearly and discriminately. They frequently noticed details and enjoyed using all of their senses as they were exposed to numerous experiences that involved sights, sounds, smells, tastes, and sensations. Many had learned not only to perceive but to express what they had experienced in words and stories, in paintings, clay, and other art materials, as well as in their play and block-building. Much of the anecdotal material in the book presents the children's spontaneous expressions of their experiences in many media.

In contrast to the children's previous confused sense of time, place, and order, there was now an almost exaggerated love of classifying things, keeping them in their proper place and order, and sticking to regularity in routines. One of the favorite activities in the nursery was "clean-up time," and the children would accomplish the job with enthusiasm in record time and to perfection, succeeding in classifying all objects, such as blocks, doll clothes, and types of automobiles down to their last detail. This activity seemed to fill a definite need for "setting of limits" and regularity which the children apparently still craved. Similarly, they enjoyed carrying out a definite and set task and were able, little by little, to set more and more distant goals for themselves.

On the whole, they were interested and curious about many things around them—the sewage pipes being replaced down the street, the insect they discovered under a rock, the carpenter who came to the nursery and how he worked. They were inquisitive about observing and experiencing things, but only some of them were spontaneously interested in finding out how and why things worked. We estimate that about half of the children had begun at times truly to explore for themselves and to do further questioning on their own. An example of this kind of questioning occurred when the group was discussing money, salaries, and how father earns money, and Shmuel asked, "But where does the man who gives father the money get the money?"

Many of the children still needed priming by the teacher before they could begin real questioning on their own initiative. In their individual sessions with the children, the teachers worked especially at arousing their curiosity, stimulating them to ask questions, and trying slowly to develop the questioning and explorative mode of tackling problems. The principle of cause and effect was very difficult for the children to assimilate and understand sufficiently to apply as a matter of course to everyday occurrences. In spite of the fact that they had become accustomed to examine and observe, there were still remnants of a passive acceptance of things as they are, with no questions asked. To a question of how or why something happened they no longer answered "just because," but on the other hand they themselves were not often spontaneously impelled to investigate. When the question was raised by the teacher, however, they were ready to consider it. This difficulty in grasping cause-and-effect relationships was sharply reflected in the dilemma of many of the children when arranging a new picture sequence puzzle or explaining the action in a picture that depicted a simple occurrence—they would describe what they saw in the picture but ran into difficulty when asked to figure out the sequence of what was happening. The teachers introduced games like "what would happen if" and "how do you know" in order to stimulate cause-and-effect thinking, organization of observations, and understanding of their significance. On the other hand, simpler laws of logic like "if this is shorter, then this must be longer" and other exercises of the type designed by Bereiter[2] were "child's play" for the children; they even seemed puzzled that the teacher should ask such simple questions.

In the area of initiative and creative thinking, tremendous strides had been made, and in these areas the D children reached or came quite

[2]Carl Bereiter and Siegfried Engelmann, *Teaching Disadvantaged Children in the Pre-School* (Englewood Cliffs, N.J., Prentice-Hall, Inc., 1966).

close to the level of the P children. Many children were rich in ideas for their play, were able to initiate and carry out their plans, and were a joy to the adults in their creative and original modes of expression and in the implementation of their ideas. They were able to choose the simplest item from the rummage box and find numerous and varied uses of it—for instance, a cardboard cone from a spool of thread became at various times a loudspeaker, a headlight, an ice cream cone, a tower on a building, a sieve for sand, and a candle. The D children sometimes used language for delightful bits of humor and imaginative expressions. They dictated their own stories to the teacher, and some of their play began to reflect imaginative fantasies.

IMPULSIVITY VERSUS ABILITY TO TOLERATE FRUSTRATION AND DELAYED GRATIFICATION

The impulsive darting about, sudden destruction of their work, and unexplained running away had disappeared from the behavior of the D children. They had become much more controlled and directed in their behavior, and their emotional reactions were much more predictable. Aggression had become more restrained, as if the children were giving second thought to their impulses. On the whole, their aggression tended to be more verbal than physical. Along similar lines, they demanded more verbal explanations from the teacher when restraints were imposed.

It was a long process until the children were able to tolerate frustration without reacting either by apathy or by temper outbursts. It took a great deal of corrective relationship and trust in the teacher before they could accept limitations and delayed gratifications in the normal limited manner of four-year-old children. There remained several of the D children who still would display uncontrollable temper tantrums, and sometimes it was impossible for us to know to what they were reacting. (This may have been inevitable because there were instances when we lacked understanding of some of their cultural values.) On the whole, however, the children had learned to wait for turns, to persevere when a task was difficult, and not give up in immediate frustration.

THE TEACHERS

It would be impossible to summarize the changes that took place in the two-year period without relating, at least in passing, the changes that took place in the teachers. When this epilogue was being formulated and was read to the teachers for further comments, some of them reacted by saying:

> But you left out the most important change of all and that was the change in the teachers. We have become very different teachers, and we also feel we have changed in our own relations with people.
>
> I have become so much more involved and aware as a teacher, so much more aware of how a child feels and thinks. There are so many new aspects that *matter* to me.
>
> We learned to think that it is not only the cognitive results that matter but rather how important it is to build relationships.
>
> I learned to reevaluate what I was doing, and now I am not afraid to throw away old precepts if I don't like them.
>
> We learned how to work together and how much we could learn from each other. The team work was a very important experience.

The most outstanding change in the teachers was in the sharpening of their sensitivity and ability to adapt to the children's changing and individual needs. In line with the changes in the children they had subtly altered their role from being the protective, accepting, nondemanding, ever-gratifying adult who was able to repeat and repeat their reaching-out attempts to the children despite many rebuffs, to the stimulators and socializers who made ever-increasing demands. The changes were reflected in such simple episodes as wiping Eli's nose countless times a day for months on end until gradually reaching the point where Eli was requested to wipe his own nose and carry his own handkerchief. It was also reflected in drastic changes of attitude such as nursing Hanna along and satisfying her deep needs for understanding and gratification until the teacher felt that Hanna had reached a stage where she could and should verbalize her needs and that she could withstand frustration enough so that the teacher could refuse to respond until Hanna broke the barrier of silence. At the beginning the teachers had been satisfied with microscopic gains. They were delighted when David had moved within a one-hour period from suspicious, passive withdrawal to actually kicking a ball. At a later period they expected the same David to be a "leader of men" and demanded of him highly social, responsible, and planned behavior.

In the activity-passivity area, for example, the teachers had withstood the test of frustration when they had not been successful in arousing the interest of the children with any of the techniques they had been accustomed to using. They then devised new techniques. They formed individual one-to-one relationships with the children and thereby were able to focus their attention and motivate them to some faint interest, some moment of activity. At other times, the teachers actually took a role in the play in order to stimulate more activity and demonstrate to the children how to play. In the homogeneous group they resorted to games in order to induce the children to *touch* the blocks and gradually demonstrated to them that blocks could be used for building. They encouraged the barest hint of spontaneous play on the part of the children by showing interest, adding materials, and asking questions. But the teachers didn't stop there. When the children had begun to be more active and to play and use materials more freely, the teachers constantly found new ways of stimulating them to further interests, broader horizons, and more adventurous explorations. The teachers had entered into an interplay with the children of stimulation and reaction which in turn inspired the teachers to more initiative and further efforts to stimulate the children in wider and wider areas.

Everyone who visited the nurseries at the beginning and at the end of the program was struck by the marked change in the atmosphere, in the activities, in the level of the children's functioning, and in the constantly changing roles of the teachers. Although we sensed that more time was needed to ensure that the progress could continue and that the changes could become truly permanent and irreversible, the teachers, parents, and the research team were, nevertheless, unanimous in feeling that the experience we had lived through had been valuable, memorable, and enriching for us as well as for the children. We fervently hoped that what had been built would not be lost and that other projects (hopefully using a similar approach) would capitalize on the achievements and capacities that our children had developed.

Bibliography

ACKERMAN, NATHAN W., *Psychodynamics of Family Life: Diagnosis and Treatment of Family Relationships.* New York: Basic Books, Inc., Publishers, 1958.

ALMY, MILLIE, *Ways of Studying Children.* New York: Teachers College Press, Columbia University, 1969.

ALPERT, AUGUSTA, "Education as Therapy," *Psychoanalytic Quarterly* 1941).

_____, "Observations on the Treatment of Emotionally Disturbed Children in a Therapeutic Center," in *Psychoanalytic Study of the Child* (vol. 9), ed. Ruth S. Eissler, et al. New York: International Universities Press, 1954.

_____, "Reversibility of Pathological Fixations Associated with Maternal Deprivation in Infancy," in *Psychoanalytic Study of the Child* (vol. 14, ed. Ruth S. Eissler, et al. New York: International Universities Press, 1959.

_____, "The Treatment of Emotionally Disturbed Children in a Therapeutic Nursery," *American Journal of Orthopsychiatry*, 25, No. 4 (1955).

_____, and SYLVIA KROWN, "Treatment of a Child with Severe Ego Restriction in a Therapeutic Nursery," in *Psychoanalytic Study of the Child* (vol. 8), eds. Ruth S. Eissler, et al. New York: International Universities Press, 1953.

BEREITER, CARL, and SIEGFRIED ENGELMANN, *Teaching Disadvantaged Children in the Preschool.* Englewood Cliffs, N.J.: Prentice-Hall, Inc., 1966.

BERNSTEIN, BASIL, "Social Class and Linguistic Development: A Theory of Social Learning," in *Education, Economy, and Society*, eds. A. H. Halsey, et al. Riverside, N.J.: The Free Press, 1961.

BIBER, BARBARA, *Challenges Ahead for the Education of Young Children.* Washington, D.C.: National Association for the Education of Young Children, 1969.

————, "The Educational Needs of Young Deprived Children." Filmed lecture for Project Head Start, Bureau of Child Development and Parent Education, Albany, N.Y., 1965.

————, "Goals and Methods in a Pre-School Program for Disadvantaged Children," *Children*, 17, No. 1 (1970).

————, "Integration of Mental Health Principles in the School Setting," in *Prevention of Mental Disorders in Children*, ed. Gerald Caplan. New York: Basic Books, Inc., Publishers, 1961.

————, and MARJORIE B. FRANKLIN, "The Relevance of Developmental and Psychodynamic Concepts to the Education of the Preschool Child," *Journal of the American Academy of Child Psychiatry*, 6, No. 11 (1967).

BIBER, BARBARA, and PATRICIA MINUCHIN, *A Child Development Approach to Language in the Pre-School Disadvantaged Child.* New York: Bank Street Publications, 1967.

————, "Educating for Individuality: A Reexamination." Paper presented at American Orthopsychiatric Association Meeting, March 1967.

BLANK MARION, "Some Philosophical Influences Underlying Intervention for Disadvantaged Children." Paper presented at the American Psychological Meeting, Washington, D.C., September 1967.

————, and FRANCES SOLOMON, "A Tutorial Language Program to Develop Abstract Thinking in Socially Disadvantaged Pre-School Children," *Child Development*, 34, No. 2, (1968).

Blockbuilding—Some Practical Suggestions for Teachers. New York: Follow Through Institute, Bank Street College of Education, [n.d.].

Blocks as a Learning and Expressive Material. New York: Follow Through Institute, Bank Street College of Education, [n.d.].

BRUNER, JEROME, *Toward a Theory of Instruction.* Cambridge, Mass.: Harvard University Press, 1966.

Child Development Guides for Teachers of Three, Four, and Five Year Olds. Albany, N.Y.: State Education Department, [n.d.].

COHEN, DOROTHY H., and VIRGINIA STERN, *Observing and Recording the Behavior of Young Children.* New York: Teachers College Press, Columbia University, 1967.

COLEMAN, JAMES, *Equality of Educational Opportunity*. Washington, D.C.: Office of Health, Education, and Welfare, 1966.

Developing Children's Powers of Self-Expression Through Writing. New York: New York City Board of Education, 1953.

DEVEREAUX, GEORGE, *Therapeutic Education*. New York: Harper & Row, Publishers, 1956.

DEWEY, JOHN, *Dewey on Education*. New York: Teachers College Press, Columbia University, 1959.

DOAK, ELIZABETH, *What Does the Nursery School Teacher Teach?* Washington, D.C.: National Association for the Education of Young Children, 1951.

ERIKSON, ERIK H., *Childhood and Society*. New York: W. W. Norton & Company, Inc., 1950.

FEITELSON, DINA, "Training Teachers for Conditions of Cultural Diversity." Paper read at Second International Congress of Reading, Copenhagen, 1968.

FOWLER, WILLIAM, "Concept Learning in Early Childhood," in *Teaching the Disadvantaged Child*, Washington, D.C.: National Association for the Education of Young Children, 1966.

FRAIBERG, SELMA, *The Magic Years*. New York: Charles Scribner's Sons, 1959.

GETZELS, JACOB W., and P. W. JACKSON, *Creativity and Intelligence*, New York: John Wiley & Sons, Inc., 1962.

GOLDBERG, MIRIAM L., "Problems in the Evaluation of Compensatory Programs for the Educationally Disadvantaged," in *Education of the Disadvantaged*, ed. A. Harry Passow. New York: Teachers College Press, Columbia University, 1968.

GRAY, SUSAN, RUPERT A. KLAUS, JAMES O. MILLER, and BETTYE J. FORRESTER, *Before First Grade*. New York: Teachers College Press, Columbia University, 1966.

GROSS, RONALD, and JUDITH MURPHY, *The Revolution in the Schools*. New York: Harcourt Brace Jovanovich, Inc., 1964.

HARTLEY, RUTH E., L. K. FRANK, and ROBERT M. GOLDENSON, *Understanding Children's Play*. New York: Columbia University Press, 1952.

HECHINGER, FRED M., ed., *Pre-School Education Today*. Garden City, N.Y.: Doubleday & Company, Inc., 1966.

"Helping Teachers Understand Children." Washington, D.C.: American Council on Education, 1945.

HESS, ROBERT D., *Language and Thought of the Child*. New York: Noonday Press, 1955.

HOLT, JOHN, *How Children Fail*. New York: Pitman Publishing Corporation, 1964.

ISAACS, SUSAN, *Intellectual Growth in Young Children*. London: Routledge and Kegan Paul, 1930.

———, *Social Development in Young Children*. New York: Harcourt Brace Jovanovich, Inc., 1939.

JOHNSON, HARRIET M., *The Art of Blockbuilding*. New York: The John Day Company, 1933.

———, *School Begins at Two*. New York: New Republic, Inc., 1936.

KAGAN, JEROME, H. A. MOSS, and I. B. SIGEL, "Psychological Significance of Styles of Conceptualization," in *Basic Cognitive Processes in Children, Monographs of the Society of Research in Child Development* (vol. 28, No. 2), eds. Jerome Kagan and J. E. Wright, 1963.

KROWN, SYLVIA, "Preschool Programs for Disadvantaged Children," *Children*, 15, No. 6 (1968).

KUBIE, LAWRENCE, *Education and the Process of Maturation*. New York: Bank Street Publications, [n.d.].

LEWIS, CLAUDIA, *Deep as a Giant—An Experiment in Children's Language*. New York: Bank Street Publications, [n.d.].

McDILL, EDWARD L., *Strategies for Success in Compensatory Education*. Baltimore, Md.: The Johns Hopkins Press, 1969.

MATTICK, ILSE, "Adaptation of Nursery School Techniques to Deprived Children," *Journal of American Academy of Child Psychiatry*, 4 (1965).

MITCHELL, LUCY SPRAGUE, *Another Here and Now Story Book*. New York: E. P. Dutton & Co., Inc., 1946.

———, *Here and Now Story Book*. New York: E. P. Dutton & Co., Inc., 1921.

———, *Our Children and Our Schools*. New York: Simon & Schuster, Inc., 1951.

———, *Research on the Child's Level: Possibilities, Limitations and Techniques*. New York: Bank Street Publications, [n.d.].

———, *Young Geographers: How They Explore the World and How They Map the World*. New York: Basic Books, Inc., Publishers, 1963.

MONTESSORI, MARIA, *The Montessori Method*. New York: Stokes, 1912.

MOUSTAKAS, CLARK, *Authentic Teacher*. Cambridge, Mass.: H. A. Doyle Publishing Co., 1966.

NAFTALI, NIZZA, *Work Sheets*. Israel Ministry of Education, 1969.

OMWAKE, E. B., "Basic Learning Begins with Play," *Teaching and Learning, Journal of Ethical Cultures of New York* (1964).

————, "The Child's Estate," in *Modern Perspectives in Child Development*, eds. Albert J. Solnit and Sally A. Provence. New York: International Universities Press, 1963.

————, "Head Start—Measurable and Immeasurable," In *Disadvantaged Child* (vol. 2), ed. Jerome Hellmuth. New York: Brunner/Mazel, Inc., 1968.

PAVENSTEDT, ELEANOR, "A Comparison of the Child-Rearing Environment of Upper-Lower and Very Low-Lower Class Families," *American Journal of Orthopsychiatry*, 33, No. 1 (1965).

————, *The Drifters: Children of Disorganized Lower Class Families*. Boston: Little, Brown and Company, 1967.

Perspectives of Learning and Teaching. New York: Bank Street Publications, 1961–62.

PIAGET, JEAN, *Child's Conception of the World*. Totowa, N.J.: Littlefield Adams & Company, 1960.

————, *Origins of Intelligence in Children*. New York: International Universities Press, 1952.

————, *Play, Dreams and Imitation in Childhood*. New York: W. W. Norton & Company, Inc., 1951.

PRATT, CAROLINE, *I Learn from Children*. New York: Simon & Schuster, Inc., 1958.

READ, KATHERINE, *The Nursery School*. Philadelphia: W. B. Saunders Company, 1958.

RIESE, HERTHA, *Heal the Hurt Child*. Chicago: University of Chicago Press, 1962.

ROBISON, HELEN, and BERNARD SPODEK, *New Directions in the Kindergarten*. New York: Teachers College Press, Columbia University, 1965.

SMILANSKY, SARA, *Effects of Sociodramatic Play on Disadvantaged Pre-School Children*. New York: John Wiley & Sons, Inc., 1968.

SPODEK, BERNARD, *Preparing Teachers of Disadvantaged Young Children*. Washington, D.C.: National Association for the Education of Young Children, 1966.

STONE, L. JOSEPH, and JOSEPH CHURCH, *Childhood and Adolescence: A Psychology of the Growing Process*. New York: Random House, Inc., 1957.

WANN, KENNETH D., MIRIAM S. DORN, and ELIZABETH ANN LITTLE, *Fostering Intellectual Development in Young Children.* New York: Teachers College Press, Columbia University, 1962.

WEIKART, DAVID, ed., *Preschool Intervention: Preliminary Report of the Perry School Project.* Ann Arbor, Mich.: Campus Publishers, 1967.

WINSOR, CHARLOTTE B., *Social Education of Young Children.* New York: Bank Street Publications, [n.d.].

ZIMILES, HERBERT, "An Analysis of Current Issues in the Evaluation of Educational Problems," in *Disadvantaged Child* (vol. 2), ed. Jerome Hellmuth. New York: Brunner/Mazel, Inc., 1968.